Tales of
the Lavender Menace

Also by Karla Jay

Dyke Life: From Growing Up to Growing Old—A Celebration of the Lesbian Experience (editor)

Lesbian Erotics (editor)

Lavender Culture (with co-editor Allen Young)

Out of the Closets: Voices of Gay Liberation (with co-editor Allen Young)

Lesbian Texts and Contexts: Radical Revisions (with co-editor Joanne Glasgow)

The Amazon and the Page: Natalie Clifford Barney and Renée Vivien

The Gay Report

After You're Out: Personal Experiences of Gay Men and Lesbian Women

Tales of
the Lavender
Menace

A Memoir
of
Liberation

Karla Jay

BASIC
BOOKS

A Member of the Perseus Books Group

Published by Basic Books,
A Member of the Perseus Books Group

A CIP catalog record for this book is available from the Library of Congress.
ISBN: 0-465-08364-1 (cloth); ISBN 0-465-08366-8

The existence of a few militant lesbians within the movement once prompted [Betty] Friedan herself to grouse about "the lavender menace" that was threatening to warp the image of women's rights. A lavender herring, perhaps, but surely no clear and present danger.

—**Susan Brownmiller**
New York Times Magazine (1970)

Contents

Note on the Text

Events in this memoir are true to the extent that my own recollections, interviews with others, and research could verify facts. People identified only by their first names have been disguised to protect their privacy.

Prologue

On the last Saturday evening in June 1995, I took part in New York's annual Dyke March down Fifth Avenue. A few blocks into the parade route, some of the more militant women blocked traffic, raising the stakes in this annual rite of defiance, since the organizers had no permit for the march. A few young friends of mine, delighted by their first political demonstration and dressed too warmly for the steamy evening, stripped off their tops, which they happily stuffed in my backpack before they charged off to join other bare-breasted lesbians. As they frolicked down Fifth Avenue, sporting their tattooed, pierced bodies, I nervously eyed every ATM machine we passed, wondering how much it cost these days to post bail for disturbing the peace.

Carrying others' clothing instead of shedding my own, I felt old for the first time in my life. But I could hardly suppress a crone's cackle when one of my young friends put an affectionate arm around my shoulder and announced, "Hey, KJ, it's okay at your age to be too uptight to strip in public."

Naturally, young people assume that anyone their parents' age is no longer sexually active. Their mistaken perception that I'm some kind of eunuch has been shaped by politically driven historical accounts that paint a picture of radical feminists as antisexual. And it's not just my young friends who make such inaccurate assumptions: I frequently address audiences across the country about the struggles of the women's and gay movements of the late 1960s and early 1970s. Whether I'm talking to the urban cool or to budding activists on a rural college campus, I find that their assumptions about this history are often framed by comedians, pundits, and other forms of popular media that aim for a quick punchline rather than complex truths. Those interested in women's studies ask: "Did feminists have sex? Camille Paglia says you didn't." The cover of a 1998 issue of *Time* magazine wondered, "Is feminism dead?" Gay audiences rhetorically inquire: "Is it true that after the 1969 uprisings at the Stonewall Inn in Greenwich Village all the lesbians were political and the gay men had fun? And then AIDS came along and the lesbians taught the gay men how to be political and the gay men taught the lesbians how to have fun?" Not exactly. Not even close.

They never ask me whether we accomplished anything worthwhile, whether things have changed for the better because of our radicalism. I suppose it's hard for them to imagine that someone like me, a staid university professor with a doctorate, once participated in sit-ins, organized demonstrations, walked in picket lines, and fought for sexual freedom. They'd never believe that, despite the risk, I enjoyed almost every action. I thought we revolutionaries were changing the world. To a small degree, we did.

But I wasn't born a rebel. Before I got caught up in the revolutionary fervor of the late 1960s, I was a well-mannered young woman attending Barnard, an elite "Seven Sisters" college. All I wanted back then, three decades ago, was a college degree and middle-class comforts. This is the tale of how a nice Jewish girl from Brooklyn became a radical lesbian/feminist. The transformation began with the brutal police response to the student uprisings at Columbia University in the spring of 1968. Up until that night, I had lived a quiet, though by no means ordinary, life.

1

Men Behaving Very Badly

I used to tell people that my jeans were by Levi, but my childhood was by Dickens. Rhoda, my mother, was what the neighbors euphemistically termed "a difficult woman." Her misery was like Texas oil: You could drill anywhere and find some. She claimed never to have recovered from giving birth to me when she was thirty-five. She suffered from serious depression, duodenal ulcers, and intestinal blockages. During most of my childhood, all I could recall of her was her closed bedroom door. She would emerge from her lair only to go shopping or play cards with her friends, while Nene Brown, our live-in housekeeper, took care of my brother (whom I'll call Paul) and me.

By the time I entered Barnard College in the fall of 1964, Nene was long gone, and so was most of my mother's grip on reality. From time to time my mother overdosed on whatever prescription tranquilizer she was currently taking and then passed out. Paul would pick her up, walk her around until she was conscious, and then unceremoniously dump her in her bed. Most of my mother's lapses into unconsciousness were accidental overdoses, but she did try to commit suicide several times. Her failed attempts were accompanied by pages of badly spelled notes detailing how our insensitivity had killed her. Ingrate that I was, I often secretly wished she'd get one suicide attempt right.

By the time I was a teenager, my mother rarely left her room, even to shop. I dreaded it whenever she did emerge, for she was prone to tantrums and hallucinations. She proclaimed that her aunts were hiding in my closet, that her cousins were urinating on her immaculate couch, that her friends were having sex on her bed. Her imagination was both terrifying and embarrassing. I was constantly uneasy about what she might do in public—what if she announced cousin Sarah's imaginary antics in some restaurant or department store? Wouldn't that liven up the communal dressing room at Loehmann's? During dinner, she would pitch a scene and occasionally a plate. She sometimes went into wild rages and attacked me with her long red nails. Fortunately, she weighed under a hundred pounds and wasn't very strong. I learned how to slap her face just enough to stop her.

My father, brother, and I coped by making jokes about my mother. We would point out to each other, but not to her, that Aunt Pearl was simply too fat to hide behind the refrigerator and cousin Dinah would never dream of having sex in our living room. Abraham, my father, said how grateful he was that my mother's hallucinations involved her own relatives, not his.

My father arranged his life so that he spent little time with my mother. He often worked seven days a week at the Waterfront Lumber Company, of which he was part owner. Marine lumber—"dunnage," it was called—was used for building bins on freighters to hold everything from grain to elephants. My father worked hard, primarily on the docks in Brooklyn. When he came home, he liked to eat dinner promptly and then go to sleep in his favorite easy chair. Every evening between ten and eleven, I would wake him up and tell him to go to bed.

Like my father, I kept out of my mother's way. I stayed out of the house as much as possible. I filled the hours between school and dinner playing field hockey, basketball, or softball. During the evenings I locked myself in my bedroom and studied. I almost never brought friends or schoolmates into the house. My brother sometimes confronted my mother during her rages, but I learned that the easiest path was to agree with whatever she said, however ludicrous it was.

Avoidance and appeasement appeared to be my best options. No one seemed to notice what was going on in my home, and I never asked for help. I didn't think anyone would understand my situation. But one day, after one of my mother's suicide attempts, our family physician advised me to leave home, as quickly as possible. "You can't save her," he said. "Get out! It's your only chance." Then he paused and added, "Don't look back."

"If you're so smart," I shot back, "why can't you help her?" He didn't reply.

But the doctor was right. In one of her mystifying rages, my mother turned out all of my dresser drawers onto my bedroom rug because I had worn sandals to the beach. Then she was appalled by the ensuing mess. "Clean it up, damn it!" she yelled. "Look at the mess you've made!" There was no point in trying to figure out her fury. I scooped up the clothes from the floor, tossed them into two shopping bags, and tiptoed out the front door. I never slept in that apartment again.

For a few days after I left, I stayed with a friend's family. Then I spotted an ad posted by another Barnard student who wanted to share an apartment about ten blocks south of the school. The area below West 110th Street was even less savory than Morningside Heights, Columbia and Barnard's shabby neighborhood, but it was a lot cheaper for the same reason. Sally's railroad apartment turned out to have two and a half rooms. The "half room" was a Pullman kitchen, a mere indentation in the hall, with an old stove and refrigerator and a couple of metal cabinets painted aqua. For some reason Sally, a stringy and taciturn history major, slept in the living room. For a mere $75 per month, the entire bedroom would be mine. Although my allowance came to less than half of the total, I calculated that I could make up the remainder through baby-sitting and other jobs. I decided to move in.

My father, angry at my leaving, threatened to cut off my allowance. After all, I was a definite asset at home. Paul was completing his undergraduate degree and was rarely around. My moving out left the burden of taking care of my mother on my father. If he chose to stay, eventually he'd have to go it alone with her. He was less than thrilled. "I'm too poor to get a divorce and send two kids through college," he sighed in resignation.

In the end he knew I'd have to leave sooner or later and that sooner was really better for me. When he came to terms with my departure, he gave me some unpainted furniture. I was all set for living on my own.

In an era when most Barnard students devoted themselves full-time to their studies, I had to divide my time among attending classes, studying, and earning enough to make ends meet. As a result, my economic needs took up the time I might have spent socializing or networking. I baby-sat a lot, and I quickly learned that the best homes were the ones with the fullest refrigerators. I also rented myself out for psychology experiments. My favorite temporary jobs were for market research companies that paid $10 an hour for my opinion. I pretended to have used almost every product, so I got called in frequently. This tactic backfired when I was asked for my views on restrooms in gas stations. I had never been in one. With a mother like mine, we hadn't traveled very far.

Although I had little time for parties, I determinedly landed myself a handsome boyfriend at my very first Barnard dance. Trent was a dashing, corn-silk blond Columbia freshman from rural Alabama. He reminded me of the few Southerners I had met, all lesbian camp counselors on whom I had had intense childhood crushes, so I fell immediately for Trent's drawl, which evoked cicadas and tough women with duck's ass haircuts.

Trent had never met a Jew. "Where are your horns?" he asked me on our first date.

"Oh," I replied glibly, "we get them filed down at birth!"

I refused to be deterred by our differences. I felt a boyfriend was a necessity. During my freshman orientation at Barnard, I heard a story about two young women who had been caught making love in their dorm room. A male student, perched atop a building on the Columbia side of Broadway, spied on them through his binoculars. The two girls were allegedly expelled, whereas the Peeping Tom was not. I never attempted to confirm this cautionary tale, but given the prevailing fear and disgust around the very idea of lesbians at an all-women's college, the chain of events seemed likely enough.

The rumor frightened me enough so that throughout college I steadfastly passed as a heterosexual. I told not a single friend or acquaintance about my earlier sexual experimentation with girls and women in high school and at summer camp. "Feminine" and trim, though muscular, I blended in perfectly with the Barnard crowd. I set, teased, and sprayed my brown hair into a shoulder-length flip as stiff and controlled as I was. I never left home without wearing makeup.

As part of my heterosexual cover, I sometimes let Trent sleep over at my apartment, though we never had sexual intercourse. He lived in the dorms, and we couldn't very well stay there. Male undergrads had to keep "a book in the door" when a woman was present. Though most guys stocked up on something slim, such as *The Communist Manifesto* or even a matchbook, there was still little privacy with roommates always wandering in and out.

Apart from dating Trent, I had no social life. Sally and I had little in common. Occasionally, we'd share meals. Our standard fare was spaghetti with Spatini—a powdered tomato sauce we mixed with water. It was pretty awful but at nine cents a serving quite a bargain. On rare occasions Sally's boyfriend, Henry, bought some dough from a pizzeria and made pizza or calzone. He was the only one of us who knew how to bake.

But even if Sally and I had been inclined to be friends, most of her time was taken up with Henry, who became an unofficial third roommate. Except for his culinary skills, he wasn't an asset. He worked full-time as an apprentice painter but chipped in very little for household expenses. And whatever he was spending his money on, it wasn't deodorant. He smelled so rank that I knew without looking when he entered the front door. "Real men don't wear deodorant," he bragged. Real men, however, apparently hit their girlfriends. Henry and Sally's frequent disputes often ended with him slamming her into a wall or a car. Sometimes he would shove her face into his armpit for extra punishment. He had an unlicensed lethal weapon there. I couldn't figure out why she continued to date him.

Once I did try to intervene in a fight. "Get the fuck offa her, you asshole!" I yelled. Matching the vernacular of an opponent was one of the cardinal rules of Brooklyn street fighting. I hoped it would work on guys like Henry from the Bronx.

"Shut the fuck up or I'll hit you, too!"

"Go ahead and try." Wisely for both of us, he ignored my dare.

By our junior year Sally had started taking drugs. At first she and Henry smoked pot together. Soon they tried anything else that might get them stoned. Counterculture magazines were full of suggestions for homegrown "highs," including sucking the air out of Ready Whip cans (don't shake first!), eating morning-glory seeds, and smoking cigarettes through holes in bell peppers that had been baked in the oven. Most of these methods didn't work.

One legal drug Sally didn't indulge in was the birth control pill. Henry and Sally were Catholic and opposed using any form of contraception. After she discovered that she was pregnant, Sally had few choices. Abortions were legal in New York State only if two doctors certified that a woman was too mentally unstable to bear a child. Alternative home remedies usually involved trying to abort the fetus by using a coat hanger, which might puncture the uterus. Some women took drops of pennyroyal oil until they aborted—or died a hideous death—whichever came first. Only one drop too many of pennyroyal separated the two outcomes. Sally opted for jumping off the bed onto the floor a lot. She took very hot baths, trying to induce a miscarriage. Finally, she went the most expensive route—a weekend trip to Puerto Rico for an abortion.

After Henry and Sally returned from Puerto Rico, they broke up.

"You killed my son." Henry was actually tearful.

"*Your* son! How the fuck do you know it was a boy anyway, you conceited asshole?" she screamed. "What about my college degree?" Back then, most colleges expelled unmarried, pregnant coeds.

"Fuck you and your education!" were his parting words.

Sally began to spend most of her time in bed. She skipped classes. She said nothing to me about what had happened in Puerto Rico. Having an abortion was so shameful that it was easier to die from one than to speak of it. I didn't know what to say to her. For an entire month Kotex filled our garbage can. Since everyone we knew had switched to Tampax (after we showed one another how to insert it), it was easy to read the meaning of the endless boxes of sanitary pads.

Our apartment was awash in Sally's blood. The brownish ooze soaked through her mattress onto the dingy yellow living room rug, stained the wooden kitchen floor, and spattered onto the black-and-white tiles on the bathroom floor. Pale and wan, she spent more and more time in bed, her face turned to the wall in inconsolable agony. She never went to see a physician.

Even when the bleeding stopped weeks later, Sally's energy didn't return, and she continued to lie in bed. Then she discovered Benzedrine, an over-the-counter cold remedy. She'd dissect several bottles at a time and eat the small white cotton balls that contained the Benzedrine. One day the cotton got stuck in her throat. After coughing for hours, she switched to buying amphetamines from local drug dealers.

The speed had some salutary side effects. Sally couldn't concentrate enough to study, but she couldn't sit still either, so she'd wash the kitchen and the bathroom down four or five times a week. Perhaps she was trying to erase her shame, her sense of guilt. Soon the apartment went from blood spattered to unbearably sanitized. I started to worry she would flunk out of school. I knew a guy who had taken so many "uppers" that he wound up writing his entire final exam on one line.

Sally decided to move back home. Latchmi, an exchange student from India, took her place. She brought with her two cats, Kali and Gandhi, and her boyfriend, Dennis. I had very little experience with pets, but I took to Latchmi's cats with great delight and reveled in their sleek, clean ways and playful personalities. I didn't have much more in common with Latchmi and Dennis than I'd had with Sally and Henry, but we studied compatibly and tried to learn about each other's culture.

I spent much of my free time with Trent. I was now a senior, and our relationship was in its fourth year. Yet I started to feel lonely. Efforts to seduce Trent had failed. In high school I had had a girlfriend, someone who shared my interest in horses and sex. I wanted a female lover again, but I didn't know how to find one. I was terrified of getting caught, but my need for sensual contact with another woman overcame some of my caution. I looked around discreetly in physical education classes and in the "HQ" section of the library where a few analyses of homosexual pathology were located. I didn't spot anyone there who appeared to be a lesbian. Some of the professors looked gay, but they probably thought I was too young for them, if they thought of me at all. I didn't know then that Kate Millett and Catharine R. Stimpson—both in the English Department—were bisexual or lesbian. I thought I was the only one at Barnard, maybe in the entire world.

I considered joining the first homophile group in the country, which had formed in 1967 across the street at Columbia. The group was founded by "Stephen Donaldson," whose real name was Robert Martin: I discovered later that many gay activists adopted aliases to hide their real identities. Supposedly, some women belonged to the group, but to me it had the off-putting air of a men's club. I could see why I was the only woman present at the one meeting I attended.

Finally, I met Kip, a Hunter student who lived in my building. She had a boyfriend—but, then again, I had one, too. She was willing to sleep with me so long as we never discussed it. She forbade me to use the word "lesbian" or even "bisexual" to describe our relationship. Perhaps she felt that if we didn't say it, it wasn't so. She told me we were merely "practicing" for our current boyfriends and future husbands. Since she was already having intercourse with her boyfriend, her argument didn't make a lot of sense to me, but pointing out the discrepancies in her logic wasn't in my best interest. We "practiced" a lot, and she sure was inventive about it. Her favorite time of the year was summer, when she wanted me to use cucumbers, zucchini, and corn on the cob as organic dildos. Better her than me. Even though I wished she would prefer my tongue or fingers to the seasonal vegetation, I didn't protest. I loved her female body, her soft face that lacked stubble, her high, round breasts. Unfortunately, after a few months she had an attack of "lesbian panic" and swore sudden fidelity to her boyfriend. I was left again with Trent.

While I was trying to figure out my sexual identity and get through college, the world around me seemed to be erupting in political turmoil. President Lyndon B. Johnson's call for a "Great Society" seemed ludicrous in the face of the social and political unrest of the mid-1960s. The war in Vietnam was escalating, while at home race riots were erupting in various cities, including New York, Newark, and Los Angeles.

For me, the most moving event was Malcolm X's speech at Barnard on February 18, 1965. His fiery rhetoric and charismatic style convinced me that there was going to be a revolution, something more violent than sit-ins at lunch counters in the South and marches on Washington. Listening to him, I realized for the first time just how much I had benefited from having been born with white skin and how much Black people might justifiably hate me for that. At the same time, by speaking at Barnard, this Black Muslim separatist was reaching out to a young white middle-class student body. Three days later, on February 21, the day before my eighteenth birthday, Malcolm X was assassinated at the Audubon Ballroom in Washington Heights. I was stunned by the propinquity of the events: I had never been in the same room with anyone who was later murdered. By my senior year civil rights leader Martin Luther King, Jr., had been assassinated as well.

Having participated in the Civil Rights Movement, leftist students, like those in Students for a Democratic Society (SDS), began by early 1968 to demand a wholly new society, one founded on the premise of universal peace and equality between Blacks and whites. In many ways Columbia University was a microcosm of the debates surrounding these issues. Undergraduates, especially those who belonged to SDS, were outraged by Columbia's affiliation with the Institute for Defense Analyses (IDA), a group that evaluated weapons and did other sorts of research for the Defense Department. Attacking IDA was a way for students to protest what they perceived as an unjust war in Vietnam. Students and community activists were further outraged when Columbia announced in 1968 it had struck a deal with the City of New York to build a gym on more than two acres of Morningside Park for the modest rental price of $3,000 per year for ninety-nine years. Columbia viewed the park, which cascaded steeply like a dry waterfall from the eastern fringe of the university down toward Harlem, as an "underutilized" space. Translation: White people didn't play there. After community protest, the university agreed to allot about 15 percent of separate but unequal space to the community, and according to the book *Up Against the Ivy Wall*, by Jerry Avorn, which came out in the wake of the subsequent student uprisings, the architectural plans called for "a back entrance on the Harlem side for the community and a main entrance facing Columbia for the University"—rather like "white" and "colored" water fountains in the South.

Despite student and community protests, Columbia persisted in breaking ground for the gym. But the students weren't about to concede defeat. On April 23, 1968, more than one hundred students, led by Mark Rudd, the charismatic head of SDS, seized Hamilton Hall to protest university policies. The revolution was on.

Word of the uprising spread quickly across Broadway to the Barnard campus. Despite general opposition to the gym and the war, few of us at Barnard, including me, knew what to think of the controversy. Barnard girls were kept in such a separate world from Columbia that for us the two campuses might as well have been miles apart. Barnard had its own faculty, library, school newspaper, tennis courts, swimming pool, and gym. Why should the issue of Columbia's gym concern us? No matter that archery and golf were practiced on the roof of the library—no one as yet had been hit with an arrow or a flying golf ball. Were the Columbia gym ever built, Barnard girls wouldn't be allowed in anyway—the Harlem community would be welcomed there long before we were.

But trouble was not something I was looking for at the moment. I had been accepted into a doctoral program in comparative literature at New York University. All I had to do was pass my oral and written comprehensives in French, which was my major, and my undergraduate days at the overrated Ivy League would be behind me.

So I was hoping that the takeover would remain an isolated incident. But soon the students seized additional buildings, including Low Library, which housed the office of the university president, Grayson Kirk. Once inside his office, the students rifled Kirk's files, smoked his cigars, and used his private bathroom.

What finally made me decide to side with the radicals were the counterdemonstrations, organized and led by white jocks. Like many of the other students, I disliked the jocks. They got an inordinate share of the scholarships and other perks, even though they hadn't won more than a handful of games in four years. Whenever those meatheads thought they had a good idea, I just knew the opposing faction had to be right. When some of them threw eggs at Black students on Hamilton's balconies and called them "niggers," I was disgusted.

In addition, the proadministration students sometimes tried to blockade an entrance with their bodies to prevent sympathizers from bringing food in. When the jocks got frustrated at the administration's inability to end the uprising, they threatened to send their future sons to college elsewhere (oh please, oh please) or tried to capture buildings that were already in the control of protesting students. It was a miracle that no one got shoved off a ledge onto the sidewalk or impaled on one of the Columbia's shiny new wrought-iron fences.

Despite the extreme tactics of both sides, a truce was declared the first weekend after the takeover. I headed to the campus to see what was going on. My first stop was Ferris Booth Hall, the student center on the southeast corner of the campus. It had become an uprising clearinghouse of sorts. Some students there cataloged donated food, while others, their fingers stained blue, ran off the latest manifestos and demands on a battered mimeograph, a machine that eventually became the true press of the revolutionary movement in this country. I walked up to a scraggly guy who had an air of being in charge.

"Can I help?" I asked.

"Yeah, man," he said, pointing to one of the cartons overflowing with canned meat and loaves of bread. "Take some tuna sandwiches over to Fayerweather Hall, and if you can't get in, toss them in through the windows. Then come back and join the other girls making sandwiches." He gestured behind him to a row of Barnard students who were slathering some white bread with peanut butter and jelly with assembly-line speed.

Some of the main entrances were open, so I was able to deliver the provisions. I took a quick look at the incredible mess the students had made. The floors looked as if a dormitory had exploded, leaving blankets, clothes, discarded food, and other detritus everywhere. Cigarette butts, roach ends, empty cans, and stained cups were piled into, over, and around a garbage can.

"What's it like to stay here?" I asked a guy to whom I handed a sandwich.

"Come back tonight and find out," he replied in an insinuating tone.

"Are you inviting me to the revolution or a frat party?" I shot back on my way out. I wondered whether I'd be safer at the latter. Though I still vividly recalled a Barnard friend who had returned from a frat party to the dorms one night with no bra and three stockings, and then passed out on the bathroom floor, it didn't seem to me that the student uprising promised women anything more inviting.

That interchange in Fayerweather Hall about summed up the roles that the "Barnard girls," as we were called, were supposed to play in the student revolution. Wherever I went that weekend, the scene was the same: Men were involved in important discussions; women were relegated to supporting roles—raising money for the cause, donating our own food for the "true revolutionaries" (or preparing theirs), and cleaning up the mess they had made of the buildings. Did I look like Dial-a-Maid? And then when we were done with all that work, we were supposed to provide emotional succor in the form of sex for the boys in the trenches.

This seemed to be typical of many actions of the Left in the 1960s. According to Jacqui Ceballos, an early member of the National Organization for Women (NOW), the women's rights organization founded by Betty Friedan in 1966, "Women at a 1965 SDS conference [were] put down with *she just needs a good screw;* the following year SDS women [were] pelted with tomatoes when they demand[ed] a plank on women's liberation." As Stokely Carmichael, the former leader of the Student Nonviolent Coordinating Committee, a black civil rights group that focused on community organizing, once put it, "The position of women in SNCC is prone!" He meant "supine," but though his linguistic ignorance accidentally put women on top, his point was clear: The coming revolution was meant to free Black men and white men, but not women. Things had clearly not changed much since the Civil War. Then many suffragists put aside their struggle for the vote to fight for abolition. After the war Black and white men got the vote, but no woman did. I began to see that men would always put our needs last.

I wanted to fight for change, but not with these men. I was becoming a feminist, even if I wasn't ready to call myself one yet. Disgusted with the political narrowness of the Columbia men, I headed home. It was one of those rare occasions when the elevator in my building was working, so I charged in. Inside the car, dressed in a frayed housecoat of indeterminate color, was the Manishewitz lady. This tiny and very elderly survivor of the Holocaust, whose real name no one knew, lived on the seventh floor. Whenever she got hungry, she would ride up and down in the elevator chanting, "Manishewitz" over and over like a mantra. It was her plea for someone to go to the Spanish grocery store on the corner and buy her some kosher food.

I went back out and bought her one small can of soup—no one I knew had actually been repaid by Mrs. Manishewitz—and returned to the building. She was no longer in the elevator. I rode up to the seventh floor to find her.

When I got there, I realized that I didn't know which apartment she lived in. Spotting a Jewish name on the door opposite the elevator, I rang the bell. The apartment turned out to belong to Daniel, a graduate student in chemistry at Columbia. He directed me to the next apartment and told me to come right back to tell him what was happening at Columbia.

Mrs. Manishewitz opened her door a crack and snatched the can out of my hand. Then without even saying, "Thank you," she slammed the door in my face. I returned to Daniel's apartment.

"You think you've got problems?" he volunteered. "When the elevator isn't working, she just bangs on my wall with a pot, yelling, 'Manishewitz, Manishewitz,' until I either buy her some or lose my mind. One day I'm gonna lace it for her."

He pointed to his stove, where a collection of pots and beakers was assembled.

"What's that—a chemistry experiment?"

"Nah, I make my own acid. It's cheaper that way. Want a hit?"

"No thanks, I've got to study."

"Stay for a while and tell me what's happening."

I perched on the edge of his bed—it was the only place to sit in the small studio apartment, since the chairs were littered with thick chemistry textbooks and drafts of term papers. After we exchanged stories of the revolution, his hand began gently rubbing my back. Okay, so my mother had warned me never to go into a man's apartment.

Spring and the spirit of revolution were in the air, and as usual I was having no luck trying to seduce Trent. Like all essentially "good girls," I considered it a failure to graduate a virgin, so I let Daniel push me onto the bed and "take my virginity," as he said, with a slight thrill in his voice. It turned out that he specialized in virgins, and when I saw his equipment, I could understand why. With a penis like a number two pencil, he'd want women with no previous experience.

"It's not how big it is, it's how you use it," he commented when he saw me eyeing him with disdain.

He used his penis every which way, but it was still tiny. He kept his erection with the assistance of the *New York Times,* which he propped behind my head and read while he performed. I thought this was a charming novelty on the order of Kip's vegetables. Finally, he got to the bottom of the editorial page and came. I went home to study, thinking, "Is that all there is?" The *Times* editorial had been more interesting than he was. I decided that sex with Daniel was not worth a second try.

I spent the weekend studying and visiting a few of the occupied buildings at Columbia. By Monday it was clear that the tensions at Columbia had escalated. The trustees had affirmed that President Grayson Kirk had the sole right to punish demonstrators, and they had indicated that the gym construction might be halted, but only temporarily.

As the stalemate continued, many courses began meeting at alternative sites. Since most of my classes were relatively small, it wasn't hard for us to form a circle in Riverside Park or on a professor's living room floor. I wondered whether the uprising would change the way we all thought about education and lead to more cordial relations between students and professors.

All utopian fantasies, however, soon came to an end. The Tactical Police Force (TPF) unit was already massing on the side streets south of

Columbia. Members of the TPF were Vietnam-era Robocops. Generally considered the toughest unit of the city's police force, they had been groomed to quell the urban uprisings of the 1960s. On April 30, at 2:30 A.M., a week after the initial takeovers, the TPF moved in to clear students and their supporters out of the buildings. Phones and water were cut off. Using a bullhorn, the police asked faculty and students to clear the entrances to Low Library. Then they charged, clubbing students and faculty members who got in their way and tossing some over the hedges. Resisters were beaten to the ground, as were some of those who simply tried to get out of the way. Students were given the option of leaving other buildings. Those who didn't were dragged, kicked, and clubbed. Even some members of the press, who were wearing passes and were covering the event, were attacked. The university had not placed any physicians on the scene; bleeding and dazed students wandered about or slumped onto the ground. Those who were arrested were herded or dragged into waiting police vans, which had been lined up on College Walk.

I was awakened by a telephone call from a friend in the dorms who had spotted masses of police moving up Broadway. "The shit is hitting the fan," he said matter-of-factly. "You'd better come now if you're coming at all."

I put aside my resentment of the male radicals. This sounded like war, and in a crunch I knew which side I had to take. I pulled on jeans, boots, a sweatshirt, and a jacket and hurried up Broadway. Just as I reached the gates at West 116th Street and Broadway, I heard thunderous shouts as the TPF suddenly attacked the students—both demonstrators and TPF supporters—who were massed on South Field in the center of the campus. Students, blinded by the headlights of the police vans and frantic to dodge flailing nightsticks, stampeded in every direction. A crowd surged toward me. Fearful of being trampled, I turned and ran back out the gates with the crowd. A throng of mounted police awaited us on Broadway, and they, too, charged. I ran in terror down Broadway and didn't stop even when I felt a sharp blow in my right ribs. Luckily, my athletic legs propelled me forward until I was safely at home. Except for my hurt side, I was relatively unscathed. I was certain that anyone who had been near the campus would be branded a "trespasser" or "troublemaker," so I decided not to tell anyone I had been there that night.

The next morning I heard that more than 700 students had been arrested in the melee and that almost 150 students had been injured. I called my father at the lumberyard to let him know I was okay, just in case he had heard something on the radio. When I told him that the cops had beaten up several of my friends who hadn't broken any laws, he asked, "What were they doing out on the campus at that hour anyway?"

The voice of Middle America had spoken. My father was expressing the sentiments of the typical parent of his generation. I hung up and burst into tears. My father and I, long united against my mother's illness, had reached a parting of the ways. He could envision the uprising only as rowdy students out past their bedtime; I had witnessed innocent men and women being clubbed by officers of the law. Part of my grief had to do with the realization that my father would have been no more sympathetic had I been one of the unlucky ones pummeled by a cop or trampled by a horse. He would still have sided with the law—or those who acted in its name—and thought I had got what I deserved.

My relationship with my father—indeed, my interaction with the world—would never be the same. I knew I could never again sit on the sidelines and hope an injustice would simply go away. The searing headlights of the police vans had burned away the blindness obscuring my political vision. That thump in my ribs had jump-started a heartbeat I didn't know I had. I saw America through different eyes now. A government that sanctioned attacks on privileged Ivy League students in the middle of their own campus certainly couldn't provide "justice for all"—certainly not for Blacks in the ghettos or in the South, not for factory workers or immigrants, and certainly not for the Vietnamese. We were all being assailed by the same fascist mentality that proclaimed, "America—love it or leave it." By the same black-booted cops or soldiers who insisted we follow their orders. By a country that valued property, including Columbia's buildings and American overseas investments, above the lives of the young and the poor. The Constitution itself had been trampled on, and it would take a revolution to right it.

A year after the uprisings I received devastating news about Trent. After graduation he had joined the air force, as he had always planned. Though we stopped dating, we stayed in touch. He would telephone when he was on leave in the States, and we wrote to each other regularly. Then one day my letter was returned to me, stamped "not deliverable." A male friend who had served in the army told me this meant that Trent was dead.

In 1992 during a visit to Washington, DC, I searched for his name at the Vietnam Memorial. Much to my surprise, there were several people with the same name. I couldn't tell which one might be my Trent. Perhaps he was none of them. My pilgrimage to the wall didn't provide the feeling of closure I'd hoped for. The multiplicity of possible Trents on the monument was unsettling. I felt suddenly, awkwardly uncertain as to whether he had indeed been killed. Perhaps he had merely got tired of writing or had met someone else who forbade him to remain pen pals with a former girlfriend.

Though Trent had supported Columbia's administration and the TPF actions, in the end he was, one way or the other, victimized by the very institutions he worshiped. If he was indeed killed, he died in an embarrassing war, one without compelling motive. If he lived, he'd have had to wrestle with the fact that he had probably napalmed Vietnamese women and children, not just Vietcong rebels. He would have returned home to people who viewed air force pilots as "baby killers." In my circle people respected student rebels and draft dodgers more than veterans. Ironically, in doing what he saw as his "duty," he chose the less honorable road.

In the end, even if Trent was alive, he was dead to me—part of the life I had led before the Columbia uprisings. I was now an entirely different person. I had left behind the polished and perfumed body and coiffed hair of a Barnard girl. My former self was gone, unrecognizable even to me.

2

Bipolar Sexuality

After I graduated from Barnard in May 1968, I worked for a publisher by day and in the evenings took two graduate classes at New York University, where I was slowly working toward a doctorate in comparative literature. I marched against the war in Vietnam and rallied for civil rights. Getting on a bus to Washington before dawn and attending antiwar demonstrations around New York City were staple activities of the era. Were it not for my negative experiences with sexist student revolutionaries, I would have signed up for one of the drives to register Black voters in the South. But I no longer wanted to work with straight white men, however well meaning they might be.

But the struggles at Columbia and the resulting police brutality also left me somewhat shaken and cautious about antagonizing the establishment; consequently, I preferred to spend some of my energy trying to solve the bewildering question of my sexual preference. For me, being bisexual was like being a Ping-Pong ball. When I dated men, I found myself unattracted to them, but ever since Kip had abandoned me for her boyfriend and taken her produce market with her, I had been unable to find a female lover. Once or twice I had gone to the Sea Colony and the Bagatelle, lesbian bars in the West Village. They were dim, greasy, and smoky—never mind that I was one of those polluting the air. When a new lesbian bar named Kooky's (pronounced "Cookies") opened on West Fourteenth Street, I decided to try my luck there.

Kooky's was reputed to be a front for the mob, which supposedly ran all the gay and lesbian bars in New York. (Craig Rodwell's Oscar Wilde Memorial Bookshop in the Village was probably the only cultural space in New York at that time owned by a gay person.) Kooky, the proprietor, had the air of a retired prostitute or a poorly put-together drag queen. She favored pastel prom dresses—the kind that required several crinolines to inflate them properly, were zippered in the back, and called for a strapless bra and a large bust to keep the dress up. Perhaps she fancied herself the Scarlett O'Hara of Greenwich Village. Her hair was shellacked into a large golden beehive that suggested she had last set, teased, and sprayed her hair in the 1950s and then left it permanently in place.

To enter the bar, I first had to get past the bouncer, who stood outside chomping on the stub of a fat cigar. Two other men sat inside the door and collected the $3 cover charge. Once I had been "carded"—I still didn't look eighteen—I was admitted to the smoky interior. On the right was a long bar where every seat was occupied by "regulars." The cheapest drinks cost $1. At a time when I could see a double feature of two classic films for fifty cents, this was an enormous sum for me.

Across from the bar were the bathrooms. When the first bar opened, a female employee sat outside the door and handed patrons exactly three squares of toilet paper on their way in. No one knows how the management decided on three squares as opposed to two or four. Perhaps the exact number of sheets was a tradition passed on from the Sea Colony. Soon the toilet paper was liberated, but the guard remained. No heterosexual bar, no matter how promiscuous its clientele, guarded the toilets in such an overbearing manner. We were constantly reminded that we were degenerates who could not be trusted to be with others of our kind in a public restroom.

On my trip to the bathroom, I used my oversized pocketbook to hide my empty drink glass, which I slyly filled up with tap water. I wasn't much of a drinker, but Kooky was insistent about pushing her wares. If Kooky thought that customers weren't downing the goods fast enough, she would saunter up to them and announce in a thick Greenpoint accent: "Drink up, goils! Dis here is a bar. If ya wanna talk, go to choich and talk in a pew!" And then she'd make the customers order another drink. The trick, therefore, was to keep a glass looking full while appearing to be constantly sipping it. Customers could pretend to be drinking vodka straight up when it was really water (though the drinks tasted mostly like water anyway). This was a risky strategy, as Kooky was not above taking a sip or a sniff of a drink to make sure it was genuine. Kooky was mean, but she wasn't stupid. If anyone contradicted her, she would remove the cigarette that dangled perpetually from the corner of her mouth, pinch it between the nails of her immaculately carmined thumb and second finger, and place it ash upward under the miscreant's chin until the customer bought another drink—or left. The bouncer and the two money collectors obeyed her orders, so even the toughest butch knew better than to be disrespectful to Kooky's face.

The constant pressure to drink, the dismal and oppressive atmosphere, and the lack of alternative spaces for lesbians to socialize in must have contributed to the high rate of alcoholism in the New York lesbian community at the time. The bar lesbians were in no position to rebel against Kooky's dictatorship. Instead, they put their energy into creating a network of friends and allies within the bar. Furthermore, what today would readily be recognized as alcoholism was ignored or considered an acceptable part of an evening out. I have since been surprised by the number of women who have confessed to me that they are recovering alcoholics.

But if Kooky and the bouncers bullied their customers, they protected them as well. They kept most straight men from wandering into the bar, which prevented fights between the butches and the men or between the bouncers and the intruders. But occasionally they let in a few men they knew. These generally weren't gay men—the bars were fairly segregated in terms of gender and race, too, not that anyone dared complain. Perhaps the straight men were Kooky's friends or members of the mob. They usually just had a few quiet drinks. Some were "dyke daddies" who would stand around the edge of the dance floor in the back and rub their crotch as they watched the women dance.

I was afraid of Kooky—what sane person wouldn't be?—but I wasn't the kind of person she noticed. But there were other things I was actually more terrified of. The drinks were expensive but watered down, and I feared there wasn't enough alcohol in them to kill the germs on the glasses, which were none too clean: A slosh in dirty water between customers was all the washing they got. It was rumored—perhaps unfairly—that people got hepatitis drinking out of those glasses. Only dapper butches drank beer right from the bottle. And then the fire exit was chained shut, probably in an attempt to keep out gate-crashers. But with all those cigarettes waving in the air, I sometimes envisioned myself caught in a nasty inferno that would leave me not only dead but also outed to everyone who knew me.

What scared me most was the prospect of being caught in a bar raid. Police were the most likely to raid gay and lesbian bars at election time, when officials were promising to "clean up" the city—meaning, they would rid it of gay people and prostitutes. A law against masquerading—that is, disguising oneself—was invoked as a pretext for persecuting gay people. When the police raided a lesbian bar, they had to release only those customers over the age of eighteen who were wearing three visible pieces of women's clothing. So I scrutinized my attire before I went out for the evening. Unisex clothing—pants that zipped like men's or shirts that buttoned left over right—didn't count as women's clothing. But even customers who evaded arrest might find their lives ruined after a police raid. If the police collected any information, such as a home address, place of work, or school, they often notified landlords, employers, principals or deans, and family members. Lesbians could be deprived of homes, jobs, an education, or even children without the benefit of a trial, without ever having been arrested—all for being in the wrong place at the wrong time.

I often asked myself whether going to Kooky's was worth the risky combination of potential arrest, bad booze, and high prices. I certainly would not have wanted my family to spot me in a police lineup with Kooky's customers. If busted, I hoped I could claim I was doing an educational research project.

But no matter what I said, I just didn't *look* as if I fit in. I had given up wearing a "flip," along with the hair spray that held it in place, and instead had grown my hair down below my shoulders in a thick wavy mass, under which dangled silver earrings. I often wore pants with boots, but I also liked loose A-line dresses or mu-mus with a pair of sandals, attire that clearly had "flower child" or "hippie" written all over it. This was not traditional femme-wear, which in those days consisted of dresses or tailored outfits. The femmes teased their hair, wore lots of makeup, and carried purses that matched their shoes. Some of them looked as if they had escaped from a bad beach blanket movie starring Annette Funicello. Since I looked so different, the first question I was often asked in Kooky's—sometimes with hostility and sometimes with simple curiosity—was, "What are you—butch or femme?" I wished they would ask my name first! To fend off these undesirable suitors, I would answer: "Gee, I'm butch Mondays, Wednesdays, and Fridays and femme Tuesdays, Thursdays, and Saturdays. On Sundays, I'm kiki [a woman who played both roles]. What day is this?" That would send most scurrying off for another drink. Often the experience would drive me to another drink as well. The more I looked around the bar, the more I thought that maybe I really was straight. There were few people I could identify with there. I never got the hang of the rules, never mentioned that I was a graduate student, and I made no friends.

Despite being shy and awkward, I did occasionally manage to strike up a conversation with a pleasant woman over a few drinks and then go home with her. We would have hot and passionate sex, but by morning we would discover we had nothing in common. The next time we saw each other in Kooky's, we'd nod a greeting, then look away.

One night I left Kooky's with a former nun. Though Mary had been out of the convent for several years, she made love hungrily with her hands, tongue, and thighs. She clung to me like a sailor to a life preserver. She seemed to be making up in one night for all those years of deprivation. I felt the same way. But after dating her for a while, I began to feel like her mistress because she already had a live-in lover in Trenton, New Jersey. Unwilling to be second best, I dropped her.

Finally, I met a woman who asked me what my name was rather than whether I was butch or femme. She offered me a cigarette, bought me a drink, and told me to call her Hal. We danced to a few Johnny Mathis singles that reminded me of bad high school parties in mildewed basements. I was not the romantic sort. But she was a good dancer, pressing her hand firmly into the small of my back and leading me competently—and sexily—around the dance floor. I put my head on her shoulder and relaxed. I could see right off that she was butch, but she didn't seem quite as macho as many of the other women in the bar. If I had to choose, it was easier for me to be femme than butch. Though she was wearing a white T-shirt under a blue long-sleeved men's oxford shirt, her hair came down over her collar, and it wasn't slicked back. She seemed completely flat-chested: I wondered whether she was wearing a binder, as some of the butch women did to flatten their breasts. I doubted that she would pass the three-pieces-of-women's-clothing test—or that she cared.

I was lonely, so when she asked me to go home with her, I did. We drove to Queens, a borough I had visited so rarely that it seemed very far away. When we got to her apartment, she started to undress herself rather unceremoniously. Much to my shock, her torso and arms were completely tattooed with the names of women. Each name had its own design—and, I suspected, its own story. Oh great. I was living a version of Ray Bradbury's *Illustrated Man:* I had apparently landed a date with the Illustrated Woman. There was one vacant spot over her heart, where I imagined my name flashing in neon colors. I must have blanched. Though writing and decor on the body are common today, I had never seen tattoos except on sailors. I had learned in college that such decorations were a sure sign of psychopathology.

"What's wrong?" she asked. She was so used to those tattoos that she probably didn't even notice them anymore.

"Sorry, it's later than I thought. Gotta go." I didn't stick around long enough for her to protest my lame excuse. I slapped on my jacket and charged out her door.

Though I dated over a hundred women after that, my experience with the tattooed butch generally cured me of picking up women in bars, though I did lapse once or twice. I continued to visit Kooky's occasionally, in spite of my realization that it was probably impossible for me to meet someone suitable. And every bad experience with a woman helped me try to fool myself into believing that I was really heterosexual. So when things went wrong with Mary and then Hal, I sauntered over to the West End Bar, a Columbia-area straight hangout, and struck up a conversation with Mike, a guy sitting at the bar. He was a blue-collar worker in a factory; he was uneducated but smart. He was rugged and handsome, the kind of guy who smoked Camels, yet still had a flashy white smile. My mother would have hated his hands, stained yellow from cigarettes and calloused from his work. A few days later we became uncomplicated lovers.

Though I could have used some help sorting out my sexual proclivities, my parents were useless when the topic was sex. Both of them seemed too embarrassed to raise the subject of the "facts of life" with either my brother or me. Once my mother tried to broach the topic. "My mother didn't tell me anything about sex," she started, "and I don't want to be like her. Sex between two people can be beautiful, and I'd like you to feel free to ask me anything you want."

"Okay, what's a blow job?"

"That's too disgusting to talk about!" she shrieked. We never mentioned the "S" word again.

My father was no more eloquent on the topic. When my brother started college, my father coughed, blushed, and finally stammered, "Son, if you have to do something, use something." His advice, which could have meant several things, would have made sense only to someone already sexually experienced.

Consequently, I floundered around on my own trying to find a suitable companion. The only real soul mate I found in the fall of 1968 was a tuxedo cat from a hippie commune a few blocks away. He was a few months old, and he had huge ears and a prominent nose. I thought he was gorgeous in an ugly way. He seemed to be living out of the commune's garbage can and on the drugs the hippies dropped on the floor. They warned me that this kitten was particularly fond of marijuana and had taken acid but was otherwise normal. I took him home and named him Ringo Lloyd Starr (the middle name was to avoid confusion with one of the Beatles). Soon Ringo seemed to be suffering from loneliness even more than I was. He started to fling himself at the door when I tried to leave and wouldn't eat while I was gone. As there had been lots of other cats wandering around the commune, I decided to find him a companion. I located a female calico kitten I thought would do. She was as retarded as Ringo was bright, but he patiently made sure she found her cat food, and he looked the other way when she tried to eat the kitty litter. I named her Pooh, the cat of little brain. Ringo was a pet I could love. He, in turn, was utterly devoted to me and kept Pooh as a pet of his own.

So I was making do without a woman lover, and all might have gone well with Mike and my newfound pets had I not gone cycling one day by myself. Even with much less time for sports than I had had during college, I often went biking around Central Park on my three-speed girl's English racer. I usually pedaled down Broadway to West 96th Street as it was safer to ride on a well-trafficked street, but one day I lazily decided I would take a shortcut east across 107th Street and into the park entrance on West 102nd Street.

I was peddling along in first gear on my red bicycle (bright colors are definitely the best for attracting the attention of wandering muggers) when I spotted a gang of six boys in my rearview mirror. The boys peddled toward me. I did the natural "feminine" thing: I shrieked. I switched the bike into third gear and peddled as fast as my legs could revolve. There I was, totally alone, peddling my way over sewer covers, flattened beer cans, bottle tops, and broken glass and around drunken pedestrians. When my leg muscles gave out, one of the boys pulled in front of me. I crashed into the back of his bike, flew over a car, and tumbled down a flight of cellar steps.

I landed face upward. I felt searing pain as my back crunched under me. I lay there wondering whether I could get up and fearing that I was about to be raped. But it turned out that I had peddled onto another gang's turf. While the two gangs fought, some adults helped me retrieve my bike and make it home.

I lay in bed all weekend, but the pain got worse. I couldn't straighten out my right leg. It was now bent at a right angle to my hip, like a chicken wing, and hot pain was shooting down the hamstring. I couldn't feel any sensation in the sole of my right foot. I hated doctors, but I knew I needed help. I called the family physician who had told me to leave home and reported that I had hurt my hip falling down a flight of steps—I didn't think insurance would pay if it turned out that I was a crime victim who had failed to report the incident. He sent me to an orthopedist, who X-rayed my hip and lower back. I knew I was in trouble when the technician brought me back in for more X rays.

"Roll over," the technician commanded as I tried to climb onto the table.

"If I could roll over, I wouldn't be here." The technician had to see the logic of this, so he rolled me over himself.

Afterward I sat in the waiting room and hoped that all I was suffering from was a sprain. The doctor finally came out. Half dragged by him, half hobbling, I followed him into his office.

He pointed to the X rays. "You have two fractured lumbar vertebrae, and a piece of a dorsal vertebrae has chipped off." On the film I could see a small piece of my spine floating in the darkness around it. "Really, I'm amazed you can walk. It's a good sign, but I don't know if you'll ever be able to straighten out your right leg. You need to go into the hospital and be put in traction."

For me, this was a horrifying suggestion, conjuring up memories of my mother's sojourns in various hospitals around the city. I was terrified and refused to go. The doctor became more aggressive. "Look, you think it hurts in your hip, but it's your back—here!" And with that he slapped me in the middle of my back, probably not all that hard, but it caused excruciating pain to shoot down my leg. The bottom of my right foot tingled, and I could feel my two smallest toes curl.

Despite the agony, I still refused to be hospitalized. Even worse than the intense pain was a vision of myself in traction in a hospital bed while my mother stood over my helpless body and lambasted me for my stupidity. As a result, I never told my parents that I had fractured my spine.

My phone conversations with them over the next few months were limited to my describing the cats' athletic activities and dodging requests to visit them.

The doctor's bullying tactics were no match for my fears that hospitalization would turn me into my mother or leave me at her mercy. He finally agreed to have some traction set up for me at home and had a brace made for my back. The contraption was a corsetlike affair that covered my torso from over my breasts to my hips. Two steel rods contoured to the shape of my back slid in the back of the brace. In scenes worthy of *Gone with the Wind*, friends laced me into the corset, which I had to wear at all times, except when I was in the shower.

I spent the next couple of weeks in my bed, with a thick board under the mattress. Mike came over with food. Sometimes he helped me limp to the bathroom or into the shower. Ringo hardly ever left the bed. He lay next to me and rested his huge head on my left thigh. The doctor provided painkillers. If I took a few, I was still in agony, but my mind became completely disconnected from my body.

Other friends came by with food for me, mostly cake and candy. As I wasn't traveling farther than the bathroom, the corset contraption started to get tighter and tighter. When I finally weighed myself again a few months later, I had gained almost fifty pounds.

One of my neighbors had recently become a Buddhist. She felt that Western male medicine, which held out little hope for my full recovery, was failing me, and she sent over a friend who was a yogi. He taught me how to meditate and gave me a book about Zen Buddhism. The yogi inspired me to become a vegetarian. It seemed right to live in harmony with nature. It made no more sense for a butcher to kill a cow for me than for American soldiers to kill the Vietnamese for "my country." Under the yogi's care, every day I visualized my leg becoming stronger; then I would try to straighten it a little bit. I'd imagine running with the wind whipping through my long hair. Gradually, I could straighten my leg out. The pain was a constant companion, but when I meditated, I could forget about it for a while.

For almost two months I spent most of my time lying on my back or on my left side with my knees bent. In this position I couldn't do much;

it was almost impossible to read, and I didn't own a television. I found myself doing a lot of thinking. I thought about how many times in my life I had been a victim of violence. There was the thoughtless violence in my parents' house, my mother's insane outbursts, and my father's frustrations, which sometimes exploded into physical abuse, such as a slap of his hand or a beating from his belt. And now there was the equally senseless violence of street gangs. As an adult I had been mugged a few times, always by men. Was it my imagination, or were men becoming more violent? Didn't they used to just grab a woman's purse and run? Once when I was commuting to middle school on the subway—I was thirteen or fourteen—I reached for some tissues in my coat pocket only to discover that a man's hand was there. Not for the Kleenex, I supposed. But when I looked up, not exactly into his eyes because he was wearing dark sunglasses, he had the courtesy to turn his head away and leap off at the next stop before I could even consider what to do. He was clearly ashamed, but now men seemed proud of their violent intrusions into others' lives.

Male violence was everywhere, sanctioned and unapologetic. The Columbia uprising had demonstrated the violence of the police. In Vietnam, American soldiers were killing people for practicing politics that was inconvenient for the U.S. government. And probably for looking different, too. True, American soldiers were being injured and killed. But a woman on the streets of New York could be injured or killed, too, and no one offered us battle pay to leave our homes.

I needed to learn to defend myself. I never wanted to be a victim of male violence again. The male Left and the antiwar movement, I realized, were addressing only small fragments of the complex puzzle of male aggression in the family, in the streets, and among nations. I decided to join the burgeoning women's movement and end male violence altogether.

☙   ☙   ☙

Aha, I see where this story is going," my young friend Gloria re-marked after reading a draft of this chapter. "Your memoir is all about bodies—bodies as sites of loneliness, alienation, physical pain. Your shift-ing identity is so poststructural. Queer theorists are going to love this stuff."

Perhaps like the monkey who picked stocks by throwing darts and beat the financial experts, I have more knowledge than I am aware of. Certainly, I write and teach theory now, but it has never occurred to me that I was living it back then. For a moment I considered whether Glo-ria is right. We did believe that identities were freely chosen, not inborn. But no one back then knew about social constructionism—we were ar-dent existentialists, weaned on Albert Camus and Jean-Paul Sartre.

"I see your point, but back then it wasn't at all about bodies, but about what people did or refused to do with their bodies. Whether you went to war or went to Canada to dodge the draft. Whether you acted as the oppressor or the oppressed. Whether you fought for civil rights or looked the other way and pretended everyone was equal. Whether you got married or were into free love. Besides, being female or Black or gay was considered a fixed group identity, not a 'performance.' Though I'm a poststructuralist now, it wasn't about theories then. It was about dreams and struggles."

I paused and sighed. "I don't know what theorists will think, but I can tell you one thing for sure. If Martin Luther King, Jr., had stood on the Washington Mall and told the crowd, 'I have a dream that . . . we will deconstruct the white hegemony,' there'd still be segregation in the South and gay liberation would be a lavender fantasy."

3

Redstockings

In September 1968 I started graduate school. Not long before, Jerry Rubin, Abbie Hoffman, and other radicals had disrupted the Democratic National Convention in Chicago. The street actions and subsequent arrests (which led to the famous trial of the Chicago 8) had demonstrated that antiwar protests and outcries against a racist society were escalating. The conflict in Vietnam was the first war that Americans had watched on television. Images of tearful Asian women and naked children running from napalm bombs and footage of bloodied soldiers on both sides of the conflict filled the nightly news.

In the wake of other political upheavals, the radical Women's Liberation Movement began to organize. Many of the founders of early feminist groups were former members of such leftist groups as SDS or had participated in the Civil Rights Movement, some by working on voter registration drives in the South.

On September 8, 1968, I read a story in the *New York Times* about a group of feminists who had rallied on the Atlantic City boardwalk the day before to protest the Miss America pageant. These angry women, the paper reported, had threatened to burn their bras and had crowned a live sheep Miss America. The sentiments of the protesters could be summed up in the title of a subsequent piece in the *Village Voice* with the headline "Atlantic City Is a Town with Class—They Raise Your Morals While They Judge Your Ass."

I discovered later that much of what had been reported in the press was pure myth. No fire had been set; no bra had been torched. If one Playtex Living Bra had gone up in foul, rubber-scented smoke, it would have taken the entire wooden boardwalk with it. In reality, the protesters had filled a garbage pail with tokens of women's oppression, including girdles, makeup, and girlie magazines. Though the press claimed that the hundred or so female demonstrators had refused to talk to an indifferent or hostile male mob, Leah Fritz, a plump, middle-aged essayist who had abandoned *Screw* magazine for feminism, cheerfully offered men and women alike leaflets about the action as she puffed on her ever-present cigarette.

Alix Kates Shulman, a feminist activist who was writing about and inspired by Emma Goldman, had got some of the protesters tickets into the pageant itself. Once inside, they unfurled women's liberation banners while the outgoing Miss America made her farewell remarks, and according to Susan Brownmiller (later the author of *Against Our Will*, a groundbreaking book about rape), they released a stink bomb as well. Robin Morgan, who had developed media savvy while playing Dagmar on the popular 1950s TV show *I Remember Mama*, had orchestrated full press coverage.

I eagerly read every detail from the sidelines, as fascinated and ambivalent as I had been during the Columbia student uprisings the previous spring. To a large degree I cheered the feminists on. After all, they were protesting on behalf of every young woman who had been taught by her mother that becoming Miss America was the pinnacle of patriotic womanly success and should be our highest aspiration. But did Miss America have any brains? Any serious professional or political ambitions? Did anyone care? In 1968 fifty women parading down a runway in swimsuits was television at its raciest. True, the contestants were partly judged on "talent"—they twirled batons, sang songs, or played musical instruments. In an "interview" they cheerily provided trite answers to

vapid questions. But everyone knew that
the bathing suit competition came on.
I certainly couldn't identify with Miss A
values she represented. Although the contest
contemporary entrants, they all seemed vi
own dresses. I, meanwhile, had slept with
couldn't even thread a needle. If this was An
wonder I felt like a freak.

Feeling different was not a new experience fo   ... nen I was in elementary school, my mother fantasized, in one gingerbread corner of
her hyperactive imagination, that I was a dainty girlchild who would
doubtlessly develop into a superlatively glamorous and feminine
woman. Then there was her real daughter, me. I preferred dungarees to
dresses. I played stickball with the boys and ignored the Ginny dolls and
their frilly outfits that my mother bought for my birthday and
Hanukkah. "Other girls perspire—you sweat!" my mother snarled at me.

Undeterred by the real child in front of her, my mother was determined to remold me into Miss America, or at least one of the models
who represented the pageant's primary sponsor, Toni Home Permanent.
Each September, instigated by Toni's promises of silky, richly waved hair,
my mother—and probably thousands like her—whipped out the lye-
drenched, noxious potion, then sent me off to school with my stiffest
curl forward. Years later just hearing the Miss America theme song made
my nose crinkle from the remembrance of curlers past. My mother, with
an absence of memory that verged on innocence, would ask me, "What
happened to your hair? It used to be *so curly!*"

So in part I felt the protesters were out there fighting the war I had
never won with my own mother and with Toni. But as I watched the action from the sidelines, I didn't entirely support the Miss America protest
either. If women's liberation was supposed to be "prowoman," weren't
feminists mocking not only Miss America but also the aspirations of mil-
lions of other women? Didn't the women who entered such contests do
so voluntarily? Hadn't the contest launched the careers of women such
as Bess Myerson? My family, including me, revered Myerson, who had

erica contest in 1945, as a woman who had broken the
rs for Jewish women in a culture that favored blond WASPs
ed Semitic features as undesirable or downright ugly. To my
y, Myerson was for Jews what Jackie Robinson, the first black player
on a white baseball team, was to African Americans.

Despite my reservations, I was excited and intrigued by the feminists' radical daring. Poring over alternative papers like the *Village Voice,* I discovered that the Miss America protesters were part of a wider movement of radical feminists. Part of me longed to seek them out, but I couldn't imagine that I would ever find time for political action. My days were taken up with work, my evenings with graduate courses, and my spare time with meditation and exercises geared to mending my fractured spine.

Moreover, just as I began to pay serious attention to what the press said about feminists, the fledgling movement was already splintering. In fact, the Miss America protest was probably the only action taken by New York Radical Women (NYRW). By January 1969 various factions were starting to emerge. Though feminists routinely blamed internal divisions on class differences, many of the pioneers of the second wave of the Women's Liberation Movement were smart and ambitious. Vying for leadership, these women undermined the ideal of equality. Shulamith Firestone—an intense and brilliant young woman who was completing work on *The Dialectic of Sex,* a treatise on sexual politics that she published in 1970—reportedly turned up at the January meeting with a speech, though no one had asked her to write one. Radical feminists believed in rotating work assignments, but many of them did not want to do the "shit work," perhaps because nearly all were white middle-class urbanites who had already cleaned up after the male Left.

By the end of January 1969 radical feminists had split into three groups: Redstockings, The Feminists, and WITCH (Women's International Terrorist Conspiracy from Hell). They agreed to meet together once a month and otherwise went their separate ways. WITCH was the only group that already had a distinct identity. Its leaders included Robin Morgan; Cynthia Funk, the heiress to the Funk and Wagnalls' fortune; Peggy Dobbins, a former member of SDS; and Florika, a former member of the New Left. Inspired by the Yippies (the leftist, anarchist group led by Abbie Hoffman and Jerry Rubin), WITCH's actions took the form of humorous and imaginative "zaps"—colorful and well-orchestrated public and political protests that always attracted the media. For an inaugural action on Halloween 1968, WITCH members dressed up as sorceresses and hexed the New York Stock Exchange and other Wall Street financial institutions. Were they effective? The market fell that day and the next. More importantly, their rowdy presence on Wall Street was an insistent reminder that not everyone was happy with the capitalist status quo.

Redstockings, meanwhile, had a more intellectual bent. It initially attracted some of the most dynamic members of NYRW, including Kathie Sarachild (Amatniek) and Carol Hanisch, activists with experience in the Civil Rights and antiwar movements; Irene Peslikis and Pat Mainardi, two visual artists; and Ellen Willis, a feature writer for the *Village Voice*. Other founding members included Barbara Mehrhof, Pamela Kearon, Barbara Kaminsky, and Sheila Cronan. The group called itself "Redstockings" in honor of nineteenth-century female intellectuals who were derided as "Bluestockings." While WITCH engaged in public theater, Redstockings set about forging a philosophy and set of manifestos.

The Feminists was synonymous, for most people, with the charismatic Ti-Grace Atkinson. She had originally been among the leadership of the National Organization for Women. In 1968 Ti-Grace was the president of the New York chapter, and many believed that NOW founder Betty Friedan was grooming Ti-Grace for a leadership role. Like me, Ti-Grace was repelled by NOW's organizational aspects. Hoping to find like-minded feminists interested in social progress for women, I had attended a few meetings in late 1968 and early 1969. I was disappointed by the homogeneity of the membership and the bureaucracy that was rigidly in place. There were endless subcommittees and reports. Although NOW was run "democratically," many radical women no longer trusted *Robert's Rules of Order* as a credible way to operate.

When I first saw Ti-Grace at a NOW meeting, she seemed to blend in perfectly. Her tall, slim body was neatly attired in prim outfits; her light brown hair was neatly coiffed. She spoke crisply, pronouncing every syllable with equal emphasis. To me, her flat, announcer-perfect American English signified someone who would be comfortable in a country club. But her ideas were truly radical. Atkinson supported the total repeal of all abortion laws (and had done so as early as 1967), defining the fetus as a "product of reproductive process in the womb from the end of the third month of pregnancy until birth"—a piece of "woman's property" that a pregnant woman should be able to dispose of at any point until she conferred "child-status" on it. NOW was more inclined to work on the "reform" of abortion laws, a process that would legalize abortion but not make it affordable for poor women. Atkinson tried unsuccessfully to radicalize NOW by instituting assignments by lots rather than elections, a philosophy she would later bring to The Feminists. The membership of NOW couldn't have been more horrified if she had tried to introduce a lottery from Shirley Jackson's short story of the same name, in which the unlucky winner is stoned to death. Frustrated by NOW's intransigence, Ti-Grace finally broke with the group on October 17, 1968, and began to form what would become The Feminists.

I was still following the actions of these groups by reading the *Village Voice* as well as *Rat* and the *East Village Other,* alternative, or "underground," newspapers. I finally joined the Women's Liberation Movement in February 1969 when two stories grabbed my attention and convinced me to join the action. First, members of WITCH pasted the city with stickers that urged, "Confront the Whore-makers" (a playful version of the antiwar slogan "Confront the War-makers"). Then the group hexed a bridal fair at Madison Square Garden and denounced the prospective brides as "slaves." I was thrilled by the boldness of the action but felt it, like the Miss America protest, was antiwoman. How could the women who attended this fair—presumably women who were already planning a wedding—not feel denigrated by being called slaves and whores when marriage had always been promoted as the positive alternative to the life of a spinster or a slut? Marriage might be slavery, but we had to offer a positive alternative before we encouraged women to abandon matrimony. And since Robin Morgan was herself married, wasn't her attack on prospective brides rather hypocritical? In *Going Too*

Far (1978), Robin noted that "the Bridal Fair protest was a new low for us in our pattern of alienating all women except young, hip, Leftist ones like ourselves. . . . We then compounded our exercise in How Not to Stage a Demonstration by releasing five white mice inside Madison Square Garden—which of course scared and consequently humiliated the brides and their mothers, not to mention the extent to which it scared and humiliated the mice." I felt there was an uneasy tension between so-called feminism and the aspirations of the average woman. Even if I didn't call myself a feminist yet, I already had a prowoman analysis of events, just as I was a lesbian long before I would embrace that label.

The second event that grabbed my attention in the alternative press was a February 13 radical feminist disruption of legislative hearings aimed at slightly modifying New York State's strict abortion laws, which permitted the termination of pregnancy only to save the mother's life. Abortion was under the jurisdiction of individual states: Some banned it altogether, whereas others had prohibitive restrictions such as the consent of several doctors. Where abortion was legal, it often required a very costly in-patient stay. Some physicians punitively sterilized women during the abortion procedure. In 1969, Cindy Cisler, one of the founders of New Yorkers for Abortion Law Repeal, wrote that over 2 million women per year were having themselves sterilized in order to avoid pregnancy. She estimated that about 1 million abortions were being performed every year in the United States, despite the availability of contraception, such as the birth control pill, which had been hailed as the great sexual liberator of the 1960s. Only one out of ten abortions was being performed legally and under sterile conditions.

When I read about the protests at the hearings, I remembered my old roommate Sally and the terrible risk she had taken by having a legal but medically questionable abortion in Puerto Rico. I also thought about Denise, a friend of mine who left college in her sophomore year because she got pregnant. Her parents locked her in their home until she delivered her baby, and then they gave the child away to relatives without Denise's consent. She was never the same afterward. She had been lively and witty. When she returned to college after her delivery, she was depressed and withdrawn. The protesters were right, I thought. Whether women had abortions or decided to bear unwanted babies, we could not win. We needed the option of safe, inexpensive, and legal abortions. It was worthwhile to fight for reasonable choices. So when I saw a flyer advertising a forum and speak-out at Columbia University on the Women's Liberation Movement the very next day—Valentine's Day—I decided to check it out. Several radical women's groups had organized the event to reach out and recruit new members.

First, Ti-Grace went up to the microphone and talked about her group, The Feminists. The group stood for unrestricted choice. It was vital, Ti-Grace emphasized, to debunk patriarchal myths about sexuality and love. She talked about sister feminist Anne Koedt's essay "Myth of the Vaginal Orgasm," which scoffed at Freud's prioritizing of intercourse and insisted that we recognize the clitoris as the main site of female sexual pleasure. Love, said Ti-Grace, is the "psychological pivot in the persecution of women." She also urged celibacy until the revolution was over. I found that an altogether unappealing idea, especially as she didn't seem to have any plans for a sexual alternative if the revolution she envisioned didn't happen in the near future. I didn't think that a reprise of Lysistrata's tactics of depriving men of sex would bring down the patriarchy. Ti-Grace talked big (and well) but was quite vague about how many members The Feminists had, and I surmised that there were probably very few.

Next, representatives from Redstockings talked proudly about their role in the disruptions of the abortion hearings and their plans for a speak-out in March. They told the audience that they stood for a "prowoman" line—that is, they would participate only in actions that benefited all women and only women. They repudiated zaps that attacked any woman at all, no matter how privileged. "All women are our sisters," Kathie Sarachild, one of Redstockings' founders, announced. I stood up and cheered from my seat. Women, they insisted, needed to learn, through a process they called "consciousness-raising," or "C-R," that they were oppressed as a class. Although Redstockings defined men in Marxist terms as a social class that oppressed women, they seemed bent on struggling with men rather than abandoning them.

I was tired of being a spectator and not a participant. After the presentations, people milled around, writing down telephone numbers. I considered which group to join. I was particularly drawn by Redstockings' insistence on a prowoman line. The group's position clearly articulated the ambivalence I had felt toward many of the actions I had read about. Redstockings wouldn't ask me to turn on another women or give up sex until after the revolution. I did feel hesitant, however, about the notion of consciousness-raising. Though the representatives claimed C-R wasn't therapy, it sure sounded like therapy. Would C-R just be endless sessions in which everyone sat around complaining about the pain of being a woman? I wasn't sure, but C-R still seemed worth looking into. If I made some friends and allies within the Women's Liberation Movement, that would make C-R worthwhile. So when the Redstockings' representatives told the two dozen women gathered around them that they would soon be opening a storefront office on Avenue A in the East Village and that they would be forming new C-R groups, I marched over to the woman holding a clipboard and added my name and telephone number to the contact sheet.

A month went by, and I heard nothing. I was wondering whether the group had disintegrated when the *Village Voice* calendar announced that on March 21 Redstockings would hold its own "legislative hearings" on abortion reform. On the morning of the event I took the subway down to a church in the Village that had donated its basement for the "hearings." An old Baby Grand piano filled one corner of the room—suggesting that the space was used for social as well as religious occasions. Redstockings had placed rows of metal chairs in a large circle, the center of which was empty.

Unlike a typical legislative hearing, there was no panel of white men sitting in judgment, no "experts" to tell women what we really needed and wanted. Instead, after Redstockings told us that we could each speak—or choose not to speak—about our own experience with abortion, testimonials began. They were moving and gut-wrenching. Some women confessed to having had more than one abortion. No woman declared that she had had one as an alternative to birth control. Some of the women spoke angrily about what they had gone through; others wept as they recounted their pain, suffering, and sense of loss. No one had taken her experience lightly. I felt lucky to have been spared an unwanted pregnancy. But as I listened, I knew that each woman's story could have been my own. If I forgot to take my birth control pills, the gulf between us would dissolve: One rape or one unplanned sexual encounter would put me in their painful place. I doubted, however, that I would have the courage of these women who stood up, one after another, to admit to having committed an act that was a felony in New York State. The courage of these feminists to dare speak about what so many women had suffered in silence moved me to tears. The event demonstrated the power of Redstockings' ritual of first-person testimonials. Even if I still felt daunted by the prospect of telling my story in public, I could see the benefits of the process.

Later that spring a representative of Redstockings finally telephoned to invite me to a gathering whose purpose was to form new C-R groups. The meeting was held in a run-down, dreary apartment in an East Village tenement. The wooden floors were gray and splintered, a few battered chairs were scattered around the living room, and the windows were so grimy that the bright sunlight took on an oily quality as it slid through the windows.

When I entered, the room was already crowded with women. All of them were white, and almost all of them were my age, though a few older women were present, too. As all the chairs were taken, I found a place in the corner so that I could sit with my back against the wall. Though I had recovered from my fractured spine, I still wore a back brace and walked with a slight rolling motion, like a sailor on shore leave. I found it excruciating to sit without any support for my back.

After a while the room was so packed that latecomers had to stand in the doorway. The meeting got going about a half hour late. First several women introduced themselves as founding members of Redstockings and told us some of the history of the group. Kathie Sarachild, whom I had seen at the Columbia speak-out, did most of the talking. She was slight, with short wavy hair and a boyish face. At first I was convinced she was a lesbian. She must have often been mistaken for one because she quickly indicated that she was straight. Even though all men are the oppressors, she told us, it was crucial to struggle with and change them. I imagined a subtitle under her: "I'm not gay."

Kathie said that she and other Redstockings, including Carol Hanisch (who had moved to Gainesville, Florida), had recently developed a manifesto for the group. Their position paper was the product of long and arduous political analysis. They, the founding members, were political pioneers, Kathie assured us. Then these unheralded seers passed out mimeographed copies of the "Redstockings Manifesto" as solemnly as if it were the Ten Commandments.

The manifesto and other handouts were carved from the same literature and philosophy that had influenced leftist men. Mao Zedong's "little red book" of sayings and bits of the philosophies of Karl Marx, Frederich Engels, Che Guevara, and Franz Fanon were the primary influences. The leaders of Redstockings, in explaining their positions to us that afternoon, maintained that women had more power in socialist countries than in capitalist societies. Redstockings, one leader pointed out, put women first. "Our oppression is just as important as that of men who are dying in the Vietnam War. It's no more glamorous to die in a war in the jungles of Asia than to perish in a back alley in Harlem from an illegal abortion," she said. Then she declared that our oppression was more serious and deeply rooted than any other. After all, the oppression of women preceded the colonization of land and other peoples, and our oppression had never stopped. Women remained isolated in their own homes. Not only did women not have other members of their group to bond with, but also we were all taught as children that other women were "competitors" for husbands, for jobs, for the cheerleading squad. Here we would all be sisters, joined in the oldest and most important struggle.

I would have never dared question the leaders of a group I wanted to join. But after the manifesto had been handed around, a woman named Rita Mae Brown, whom I knew slightly from NYU, pushed into the center of the room from her position in the doorway to take issue with Redstockings, even though it was her first meeting. Why, she demanded, didn't Redstockings have a position on gay women? She began to argue that lesbian relationships were as important for a feminist group to embrace as the struggle to change men.

When I had first met Rita the previous fall, she had had long black hair that fell far below her shoulders and sparkling mischievous eyes. Now her hair was cut short, which emphasized her hard jaw and sharp cheekbones. People often described Rita as beautiful. She was lean and darkly attractive, but that wasn't the heart of her appeal. Hardened New Yorkers were magnetized by her combination of intelligence, boldness, and wry humor. They didn't notice that her charm was as carefully contrived as her southern accent. She would stretch out vowels whenever she wanted to make a point. I found it unlikely that someone who had moved from Pennsylvania to Fort Lauderdale (not exactly the heart of Dixie) as a teenager would pick up such a thick drawl. But, authentic or not, Rita had a presence. When she entered a room, she didn't let anyone forget—ever—that she was there. She spoke her mind, sometimes aggressively, alternately coaxing or bullying us all in the direction of her own needs and issues.

Rita alone had the courage to speak up at that Redstockings' meeting, long before anyone else in New York's feminist circles dared to be openly gay. Back then, apart from early activists such as Phyllis Lyon, Del Martin, and the other pioneering women of Daughters of Bilitis (DOB), few dared to admit in a public setting that they were lesbians. It was one thing to hang out in a gay bar where everyone simply assumed similar sexual proclivities or to be open in a gay student organization. It was quite another to announce one's lesbianism and then demand it take center stage in a room full of straight feminists who were likely to be heterosexists (the word "homophobia" came later) and who had just issued an ultimatum to keep on sleeping with men as part of a program to mend the oppressors' ways. Rita's sharp challenge made Redstockings' program seem quixotic to the point of being delusional: Were these women the oppressed or the oppressors?

After Rita had finished speaking, I sat there as if I had been hit by lightning. I wouldn't have labeled myself a "lesbian" or even a "bisexual." I couldn't have said the word "lesbian" if there had been one kissing me right then. Yet though I felt cowardly in the face of her outspokenness, I was also struck by the degree to which Rita resembled me—not physically, though we both had dark hair and tanned complexions, but in more fundamental ways. Rita was also a graduate student at NYU. She didn't look like a bar dyke and wasn't obviously butch or femme. She was interested in politics instead of the latest baseball scores. The more time I had spent with the denizens of Kooky's, the more I wanted to disassociate myself from them. I found in Rita an unsettling mirror of all that I could be and all that I feared I was.

The leaders of Redstockings were disturbed and threatened by Rita's behavior. They turned the conversation back around to men as our oppressors. Still, they looked uncomfortable. After all, Rita was calling *them* her oppressors when they were insisting that women like them (and us) were the most oppressed people on earth. One of the main tenets of the "Redstockings Manifesto" was, "We identify the agents of our oppression as men. . . . All other forms of exploitation and oppression (racism, capitalism, imperialism, etc.) are extensions of male supremacy: men dominate women, a few men dominate the rest." Although the group's members identified with "the poorest, most brutally exploited women," they would have found it counterproductive, to put it mildly, to be forced to contemplate the ways that working-class women, disabled women, or Third World women (as we called women of color) were far worse off than someone like Kathie, who had attended Radcliffe College. By formulating a Marxist class analysis that emphasized unity among all women and foregrounded sexism as the tool to analyze other oppressions, they had hoped to quell demands by other women that double and triple oppressions receive priority.

I was thrilled at Rita's daring, but I pitied the leadership. The original members of Redstockings had worked so hard to hone their philosophy and embrace new members, and now their worst fears were being realized. They were not being lauded as the pioneers they felt themselves to be. Rather than gratefully following their lead, new members such as Rita Mae Brown were rudely challenging their painstakingly crafted manifesto and lumping them with the oppressor they had struggled to understand and conquer.

But what could they do in the end except invite Rita to join their founding C-R group to help them fight their heterosexism? The rest of the meeting was devoted to assigning us to groups of eight to ten women who would meet one night or weekend day each week. A delegate from the founding Redstockings cell—Group X as they liked to call themselves after women's determining gene—would instruct each new group so that it would follow correct C-R procedures.

I left the meeting feeling exhilarated. There may have been disagreement, but all the arguing was done by *women*. There were no men here to order us to make sandwiches and to clean up while men did the heavy thinking, the way the Columbia "revolutionaries" had done. I believed that Redstockings' combination of feminism and Marxism was a stroke of genius. Analysis of oppression had to precede actions in order to avoid the antiwoman tone that some earlier feminist protests had taken. We had to understand the roots of our oppression in order to unravel it and to overthrow our chains. This group had everything: smart, articulate women; lesbians interested in politics; a political agenda; and concrete goals. I clutched the mimeographed handouts to my chest and couldn't wait for my first C-R group to meet.

෮෭ଃ   ෮෭ଃ   ෮෭ଃ

In December 1997 I attended a Veteran Feminists of America awards dinner, where I was one of the honorees. The event was the feminist equivalent of a college reunion: I knew at least half of the women personally and almost all of the women by name. After all, in 1969 there were probably fewer than five hundred radical feminists in the entire United States.

After dinner each honoree had five minutes at the microphone to represent her group or action. I listened as many of the women recited what novelist Suzy McKee Charnas would call a "self song" about their string of victories in battle. The shared memories were fun, but those who threw in calls to continue the struggle made it clear that their ideology hadn't shifted much.

Carol Hanisch of Redstockings handed out photocopies of her "Resolutions of 1997." Carol's "wish list" for equality in work, dress, education, and employment had changed little from her writings of the late 1960s. Oh yes, there was a mention of AIDS, and there was a new concern for elder and health care. Not surprisingly, the word "lesbian" didn't appear once. Even though her statement mentioned "women privileged by race or class," she still chose not to see that heterosexuality is quite a bonus in a country where the number of hate crimes against gay men and lesbians is alarmingly high.

The decades-old chasm between the straight feminists and myself opened once more in front of me. It's not simply that I'm a lesbian and they're not, though that's certainly part of it. Even with many lesbians present, some of the straight feminists still couldn't get the "L" word out of their mouths. The nongay feminists didn't seem to hate lesbians or distrust us anymore, but I got the feeling they would like us to shut up or disappear. Our queer values and goals are disruptive and embarrassing for those who still want to focus only on abortion rights or anti-pornography legislation. Lesbian erotica is flourishing; maybe straight feminists view us as part of the problem. Perhaps many have forgotten that silence—the conscious or unconscious erasure of lesbian issues—is a form of oppression.

But decades later I was no longer angry at them. Not to change is a form of death, and I saw all too many feminists standing before me frozen circa 1969. Dogma is certainly cheaper than cryonics. They had become Snow Whites (whom we had all despised back then): Now they were the living dead, relics of an uncertain past, feminists under glass.

One person who did change radically over time was Rita Mae Brown. In 1969–1970 she demanded that members of the women's movement tithe their income just as some Southerners gave 10 percent of their money to their churches. Rita was poor then. After she became rich, tithing lost its appeal to her. Her stories of family origin shifted as well. In *Out of the Closets* (1972), which I coedited, she maintained that she was an orphan who didn't know her racial or ethnic origins, but in a recent memoir, *Rita Will* (1997), I was startled to read that she is an abandoned love child with aristocratic ancestors. Now she writes that back then she was more interested in cats, dogs, and horses than in feminists. Perhaps the mystery and the contradictions were part of her undeniable appeal. We all laughed so hard at some of her hilarious accounts of her childhood—anecdotes that appeared almost verbatim in her 1973 novel *Rubyfruit Jungle*—that no one noticed or cared about small discrepancies.

Rita was our Jay Gatsby, someone who had totally reinvented herself once she landed on New York's shores. It was part of her charm, and also part of her failure, that she could always articulate the politics of the moment—demanding radical behavior and separatism when this ideology suited her ends and dropping these feminist goals when she wanted to sell novels and screenplays to a mainstream audience. She modulated her politics as fluidly as her accent. Her chameleon qualities became part of the reason she survived and flourished while so many of the other women I met through Redstockings seemed to suffer from a marked inability to change with the times. Although I recognize the value of her unique contributions to the lesbian and feminist movements, I also realize that probably none of us knew who she really is.

4

A/K/A Jay

The night before the first meeting of my consciousness-raising group I was too excited to sleep. I sat up reading the "Redstockings Manifesto" over and over as if I were going to be quizzed on it. I wondered what we would discuss. I fretted about what I would say about myself. If C-R turned out to be a do-it-yourself form of therapy based on self-confession, I would probably be unhappy enough to leave the group. After all, as a child my survival had depended on protecting family secrets. My brother, Paul, and I had had different protective strategies. He coped by reticence, occasionally punctuated by abrupt commands intended to defend his space: "Shut up! Get outta my room!" My approach was the opposite. I developed an easy, jocular demeanor intended to short-circuit inquiries about anything personal. Even as a small child I understood that no matter how odd I considered my mother, others would think her stranger still. No one would question a lighthearted, smiling child; no one ever did.

On some level feminism frightened me. It seemed invasive. It demanded a certain complaining I didn't want to engage in. I didn't want to hate Mike, my father, or other men. I also didn't fully believe that women were as oppressed as men. Doing housework was a bore, for sure, but it wasn't as lethal as being shipped off to Vietnam or being sent to jail or exile in Canada for refusing to kill others. I had seen women suffer terribly because of their gender, but no one I knew personally had died from it. We hadn't been enslaved like the Hebrew people in Egypt or the Blacks in the South. I didn't want to think of myself as victimized because of my gender. And even though Kathie Sarachild wrote that antifeminists dismissed consciousness-raising because they viewed topics like housework as insignificant, some of us who sided with Redstockings approached such issues with a queasy feeling that they didn't stack up against the larger atrocities of the world.

Now in the spring of 1969 I worried that I wasn't really political enough to make a commitment to feminism. My career and my sexuality were still both uncertain. I liked working in publishing, though I didn't see how I could rise from my menial position as assistant editor to any job worth having. My relationships seemed equally limited. I was still sleeping with Mike, the trophy boyfriend I had nabbed off a barstool. We had a purely sexual relationship. What I liked best about him was how little mental space he absorbed, how little emotional commitment he demanded. I was grateful for the compassionate care he had rendered when I was immobilized by my fractured spine, but I knew better than to confuse gratitude with love. I assumed that I would never feel close to a man or a woman, that prolonged exposure to my parents had made me immune to the type of sentiment that led to marriages like theirs. I was comfortable with my relationships the way they were. I didn't mind sharing a bed with a man or a woman; I just didn't want to spend my life with anyone. I preferred to be alone much of the time and liked the notion of commitment even less than most men did.

Our first C-R meeting took place in the late spring or early summer in the same dingy Redstockings' apartment in the East Village, except this time there were only ten women present. There were eight "recruits," including me. The core Redstockings group was represented by Kathie Sarachild and Alix Kates Shulman. All eight of us arrived at the same time. We stood around gawking at one another like grade-school children thrown together on the first day of school. I felt oddly shy and wondered whether I should make a quick exit.

We sat in a circle and listened eagerly as Kathie gave us instructions. Once we had chosen a topic, we were to start with anyone who wanted to speak first as long as we avoided always beginning with the same person. Each woman was to speak on the topic and to narrate her personal experiences. The listeners were allowed to ask questions to clarify each account, but we were not to challenge the truthfulness of any statements, nor were we to psychoanalyze a woman or her motivations. In "Notes from the First Year" (1968), Redstocking Pam Allen termed this approach creating a "non-judgmental space."

After each woman had spoken, we were then to seek the common core of our oppression as women. For the first few weeks we would analyze our experiences in relation to the "Redstockings Manifesto" to ensure that we were in total agreement with every word of it. As Kathie Sarachild wrote in the 1978 Redstockings collection *Feminist Revolution,* "The aim of going around the room in a meeting to hear each woman's testimony . . . is to help stay focused on a point, to bring the discussion back to the main subject after exploring a tangent, to get the experience of as many people as possible in the common pool of knowledge." The idea was not to be "nice" or to provide "therapy" or to "change women." The whole point was to develop knowledge to overthrow male supremacy.

Before we started speaking, Kathie and Alix gave us a quick history of consciousness-raising. Redstockings did not really invent C-R; the group borrowed the concept from Che Guevara and other Marxist Cuban revolutionaries who were organizing peasants in South America. They, in turn, had adapted a Communist Chinese strategy called "speaking bitterness." When the Communists first attempted to organize the peasants in mainland China, they asked the peasants to speak about their own experiences as oppressed individuals. In the process the peasants understood that they were oppressed as a class, that their suffering was widespread, and that the masters profited from their pain. These understandings galvanized the peasants to revolt.

The same technique, Redstockings assured us, would liberate women. When the world's majority realized the degree to which we were enslaved, we would rise up and overthrow the patriarchy. When women refused to accede to men's demands, men would be forced to grant us equality. Redstockings had developed a nonviolent strategy for revolutionary change. We had to be careful, Alix and Kathie explained, because the government was surely watching our every move. In order to be safe, we would know only the Redstockings in our own cell, and each cell would send only one representative to a monthly meeting. There were no mass membership lists for mailings. If and when we organized demonstrations, each representative would pass information along to her own cell. No one person would know enough other people to endanger the entire group.

After carefully laying out these and other precautions we had to take to protect the group, Alix moved on to the heart of the meeting's business. She read us the first point that we needed to discuss. "Women are an oppressed class. Our oppression is total, affecting every facet of our lives. We are exploited as sex objects, breeders, domestic servants, and cheap labor." We all looked nervously at one another, hoping someone else would volunteer to begin. Finally, Celeste raised her hand. She identified herself as a grandmother in her early fifties. She began to talk about her life as a mother, about which she seemed to feel more nostalgic than bitter. Despite having told us not to interrupt, Kathie kept breaking in to suggest that Celeste was "resisting" consciousness-raising. She claimed that Celeste was "editing" her narrative and leaving things out. Kathie was an intense and astute listener. She also worked as a film editor; perhaps she viewed omissions as a series of discarded clips on the cutting-room floor. Maybe Kathie's points were right, but her approach came off as belligerent. (She would have said "assertive.")

I identified with Celeste. Why should Celeste and the rest of us have to lay our lives out to total strangers? Why was Kathie allowed to interrupt while we were supposed to listen attentively but silently? One of the ideas of consciousness-raising was to give power and space to the "quiet woman." I felt that if I was harshly challenged, I would be more likely to leave than to join a revolution against men. I wondered whether the Redstockings' rules were meant for us but not for the "leaders." I later discovered that some of the members of Group X had interrupted so much that the group had decided to use bingo or poker chips to limit discussion. Each time a woman spoke, she had to turn in one chip. When she was out of chips, she had to shut up.

By the time it was my turn, I realized what was expected of me—some angry account of how I felt oppressed by the men around me. Actually, I felt I had lived a somewhat privileged life in regard to men, but that perspective was going to cause an accusation of "resistance to consciousness-raising." So instead I offered a brief narrative of being "hit on" by guys in college and afterward. Even saying that little made my heart pound. I was chided for being too cautious and mild in my account. Surely, something worse must have happened to me. I tried to look innocent and blank.

After we had finished going around the circle, we struggled to locate the nexus of our very disparate stories. Though we all came from very different places in life—other members included Elsie, a middle-aged social worker; two women who worked in the art world; a retired grandmother; an office manager; a budding screenwriter; Michela Griffo, a graduate student; and me. We were all white and middle class; as a result, it was easy for us to empathize with one another's stories. Comments about the oppressive behavior of fathers, husbands, brothers, and male bosses would elicit a round of appreciative head nodding from all of us as we recognized ourselves in each other's narratives. I felt less alone, and I really did begin to sense my commonality with other women.

We dubbed ourselves "Group A" and agreed to meet again every week. Alix informed us that she was going to be our guide through the process of C-R. I was pleased that we would get Alix, not Kathie. Alix's comments were as perceptive as Kathie's, but Alix radiated sympathy and genuine concern, whereas Kathie appeared indifferent to individual pain in her quest for political "truth." Alix was a beautiful woman in her late thirties with long dark hair, radiant skin, and the sculpted cheekbones of a model. But although Alix certainly could have entered pageants—and won—she wasn't the beauty-obsessed woman she would later write about in her first novel, *Memoirs of an Ex-Prom Queen,* which she published in 1972. Like Kathie, Alix was fully focused on the political struggle against male domination.

Alix turned out to be a graceful and gracious guide to C-R. For the first two weeks she led us gently through the "Redstockings Manifesto." Alix stuck carefully to the principles: Each of us, in turn, made our individual contribution to the evening's topic and then worked together to see how our individual stories were part of our collective experience as women. Alix was never harsh or critical if someone enthusiastically interrupted a narrative with a comment that just couldn't wait. We discussed the ways in which we had been forced to submit to the will of men through "brainwashing, stupidity, or mental illness," and we cataloged the "continual, daily pressure from men." We discussed the ways in which men profited from our oppressed state. We never considered that to a degree we were being indoctrinated by the ideology of the "Manifesto." We never talked, for instance, about how much better off we were than poor women or women of color. We never discussed the fact that we, too, profited from the inequalities of the world or that all our talk was unlikely to change anything.

Once we had finished analyzing the manifesto, we went on to investigate other topics in the order laid out by Redstockings. We dissected our relationships with men. We discussed how we had been raised differently from our brothers. We spoke of our parents' marriages and of their expectations for ours. We debated the pros and cons of being single or married. We laughed at our dating experiences, and we talked about how we were treated at school and work. In the second month we discussed our relationships with other women and what kind of women we were and hoped to become. We compared how we felt about our bodies and discussed our strategies for keeping them safe from men. Some women wore drab or bulky clothing so that men would leave them alone. Some had dieted their bodies away; others had covered them up in protective layers of fat. We all avoided certain streets where men routinely harassed us. We often shared ways in which we had resisted oppression: I had once heaped ten spoons of sugar into the coffee of a male coworker who demanded, "Get me some coffee, will you, hon?" Alix had come up with a pioneering marriage contract that spelled out each party's responsibilities. Because Group A was as confidential as group therapy or a twelve-step group, I cannot divulge exactly what others said during those meetings. During those sessions my life and my attitudes changed, totally and irrevocably. Like a sculptor carving marble, each discussion reshaped my mind in small but indelible ways.

For instance, many of us grappled together and by ourselves with the implications of naming. The most obvious manifestation of this power is the fact that in most countries women bear the surname of their fathers and then of their husbands. A woman "loses" her name when she marries, but in fact she has never had her own name, only her father's. Worse still is the possibility of not having a father because to be "illegitimate" is to lack the imprimatur of patriarchal approval.

Many of the women in Redstockings changed their names in rebellion against the patriarchy, often choosing to use their mothers' names. In addition to being a symbolic gesture, adopting a nom de guerre made it just a tad more difficult for the government to figure out who we were and where our paltry bank accounts were stowed when it came time to incarcerate us. As much as I wanted to drop my patronymic, however, I wasn't eager to claim my mother's name. Instead, I decided to substitute "Jay," my middle initial, for my last name.

When I tried out my new name, Karla Jay, it felt immediately like a more accurate representation of who I was. I realized changing my name was not only about challenging the patriarchy—it was also about untangling my own identity from my family history. I understood for the first time that I had, in fact, always detested my birth name, Karla Jayne Berlin. Well, not all of it. Karla seemed to me an original first name, and I felt comfortable with it. My father hated his own biblical name, Abraham, and preferred to be called Eddie or Butch. His first thought was to name me Gale because I had been born in a blizzard. My mother objected, so he chose my name from a list of freighters he spotted in the shipping news that he read every day in conjunction with his work. I'm lucky, I suppose, that a ship with a name like the *Brunhilde* didn't dock then. Fortunately, the *Karla Dane* steamed into or out of port the week I was born, and my father was determined that would be my name. My mother persuaded him to change my middle name to Jayne instead of Dane, with the addition of an elegant *Y.*

But if I liked my first name, I hated the surname Berlin. For one thing, I'm not German. My ancestors came from the finest shtetls in England, Austria, and Ukraine. My paternal grandfather was from England, and for a long time I supposed that he had been assigned the name of a city when he entered the United States; immigration agents had a way back then of altering what they considered unpronounceable names. Years later, I discovered that my grandfather had changed his name himself. Growing up as I did after World War II, I hated and feared Germans, who had annihilated any relatives I might have had left in Europe. I didn't want to be associated with a bunch of Nazis. Because I attended elementary school during the Cold War, I was often teased about the Berlin Wall. Some children would ask whether my first name was East or West. I didn't find it amusing. Moreover, Berlin was a name that no native Brooklynite seemed capable of pronouncing correctly. Most of my friends pronounced my last name as "Boiling," although they said, "The water is berlin." (People put "earl" in their cars, and "Oil" was a boy in my class.) It was impossible to fight an entire culture—all I could do was "berl" in rage.

I wasn't particularly fond of my middle name either; people often assumed it was hyphenated to my first name. My mother and even Jessica, my best friend, called me Karla Jayne to get my attention when they were angry. As far back as I could remember, I had used my middle initial in place of Jayne. But I did like the "Jay" part. Some of my fond association with the word was based on pleasant times in summer camp. During my first summer there I was only five. I was placed in J-Bunk—probably an abbreviation for Junior Bunk—a place for children considered too young to be away from home for two months. J-Bunk was my first taste of freedom, a fun-filled life in the Catskills. Furthermore, Jay rhymes with "gay."

Changing my name was also a way to "divorce" my parents, to let them know that I had never accepted them in that role. As children my brother and I both fantasized that we had been adopted. I imagined that my mother had found me in Schrafft's, on Flatbush Avenue, a restaurant where Irish waitresses in prim black uniforms with white aprons and white lacy collars served premium ice cream in fancy dishes. I fantasized that someone from a finer family than ours had abandoned me somewhere in the vicinity of the rolls, leaving me with a lifelong urge to eat bread.

I didn't change my name legally until 1978. I felt that it would be a paradox for me to petition a male court to change a name that patriarchal law had imposed on me in the first place. But after I had coedited three anthologies as Karla Jay, only old friends, relatives, and people at work knew that I had any other name. I felt fragmented and decided to hire a lawyer to execute a legal name change.

I have now spent a full three-fifths of my life as Karla Jay. In the rare instances when I run into someone from my childhood or high school who still calls me Karla Berlin, I have the distinct feeling that they have mistaken me for someone else.

But the changes wrought by C-R went well beyond my name. C-R totally altered my vision of who I was and where I was going. It gave me a political tool, a class analysis through which I could (re)view and come to terms with my Dickensian childhood. I trusted C-R in a way I would have never been able to accept psychoanalysis as a process for understanding my own life. Psychiatry had failed my mother, in part because she was a woman. Since mothers weren't paid for their labor, her contribution to society couldn't be measured in capitalist terms. Consequently, the perceived value of enabling her to function normally was less than that of any working man. Also, because she was now almost a senior citizen, she had even less intrinsic worth as a psychiatric patient because she would no longer reproduce or raise children. Perhaps the situation would have been different had we the money to keep her in private institutions or pay for extensive analytical help.

But now in Redstockings part of my evolution was a dramatic shift in how I viewed my family. As a child I had idolized my father. I listened eagerly for his rapid step in the hallway, the jingle of keys in his pocket, the tuneless melody he hummed. He often worked seven days a week, but when he had a day off, usually in the winter, he would take my brother, me, and sometimes my best friend, Jessica, to Coney Island, where he would buy us lunch at Nathan's and amuse himself by watching members of the Polar Bear Club plunge into the frigid Atlantic surf. Paul played skee-ball, while I went on rides, the wilder the better.

I had worshiped my father as my savior. If he had left me in the hands of my mother, I would have been doomed to live in a madhouse with no protection. Whenever he argued with my mother, he insisted that he stayed only "for the sake of the children." I believed that he sacrificed his happiness for mine, and I adored him all the more for it.

In my C-R group I forced myself to consider the side of my father I had never wanted to acknowledge. Whenever my father threatened to leave my mother, as he frequently did, he would say: "I'll take Paul. You can have Karla." He would have abandoned me, his only daughter, but would have felt obliged somehow to raise his son alone despite his heavy work schedule. Perhaps he simply felt that a man could nurture his son, whereas a woman, even one like my mother, should accept responsibility for raising her daughter. But as a child, I saw his willingness to save Paul while abandoning me as one more proof of my female inferiority, and I lived in dread of the day that my father would act on his threats.

There were times during my adolescence when he actually did leave home. He would pack a suitcase and move to a hotel. There weren't too many hotels in Brooklyn, so he wasn't very hard to locate when I needed to find him—he was usually at the St. George in downtown Brooklyn. Anyway, I could always telephone him at the lumberyard where he worked. I felt sorry for him, having to put up with my mother all those years, but after he'd be gone a while, I would beg him to come home. Though I had acted as my mother's parent since Nene, our housekeeper, left when I was eleven, it seemed unfair, even cruel, to make a teenage girl cope with what she could not. Years later relatives told me that sometimes he was not alone in the hotel. No one ever elaborated on whether he had a girlfriend or simply hired prostitutes.

Now that I was recounting the story to my Redstockings C-R group, I realized that he had never intended to leave permanently. Why, I wondered, had he married and stayed with a woman like my mother? He once told me that friends of his had investigated her before his marriage and had warned him not to marry her—that she had a history of mental illness. He dismissed their accusations as jealousy. Perhaps he thought that his friends couldn't believe that a short, fat, homely man like him had won the hand of a slim and glamorous woman.

Our family physician had stated, when he urged me to leave home, that my father's decision to stay with my mother must mean he was just as crazy as she was. At the time it was too awful a truth even to contemplate. Now, years later, as I sat in my C-R group and asked myself the pertinent Redstockings' question about who profited from my mother's mental illness, the answer seemed all too obvious. My father did. Her inability to cope with the stresses of the world was part of what attracted him to her to begin with. From the days of my early childhood when she locked herself in her bedroom, it was apparent that she could never leave him. She couldn't cope with the outside world. She didn't even know how to pay bills anymore. She was virtually unemployable and didn't know how to drive. She had few friends and almost no relations. She was his Rapunzel, sealed in the tower of her hallucinations. Only he, the prince, had the key. The more she attacked herself, and then us, the more miraculous his protection seemed. The more she acted the part of the dragon, the more he appeared to be the knight in the eyes of his children and friends.

Now that my brother and I were long grown up and able to fend for ourselves, it was clear that my father lived with my mother because he chose to. Why? In the late 1980s, only a few years before he died, one of his sisters told me that his childhood had been different from (and perhaps more difficult than) what I had been led to believe. My paternal grandfather was a tireless rake who stopped chasing women only when relatives of a girl he had seduced disfigured and blinded him with lye. My once-handsome grandfather lingered for almost a decade as a hideous invalid. When my father spoke of his family, he often predated his father's death to the moment of the lye attack. Because of my grandfather's inability to work, my father had to support his mother and sisters from an early age. His refusal to leave my mother may have been a reaction to the libertine behavior of his own father or a fear of its dire consequences. Perhaps my grandfather had given my father the habit of sticking by errant relations.

The other members of my Redstockings cell made me wonder how my mother had got that way. To decide that she was born crazy, a product of defective genes, would have put my own sanity in question. I realized that I knew very little about my mother or her own mother, who had died when I was two. I began to ask my mother about herself, and over a period of years she told me bits and pieces. I gathered other information from some of her relatives.

Like my father, my mother had fictionalized some of her family history. My maternal grandmother, I learned, had also suffered from mental illness, so perhaps there was a genetic or learned behavioral component to my mother's illness, whose exact diagnosis I never knew. As a small child I was told that my grandmother had been run over by a motorcycle. According to the official version, the accident led to her death from a cerebral hemorrhage when she was fifty-two. Later I discovered that she had in fact died in the mental ward of a Brooklyn hospital. No one would tell me why she had been committed. My mother once muttered something about "blackouts," and one of my maternal relatives hinted at "spells" that sounded vaguely Victorian. It couldn't have been easy for my mother to grow up with her own parents, and I wondered how much of her behavior was learned from her mother.

In 1973, when I was in my mid-twenties and still unattached to a man, my mother kept urging me to get married. I pointed out to her that she hadn't wed my father until she was in her early thirties. She revealed that she had been married once before then, something that no one had ever mentioned. As a teenager, she had wed her high school sweetheart, Meyer Lipman. Meyer had been diagnosed with a potentially fatal heart condition, but choosing love over common wisdom, my mother eloped with him. When he became ill, she moved him to Florida. She hoped that her devotion and the warm climate would prolong his life. He died anyway, and his family blamed her for his death.

To make her point, my mother invited me into her bedroom and opened her hand-carved mahogany jewelry box. From the hidden recesses of the bottom velvety tray, she carefully extracted a minuscule wedding band and a pin from Erasmus Hall High School with the initials "ML" carved on the back. She placed them in her right palm and held out these relics of her former life for my inspection. I picked up the tiny ring. She would never fit into that ring again, but she had kept it all those years as a tangible proof that she had once had—and lost— another life.

When I was a small child, my mother was still a glamorous woman. She combed the sales racks and picked up fashionable bargains. Whatever her faults, she had impeccable taste. She turned men's heads on the street, and on a few occasions strange men flirted with her right in front of me. She'd point to me and cut them off. I imagine that as a beautiful twenty-year-old widow my mother must have been the object of many unwanted advances from men who assumed that they could sleep with her because she was no longer a virgin. She had married once for love; now she intended to marry for money. And so she chose my father. But as my brother and I grew up, his fortunes declined. Her children didn't turn out the way that she had imagined. Her son was unathletic and refused to become a physician. Her daughter was a "man-hating feminist" who didn't shave her legs.

Though each member of my C-R group experienced private epiphanies just like mine, there were limits to the powers of consciousness-raising. For one thing, we came from different ethnic and religious backgrounds, and our diversity created inevitable barriers to unity. According to one woman I spoke to later about Group X, Barbara Kaminsky was vocal in Group X about the need for class analysis. She reportedly said that she wasn't going to do consciousness-raising with richer women who weren't willing to share money with her. Many of the Redstockings didn't like to discuss their own privilege—their Seven Sisters educations, their well-paid jobs, the leisure a few might have gained from patriarchal inheritances, or their husbands' jobs that enabled them to write and organize.

Even more seriously, hard-core Redstockings would never admit that there were any possible flaws in the process of consciousness-raising itself. Each topic would elicit painful memories and experiences for at least one of us. It must have been excruciating for some members of my

C-R group to discuss date rape, childhood abuse, parental incest, and a host of other iniquities that had been perpetrated on them. Even more horrifying was to lay those issues out for a group that would use them as a part of a larger political agenda but that lacked the analytical tools to grapple with the effects of that pain on a particular woman. Expressions of support did not substitute for the kind of professional intervention some group members needed. The fact that any atrocity was considered part of a larger global pattern of abuse was often of little consolation to the woman who had bared her soul. Sometimes women who spoke of horrifying experiences seemed too dazed to even understand the implications or magnitude of what had happened to them. Sometimes they seemed to be drowning in a sea of personal pain. Either way collective political analysis seemed a distant, difficult, or downright irrelevant way to approach their suffering.

We were unprepared and untrained to negotiate trauma. Many of us had been rejected or betrayed by our families, friends, or lovers. Most of us were in our early twenties, and few of us had really figured out how to work through our problems. My own reaction to violent expressions of pain or anger was to shut down or withdraw emotionally with the smooth speed of a merchant slamming an iron gate in front of his store. In a second, I was in a safe distant zone, while the shell of my body sat like an attentive statue.

When we failed to deal with individual pain except as part of a larger political issue, several original members of our cell drifted away. Some joined twelve-step groups such as Alcoholics Anonymous or became goddess worshipers. Others sought personal salvation in their work. These days, critics such as Celia Kitzinger and Rachel Perkins, in their book *Changing Our Minds* (1993), lambaste twelve-step groups and other therapies and nostalgically suggest a return to feminist process. The unpleasant truth is that back then we simply didn't know how to alleviate the suffering of our sisters and the addictive habits they embraced to cope with their pain. I'm not convinced we'd do any better now.

Those like me who could intellectualize about our experiences and dissect them with the objectivity and precision of a surgeon were the ones who found the C-R process beneficial and who stayed on. Though

I would have supposed that such sharing of a person's deepest secrets would lead to intimate friendships, in fact we shared little outside of the group except for political actions.

The founding members of Redstockings saw C-R as a panacea for the world's ills and would never admit that there were limits to the process. Those of us who had not formulated the ideology were less wed to its tenets. Sometimes at the monthly meetings of cell representatives, we suggested that procedures be altered slightly. But some of the founding members reacted as if we were tinkering with divine revelation. They insisted that newer members just didn't understand, but that after we had been Redstockings as long as they had, we would see that they were right. They wouldn't—or couldn't—admit that this assertion was ridiculous, for no matter how long women like me were in Redstockings, the founders would have always been there longer.

In truth, many of the founding members wanted to be acknowledged as pioneers, but feminist politics of equality forbade them from declaring themselves our "leaders." We newer feminists did have a lot to learn from them, and we were grateful for their ovular work; we didn't simply want them to step aside now that they had laid the groundwork. Yet they were bitterly opposed to sharing power. The founders rejected any push for change as treason; dissenters were simply made to feel so unwelcome that they left the group. By late spring 1969 Linda Feldman, Barbara Mehrhof, Pam Kearon, and Sheila Cronan had all left Redstockings for The Feminists. Shulamith Firestone left in the fall to found New York Radical Feminists with Anne Koedt, who had quit The Feminists. Our leaders covered up the defections by inflating the number of Redstockings. They hinted—remaining vague and mysterious in the name of security—that the group had two hundred members, but I believe there were only fifty or sixty and perhaps a total of two hundred women actively involved in radical feminism in New York City.

Those of us who remained in Redstockings struggled with a double standard of behavior that divided founders from newer members. We were often assured that we were all sisters and that chores would be divided up by lot or some other equalizing means. Yet newspapers and other media always interviewed the same founding members of Group

X, who spoke on behalf of all Redstockings with no apparent qualm. Those in Group X would often point to the exigencies of time as the rationale for hogging the limelight; after all, the press telephoned them one day for a story that had to appear the next. The fact that one or two phone numbers were synonymous with Redstockings gave those women an inordinate amount of power they denied having.

The leadership did dole out a few of the less glorious chores to new members like me. After a few months I was sent on my first speaking engagement in southern New Jersey, where I addressed a local group of feminists about how to form a consciousness-raising group. I felt both nervous and important. I had never given a public lecture, unless I counted in-class reports in high school and college courses. The group was friendly and receptive, and I stayed in the home of one of the members. By my humble standards, her residence was luxurious, but when I woke up in the morning and saw sheep grazing outside my window, I suspected I was the official Redstockings emissary to the boonies.

Redstockings was much more talk than action, but we did some organizing, mostly around abortion issues. I recall getting tickets, along with a number of other feminists, to sit in the audience of a television talk show that was to be aired live, as many shows were back then. The topic of the show was abortion, and we were passionately interested in making sure that the call for free abortion on demand was going to be aired, if only from the audience. As the show geared up to begin, it became clear that the women on the stage, all of whom had had abortions, were not going to be shown to the home audience. The lights were dimmed around their faces, hiding them. Unfortunately, this technique sometimes didn't work very well, and television mystery guests were recognized by family and friends. A wig and strange glasses provided a better disguise. The implication was that these women were criminals who had to hide their identity out of shame. We were appalled. As the show started, some of the feminists jumped up and yelled, "I've had an abortion, and I'll show my face." They tried to replace the women on the stage, but the security guards kept the women back. A compromise was reached during a commercial break, and feminists were allowed to present their testimony from the audience.

One Mother's Day, in 1969 or 1970, we dutifully lined up outside WNEW-TV (a local independent station) to get tickets to the *David Susskind Show*. Susskind, whom we all thought of as a jerk, was the grandfather of the television talk show. (Compared to most talk shows today, he seems most enlightened.) He featured panels of people discussing timely topics, and he came up with some truly improbable combinations, such as Susan Brownmiller, Germaine Greer, John Simon, and Anatole Broyard on the same show. For the Mother's Day show that Redstockings attended, Susskind had invited a panel of five men to discuss the wonders of marriage and motherhood, which in those days were an inviolable combination so far as talk shows were concerned. When Susskind turned to the audience for questions, Elsie, one of the Redstockings planted in the audience, asked the panelists how they helped their wives out around the house. There was one of those long television moments of dead air. In those days men generally believed that taking out the garbage was their major contribution to the smooth functioning of a household.

Members of Redstockings talked about organizing around other issues, but I don't recall that we actually did anything. At one point a strike by telephone operators seemed to be in the works, and we discussed supporting the women on the picket lines. The operators, almost all of whom were women, were paid poorly. There were frequent complaints in the alternative papers about the mistreatment of these women, who could be fired for leaving their switchboards without permission, even if they had to go to the bathroom desperately. I can't recall whether the strike actually materialized, but in the end Redstockings did nothing to back these women. Redstockings was better suited for political analysis than political organizing.

Lesbianism was a more widely discussed issue than class and labor. Rita Mae Brown's vociferous arrival in Redstockings had sparked discussion in Group X, although reactions were mixed. Irene Peslikis, for one, was emboldened to admit to a long-term lesbian affair that Group X knew nothing about. But other members of Group X, echoing Betty Friedan's assertion that lesbians were a "lavender menace," began to blame gay women for causing dissension in the group and accused them of being "antifeminists." Kathie Sarachild wrote in *Feminist Revolution* that "many lesbians complained that they were excluded from the movement in the beginning often by simple virtue of the fact that the women in it spent so much time talking about such boring or irrelevant or disturbing to them subjects as sex with men, getting men to do the housework, and such related problems as abortions and childcare."

What she and many other heterosexist Redstockings overlooked was that lesbians had been raised in families with men, had usually had sexual relationships with men, had worked with men, and sometimes lived with male roommates. Several lesbians I knew had children from previous marriages. What the straight women couldn't see was that many Redstockings talked about men all the time the way dieters obsess about food. There were times when some of us, including a few of the heterosexuals, felt it would be more productive to focus on ways in which women could interact with one another positively.

The currents of homophobia made many newer members, including me, reluctant to mention homosexual experiences to the group. Only when Michela Griffo came out to Group A and it accepted her lesbianism did I feel that group members would embrace mine, and they did. My admission of "bisexuality," which came as a surprise to no one except me, even brought me a few suitors, especially as word spread throughout the Women's Liberation Movement that I was "one of them"—that is, a lesbian.

And much to my amusement, I suddenly found myself being courted by several nongay women. Some simply wanted a "homosexual experience." They saw it as an extension of their consciousness-raising, an experience that they could much more easily embrace than becoming Black or lower class. Others defined themselves as "political lesbians." Unlike "real lesbians" such as myself who had had sexual experiences with other women prior to feminism, these women had not been born queer but decided to sleep with other women as an act of political solidarity until the revolution was over. Sex with other women was a cut above a relationship with the terrible enemy—men. Presumably, once men had given in to feminist demands, the political lesbians would return to their "normal" sexuality. Obviously, most of the women who pursued me were not Redstockings leaders, who were struggling with men, orgasm by orgasm. However, there were a few sister Redstockings as well as members of New York Radical Feminists and The Feminists who were more than a little bit curious.

Rita Mae Brown had a reputation for sleeping with straight women, mostly in the NOW leadership. In a recent memoir, *Rita Will* (1997), however, she dismissed these rumors and called those feminists "big-boobed babe[s]." Michela had a gorgeous model for a lover, and she was faithful to her. Since I was the only other openly gay woman in Redstockings, I guess that left me.

My teenage lesbian affairs had been easy and guiltless, in part because my sex partners and I never admitted, even to each other, that we were really lesbians. Straight feminists behaved in a completely different manner and came with their own set of complications. One woman batted her eyes at me so much that I wondered whether she wore ill-fitting contact lenses. Luckily, since such women often expected me to ask them to bed or to make the first move, I could pretend not to notice their interest. If any of these women had spent even one evening in Kooky's, they would have noticed that I was no butch. I slept with a few of the women I found irresistibly attractive or bright. I've always found intelligence and wit much more of a turn-on than appearance, especially as I've never been attracted to a defined type.

Although it was a sudden treat to have an assortment of women to choose from, the sex invariably disappointed me. Regina and Marly represented the two extremes of lesbian/feminist sex in the late 1960s—both depressingly unsatisfying for me. Regina rushed into my bed and then played dead better than my neighbor's dog. Making love to her felt rather as I imagine necrophilia might. Since Regina wasn't really a lesbian, she came to the experience with a cerebral image of what she had already decided "feminist sex" could be. If I had ever whipped out a vibrator, which in those days was battery powered and made of hard, cold, white, phallic-shaped plastic, Regina would have denounced me for imitating the patriarchy. As it was, almost anything except oral sex was too patriarchal for her, so finger-fucking, tribadism, and other common techniques tended to remind Regina in some unpleasant way of her ex-husband. Afterward she snorted, rather triumphantly, "So that's all there is to lesbian sex!" If that's all there were to lesbian sex, I'd be heterosexual, too.

Marly approached sex like a ravenous animal. Obviously, a sexless revolution had gone on far too long for her. She took to lesbian sex with wild abandon. Squealing with delight at the similarity of our bodies, she left me covered with passionate hickeys and scratches. The first time Marly came, she yelled, "Oh God! Oh God!" and wrought further damage on my hair and back. Never one to miss an opportunity for repartee, though I'm polite enough not to talk during sex if my mouth is full, I retorted, "Just my luck, I do all the work, and some man gets the credit!" That shut her up fast.

In each case the morning after brought two equally unattractive reactions. Regina launched into full-scale homosexual panic, worrying whether she was indeed a lesbian. She accused me of seducing her. I closed my eyes so they wouldn't roll spontaneously in disbelief. Ringo, my cat, would get angry if anyone raised her voice to me (and he hadn't even met my mother). He waited until Regina's back was turned and dragged her bra through his litter. Then he turned over the garbage, extracted an eggshell covered with coffee grinds, and deposited it in her lap.

His behavior diverted Regina's attention from her panic. Her fury was now focused on Ringo, who sat in the middle of the rug and made his eyes as saucerlike and innocent as possible. How could I argue with Ringo's instinctively accurate assessment? I showed my now ex-lover to the door.

More terrifying to me than lesbian panic, however, was love. Marly's eagerness to become my other "half" dwarfed lesbians' U-Haul sensibilities. Her behavior might have simply been her blissful reaction to a first lesbian experience. It suggested some utopian vision that we could double up and defeat the patriarchy all the more swiftly—after all, "an army of lovers cannot fail," the motto of Sparta was supposed to have said. But whatever Marly was implying, I didn't want it. I reminded her that possessive and exclusive behavior was a remnant of patriarchal ideology. This time, Ringo, his tail at full mast, showed her to the door.

After a few such experiences, I decided that I would never intentionally bring another straight woman out. A better strategy was to leave the initiatory acts to others. Then if the straight women liked the sex and became gay, I'd still be around.

Despite this newfound community of women, which helped me come into my own politically, intellectually, and emotionally, I still felt lonely and out of place. I longed to find lesbians more like me. Where could I place my ad? Real lesbians wanted, some experience needed. Just when I was giving up hope, the Stonewall uprisings happened. My prayers were answered.

❧   ❧   ❧

I wish I could say that C-R and feminist politics led me to a great epiphany about my parents, one of those shining moments of reconciliation and love that populate soppy movies. That never happened. I can't say that I loved my mother or even that I forgave her for what she had done to me, but as a result of C-R, I did understand her and was able to care for her later on.

After my mother died in 1984, I discovered that, though my father was thrilled to have a daughter, he did not believe that I was his biological child. His claim that one of his best friends was my "real" father may have been simply the delusion of an old man with Alzheimer's, but it seemed to explain his disparate treatment of my brother and me. The last time I saw him early in 1993, he was a shrunken, bitter man in his nineties who was tired of living and waiting to die. My partner, Karen, and I visited him in a Florida nursing home. The activity wore him out, and he began to nap. Before I left the room, I leaned over him and kissed him on his cheek. "Bye, Dad, I'll come back to visit soon."

"I'm not your father. I never had a daughter, just a son." Those were his final words to me. He died a few days later.

5
Stonewall Girl

The Stonewall uprising and its aftermath have already left the confines of history and entered the rarefied air of legend. What happened during and after the raid that night has become the subject of several books, documentaries, and even a fictionalized film featuring a trio of lip-syncing drag queens. Though a Broadway musical version that will dwarf both *Cats* and *Rent* is probably in the works—call it *Phantom of the Stonewall*, if you will—the events of that evening are murky at best.

Hearing people reminisce, I get the impression that everybody was there except me. From my window on the Upper West Side, I alone failed to witness history in the making. No one rang me up to announce an irresistible riot, probably the best one since the turmoil at Columbia University. It was just my bad luck that Friday night, June 27, 1969, to be the only gay person in New York not dating in the Village or showing friends from out of town the wonders of Christopher Street. Even a suspiciously large number of lesbians claimed to have been present at the historical flashpoint, despite the fact that places like the Stonewall actively discouraged women from entering their premises.

For most gay men and lesbians of a certain age, the police raid at the Stonewall Inn is like the John F. Kennedy assassination—they can recount where they were at the moment of the shooting. Unfortunately,

I can't. Since I didn't own a television, I was probably in the Thalia watching a battered version of Marcel Carné's *Children of Paradise* for the tenth time and waiting with bated breath for the final reel to catch fire yet again. Or I might have been re-viewing Ingmar Bergman's *Persona*, about the nearest thing to a lesbian film I had ever seen. Never mind that the plot centered on a psychotic breakdown—I would have run off with Liv Ullmann or Bibi Andersson in an instant. There weren't too many lesbians who looked like film stars in Kooky's. In the dark Thalia I fantasized about myself battling with the Illustrated Woman for their attention.

The more pressing news of the week was the death of Judy Garland, the tormented singer who was an icon of my parents' generation and of my own. *The Wizard of Oz* was an annual television event in America's living rooms. Children like myself, who knew we were "different," even if we couldn't put a name on our outsiderness, could identify with the Lion, the Tin Man, and the Scarecrow. All they wanted was to be fixed, made whole—in short, to fit in.

Almost every gay man of my generation—and a few lesbians as well—worshiped Judy, the first megastar readily identifiable by one name. Some gay men spoke in reverent tones of wanting to perform a drag imitation of her as if her life were a passion play. Male homosexuals were mesmerized by each broken love affair, illness, and suicide attempt. Judy's tragic life was proof that love was hell for everyone and that the price of romance was drugs, drink, and death. On June 27, 1969, the day of her funeral, an estimated twenty thousand people—many of them male homosexuals—stood outside the Campbell Funeral Home on Madison Avenue, despite the extreme heat, and wept as their idol was laid to rest.

Many people have said that Judy's suicide put the crowd at the Stonewall in a particularly testy mood that night. Maybe the heat added to the mix as well. The only typical event of the evening was the police raid. The mayoral election was revving up for fall 1969, which meant that John V. Lindsey was sprucing up his reputation as a defender of public morals. Maybe the owners of the Stonewall had simply forgotten to pay off the cops that week. Or perhaps, as Martin Duberman suggests in his 1993 book *Stonewall,* the police were trying to intimidate the proprietors into even bigger payoffs, or perhaps the new commanding officer had ordered patrolmen to stop taking payoffs altogether.

As best as I can reconstruct the story, this is what happened. The Stonewall was basically a white working-class bar with a reputation for having a crowd that "did drugs." A few transvestites hung out there, but the legend-makers added a cast of thousands; two of every kind seem to have been there. Some say a lesbian who was visiting a friend in the Stonewall was the first to resist, or she may have thrown an object at a police officer. Yet this woman who launched what has been called "the hairpin drop heard around the world" has remained ominously anonymous. Others say there were no lesbians in the bar. Not surprisingly, all the extant photos of the uprising show the same campy, fey young white boys, the kind of street kids most associated with the place.

Contemporary accounts of the event are the most accurate. At the time I followed Lucian K. Truscott IV's news coverage of the uprising in the *Village Voice.* His version appeared just days after the event. According to Truscott, the Stonewall uprisings began as a small and almost cheerful raid, with a total of six cops involved. After all, most gay people knew that if they had proper identification and clothing, they had to be released. The Stonewall, like most New York bars, also flashed red or white lights to warn customers of potential police action because same-sex dance partners were subject to arrest. Truscott wrote: "A crowd started to gather on the street. It was initially a festive gathering, composed mostly of Stonewall boys. . . . Cheers went up as favorites emerged from the door, striking a pose and swishing by the detective with a 'Hello there, fella.' Wrists were limp and hair was primped." When a police van pulled up, the crowd was not amused; curses and boos turned to violence as the crowd began to throw everything in sight at the cops and at the Stonewall—beer bottles, soda cans, spare change, and bricks flew at the police officers, and someone tried to hit them with rolled-up newspapers as if they were errant dogs. When the police took refuge inside the Stonewall, the crowd attacked the door with a parking meter. The Stonewall was set on fire, and the crowd was hosed down by the cops, who were still inside. (They had most likely nabbed a fire hose, abandoned by a fleeing fireman.) Police hauled in whomever they could snatch up. By accident, they grabbed folk singer Dave Van Ronk, who had just emerged from the very straight Lion's Head next door. Ronk was charged with "felonious assault of a police officer."

By the next day I had heard the story on the radio and read it in the newspapers. The media attention attracted crowds of people who wanted to see the damage. Those who had been involved in the riot returned to admire their own handiwork of the previous night. The leftist Pacifica radio station reported that a number of campy and angry signs were posted on the boarded-up windows of the bar, such as "There is all college boys and girls in here" and "Support Gay Power—C'mon in, girls." I laughed out loud when I heard the story. There was a festive spirit as well. According to mythology, street kids sang and danced in a chorus line:

> We are the Stonewall Girls,
> We wear our hair in curls,
> We have no underwear,
> We show our pubic hair.

But by Saturday night the Tactical Police Force was lying in wait for troublemakers, and the cops stampeded into this crowd with even more venom and anger than they had at Columbia the year before. Now it became a game of "cat and mouse." The TPF would attack, and the gays would retreat, only to sneak back once the cops were out of sight.

On Sunday, excited by the media reports, I decided to head down to the Village to see for myself what had happened. I got off the Broadway local at Christopher Street. From the other side of Seventh Avenue South, I could see signs of a heavy police presence: police vans on the side streets; horse manure in the gutters. I decided that I would walk across Christopher Street, and if the cops stopped me, I would say that I was headed someplace specific, such as the Bigelow Pharmacy on Sixth Avenue. People didn't usually think I was a lesbian, so I would act dumb about what was going on. But when I stood on the side of Sheridan Square opposite the Stonewall, I couldn't help but stop and gape.

Instead of radical banners and rowdy demonstrators, all I saw was a sign tacked onto the boarded-up windows of the Stonewall Inn. Written by the Mattachine Society, the sign asked people to behave themselves. It wasn't quite what I had expected.

Just then I saw a poke of TPFers headed my way, and I beat a hasty retreat back up Christopher Street—I had learned all too well at Columbia that the wheels of justice tended to grind the innocent along with the guilty. Since I had started graduate school, I had developed a great fear of being arrested, as I believed that even one conviction would ruin my chances of teaching at a university. If I were going to get busted, it would have to be for something I fervently believed in. I was saving myself for the revolution, but this certainly didn't look like it. I got back on the subway and went home.

The riots and other acts of scattered resistance continued through Wednesday. I didn't know what to make of the unrest. I wish I could say I had the same prophetic vision that everyone else seemed to possess. Others knew as soon as they looked at those boarded-up windows that everything was suddenly going to be different. Poet Allen Ginsberg told Truscott that week that the men in the Stonewall were "beautiful," that "they've lost that wounded look that fags all had 10 years ago." Although I found it admirable that these men had had the courage to resist a routine, if nasty, police operation, deep in my heart I felt that it would be business as usual at every gay bar all over town by the following Saturday. Lesbians and gay men sometimes defended their turf in a bar with the ferocity of cornered bears, but they fought back because they had no place else to run to or hang out in. I didn't equate that type of fighting with the political activism I had learned in Redstockings. There seemed to me to be a great difference between conscious political action that happened because members of a group or a community agreed on a common core of oppression and decided to overthrow it and the kind of spontaneous upheaval that had occurred at the Stonewall.

Both the TPF and the Mafia could outgun us any day. What were these resisters going to do in the end when they became tired of prancing in the streets and playing hide-and-seek with the cops? Though people who witnessed or were somehow involved in Stonewall—Jim

Fouratt, John O'Brien, Ed Murphy, Craig Rodwell, Martha Shelley, Sylvia Rivera—became involved in the Gay Liberation Front (GLF), I have met *only one* of the campy young men whose images flashed across newspapers and television screens that week. Like the lesbian who allegedly started the uprising, very few of the participants have come forward to claim the credit that they're due as forefathers of the gay revolution. What happened to our Paul Reveres? Did they simply take a midnight ride the following weekend to another bar or a hipper party? With the Fourth of July coming, did they decamp to Fire Island because no respectable gay revolution could occur until after Labor Day?

If my assessment seems too harsh, perhaps it is in reaction to our completely uncritical glorification of Stonewall as a monumental event, a revolutionary moment. In some ways the events that night weren't at all sudden or shocking. They were made possible by many years of committed activism by Mattachine, the Daughters of Bilitis, and other homophile groups that helped create and sustain thriving gay communities and political awareness. They were made possible by the passion of activists who had gained expertise in the women's movement, the civil rights struggle, student uprisings across the country, the antiwar movement, and socialist or communist groups. Stonewall happened because Rosa Parks had refused to give up her seat to a white man and lived to tell the tale, and because Martin Luther King, Jr., had walked peacefully down many southern streets and been assassinated for his efforts. The Stonewall uprising was not so spontaneous after all; it arose out of the courage and vision of participants in other movements.

Stonewall was a catalyst or a flashpoint, and its historical significance rests on incidental factors, such as time and place. If Stonewall hadn't happened, I am certain that the seething resentment of some elements of the gay community at social injustice would have caused eruptions in another locale. The tenor of the country was such that it was impossible for a radical gay and lesbian movement *not* to emerge at that pivotal moment in time. Had this same bar rebellion happened in a small city instead of in the media capital of the world, it might have passed unnoticed. If not for the central role of the media and the committed activists who began to form the Gay Liberation Front shortly after the riots, the Stonewall fracas would have been quickly forgotten.

Fortunately, some women and men were incensed enough at what had happened that they could not let the matter drop. A handful of activists, including WBAI (Pacifica Radio) show host Charles Pitts, Bill Katzenberg (an SDS member), and Pete Wilson (a former member of the League for Sexual Freedom) set up a meeting on July 24 at Alternate U. This radical haven of hip education was located on the second floor of a building at the corner of Sixth Avenue and Fourteenth Street. Some of those who attended the meeting represented the diversity that would both enrich and plague what was to become the Gay Liberation Front. In some ways the roots of the GLF's destruction were inherent in the conflicting constituencies represented at the very first meeting, groups much more divergent than those I had been a part of: drag queens, bar dykes, street people, feminists, radical students, leftists, socialists, Marxists, Maoists, anarchists, libertarians, hippies, and former Yippies. As in Redstockings, conveners of this organization tended to have strong personalities and to be eloquent, persuasive, and dogmatic.

There were a few people who had experience in the homophile movement. Foster Gunnison, a cigar-smoking libertarian, had been involved in homophile networking conferences in the 1960s. Martha Shelley had been the president of DOB-NY in the fall of 1968. By the time I met Martha at GLF, she had become quite militant and was the kind of radical who liked to urge others to take up arms for the struggle. She looked the part, too: Small, round, and compactly built, all she needed was a beret over her dark curly hair to look like an induction poster for Che Guevara's army. Ellen Broidy had previously been involved with the gay student group at New York University. Craig Rodwell (known back then as Craig Phillips) had worked in Mattachine. He and Randy Wicker (Charles Hayden) had picketed the draft board on Whitehall Street, an action rather too radical for others in Mattachine. In 1967 Craig had opened the Oscar Wilde Memorial Bookshop, the first store of its kind for gay men and lesbians. A tiny square space on Mercer Street in the Village, the store's stock consisted mostly of tangentially gay material published by mainstream presses. Craig, a Christian Scientist, was clean-cut and trim. He was the sort of man who didn't "look gay" at first, but as soon as he opened his mouth, his queen's vernacular immediately tagged him as homosexual.

Others came from different political backgrounds. John O'Brien, Ron Ballard (one of the few Black men in GLF), and John Lauritsen were Marxists. Some had been ejected from socialist groups for their sexual preference, as the "party line" was that homosexuality was a capitalist disease. Susan Silverwoman (Silverman) was only nineteen years old and had not yet identified as a bisexual, but she attended early GLF meetings and ran the programming at Alternate U. Jim Fouratt had been succinctly described by Tom Burke in *Esquire* as "a tense boy with leonine hair . . . a New Left celebrity, seminarian *manqué*, the [Yippie] radical who burned the real money on the floor of the New York Stock Exchange as a war protest." Jim was slender and boyish at a time when such androgynous looks were the craze. He generally dressed in a T-shirt and tight black leather pants (under which even the casual observer, such as myself, could note that he wore no underwear—I wondered on several occasions whether his pants smelled bad or, if not, how he kept them from reeking). He was a hardened activist, the type who could shout down others in the room until his view prevailed.

Then there were people who came to gay rights activism from even farther afield. Lois Hart, for instance, was undoubtedly one of the most charismatic and forceful women in the group, someone we later dubbed the "Mother Superior" both for her religious leanings (she was a former nun and a follower of the mystic Meher Baba) and her "touchy-feely" maternal bent. Lois could come off as a warm and caring John Lennon figure and even wore similar granny glasses. She was also shrewd; some might have said calculating. Pat Maxwell looked like a butch street dyke but had once been a teacher at a Summerhillian school in Illinois and had lost custody of her children because of her lesbianism.

Most of the people were young, white, and unemployed. Most were students or recent college graduates like myself. But some of the participants were simply what radicals referred to as "street people"—generally lower- or lower-middle-class women and men without any prior political experience, who came because they were incensed about the Stonewall riots or because they knew someone who had participated in them. A "street queen," for instance, was very different from a college professor who might dress up in a gown for a Halloween party. Jerry Hoose was a self-described "truck boy." I had no idea what that was, so one day I asked him. He explained matter-of-factly that he liked to have sex in the back of the empty trucks that were parked under the Westside Highway (which was an elevated roadway at the time). There in the empty cargo space—still reeking, I presumed, of the meat it had carried to the wholesale markets lining West Street—Jerry found his pleasure with men he couldn't see and vice versa. "Isn't that dangerous?" I asked a mutual friend. "I mean, you might get arrested—or killed!"

"Yes," he replied dryly. "That's the whole point."

I still didn't get it, but I was glad I was a vegetarian. I wouldn't want to eat the hamburger that had been in trucks that doubled as orgy rooms.

Another street type was Marty Stephan. A burly white woman who sold tokens in a subway booth, Marty looked as if she drove one of the rigs Jerry favored. She was someone who had spent a lot of time in the bars, and she relished her butchness. She called her lover her "wife," and this unnamed woman dutifully walked ten steps behind Marty. Ellen Broidy once accidentally let Marty into her apartment and slammed the door on Marty's wife because she had fallen too far behind. Marty was kind and generally well liked, but she seemed so apolitical that I never figured out what had brought her to GLF. People like Jerry and Marty were somewhat at a disadvantage when the rhetoric flew, though Colonel Robert and his famous parliamentarian rules never ran a single orderly moment at GLF.

There were a few street transvestites who worked primarily as prostitutes. They generally wore makeup, had long hair, and referred to themselves with female pronouns, but they usually wore pants, not women's clothing, as later film versions suggest. I became friendly with two transvestites. Sylvia Rivera, a Latina street queen, would hold forth at GLF meetings, gesticulating wildly and punctuating her own comments with Dietrich's guttural laugh as she presented her views in forceful, if ungrammatical, New Yorkese. Her friend Marsha (sometimes "Marcia")

P. Johnson was a sassy and funny Black transvestite. Martin Duberman wrote in *Stonewall* that she once told a judge after she had been busted that the *P* stood for "Pay it no mind." The laughing judge demanded no bail.

Hopeful (but not certain) that something was going to happen after the Stonewall riots had subsided, I went to my first GLF meeting at the end of July, which was probably the group's second meeting. I had seen an ad for it in the *East Village Other* or *Rat*. At first I didn't know what to make of this colorful, boisterous group. The chairs were pulled into a loose circle in which everything seemed to be spinning, like Yeats's gyre, chaotically out of control. Everyone was shouting about what should be done without listening to what others had to say. I was initially put off by the fact that out of maybe fifty participants, there were fewer than ten women present, but those who were there—Arlene Kisner; Lois Hart and her lover, Suzanne Bevier; Ellen Shumsky (who was then using Bedoz as her last name); Ellen Broidy and her lover, Linda Rhodes; Martha Shelley; and Susan Silverwoman among them—were articulate and political. Unlike Redstockings, where only Rita Mae Brown, Michela Griffo, and I spoke up about our sexual orientation, these women were loud and proud. These eloquent and persuasive women contrasted vividly with the women I had met in the bars. Sitting in the meeting, I could see new possibilities for my life: Maybe there *were* other women like me who were political, had a feminist consciousness, and wanted to sleep with women.

The group as a whole shared my politics. The members of the GLF were hell-bent on changing society, not ourselves. As the first issue of the GLF paper *Come Out!* put it so boldly, "We are going to transform society at large through the open realization of our own consciousness." The organization was grounded in leftist politics minus the homophobia I had encountered in Redstockings. The GLF also seemed more committed to action than Redstockings—there were discussions about picketing the *Voice*, which had refused to run a GLF ad because the *Voice* considered "gay" to be an "obscene" word.

But while I was drawn to the politics and the energy of the group, I was put off by some of what I found there. I had never met a real drag queen before—though it was sometimes whispered that Kooky was really a man under all that hair and garish makeup. Redstockings and other feminist groups strongly believed that such men were an offensive parody of "real" women—that is, those of us who were genetically female and sentenced to a life of oppression because of our gender. Such men could simply discard women's clothing and reclaim male privilege. Feminists believed that transvestites caricatured the very worst of femininity by donning pounds of makeup and by wearing the very kind of clothing we were fighting to free ourselves from, especially short, tight, revealing skirts or dresses and stiletto heels. Drag queens adored tragic victims such as Judy Garland and glamorous schemers such as some of the characters played by Bette Davis and Joan Crawford. Real female heroines like Amelia Earhart or Eleanor Roosevelt were of no interest to them. Have you ever seen a drag version of Susan B. Anthony? Case closed, or so I thought back then. Now in the postmodern cyber age where a person on the Net might be a man, a woman, or an alien space creature (and maybe all three), I have embraced the liberating aspects of claiming and shedding birth identities and sexualities. I envy the fluidity of a young man I know who feels comfortable in business suits at work and evening gowns at night. But at the time drag struck me as sexist.

And what was I to make of Jerry Hoose and the other men like him who told me unabashedly of their sexual encounters on the piers, under the highways, and in the tubs, where in one night they had had more sex partners than I had had in my entire lifetime? On the one hand, I had to admit a bit of envy at their plentiful sex lives. On the other hand, I was appalled at their celebrating what feminists denounced as "sexual objectification." Though some of the men opposed becoming fixated on specific body parts, others reveled in it like a warm bubble bath. They could recite their type for me down to his delicate toenails—height, weight, age, coloring, race and ethnicity, body hair, penis size, and circumcision status. If the physical attributes didn't add up, it didn't seem to matter at all to them what personality, sense of humor, or mental abilities that man had. Whatever I thought about Jerry, at least he wasn't rejecting anyone based on looks—the trucks were completely dark inside.

It was easy for some of the others to denounce him while they worshiped ten-inch dicks.

In many ways most of the GLF and I were in sync regarding gender politics. A good number of us, including me, were into androgyny or "gynandry" (if you approached the issue from a gynocentric viewpoint). Many of us believed that the best way to eliminate the male/female divide was for all of us to look and act as much like one another as possible. Men were encouraged to wear their hair long and to sport jewelry such as beaded necklaces. Facial hair was discouraged. On a few occasions Allen Young, a leftist journalist who worked for Liberation News Service, was chastised for wearing a mustache or beard and heavy work boots, which he preferred to regular shoes: Both were too macho. In contrast, short hair was favored for women, and I was applauded when I finally cut my hair in 1972, though the decision was based on an attempt to rid myself of rampant split ends rather than on political considerations. Most of the lesbians favored bell-bottom denims, boots, and flannel shirts with a T-shirt underneath. After all, we were dressing for the revolution, not *Vogue*.

Despite the push toward a gynandrous center, the sexism of some of the men was—for me, at least—the biggest obstacle toward immediately and completely immersing myself in GLF. A number of the men were more oppressive to women than any heterosexual guy I had known. A few of the men looked at me with such unveiled contempt that I started to give credence to the old adage that some men were gay because they hated or feared women. I'm sure that these guys would have preferred for the women to leave so that the GLF would become an all-men's group, sort of like a political bathhouse, where they could get naked with one another. If we were going to be there, however, a few men thought we might as well make ourselves useful by baking some cookies and making coffee. Some of the other women and I were constantly correcting men who called us "girls." "I'm a woman, not a 'girl.' How would like me to call you 'boy'?" we'd remind them over and over.

Fortunately, these men were in the minority. But aside from chiming in to correct them, I was quiet at first, and I recall that I didn't attend any meetings or dances in August, if there were any! Centers of movement activity like the Alternate U were not air-conditioned. Though the summer may be prime time for riots in inner-city ghettos, I can assure government officials that no revolution will ever occur in the New York gay community in August, unless queer tourists suddenly take up arms. The natives flee to the beaches and the mountains, at least those who can afford to get away. So after my initial association with GLF, I began to drift away.

Meanwhile, I had other things on my mind. When fall arrived, I decided to find a better job. I quickly landed one as an assistant editor at Collier's. Thanks to my language skills, I was assigned to write and edit articles on French-speaking countries for the annual *Collier's Encyclopedia Book of the Year in Review*. One day when I thought I was losing my mind as I looked through the company's racks of foreign journals for information about the smuggling of peanuts over the Senegalese border, I glanced into the indexing section and spotted a nervous fellow plucking out his long hair, clump by clump. Here was someone who looked exactly how I felt. We struck up a conversation.

"Hi, I'm Karla from editorial."

"I'm Samuel. I do the indexing here." We twitched in sync as we kept an eye out for patrolling supervisors.

He was just my sort of guy. So what if he was straight? He was a leftist vegetarian with anarchist leanings, and we quickly became soul mates. We went out to lunch together and discussed politics while we smoked bidis, a legal Indian cigarette made from male hemp plants.

Samuel and I shared a lot—a love of culture, the belief that the company should unionize, and a commitment to taking actions, both covert and overt, to change society. He was much better at subversion than I was. One of his tricks was to cross-reference people in an index where no supervisor would bother to look. Who, for instance, would try to find Richard M. Nixon cross-listed under "Dictator, American" or Lyndon B. Johnson under "Cattle Rancher, Texan"? Occasionally, he slipped a hilarious entry by the ever-watchful bosses. If I could have been attracted to a man because of his beliefs, it would have been Samuel. Somehow, my lack of sexual attraction to him helped convince me I really was gay.

In the end it was through Samuel that I went back to the GLF. I told him of my bisexuality and current boyfriend. He seemed not to be threatened by either my bisexuality or my feminism. He had followed the activities of various feminist groups in the same papers as I had. In fact, one day in September he brought in the *East Village Other* and *Rat* and showed me an article about a Gay Liberation Front demonstration in front of the *Voice*. It reported that by the end of a day of picketing, *Voice* publisher Ed Fancher had decided that the words "gay" and "homosexual" weren't so bad after all and could be used in classified advertising. It was the first major victory for GLF. And sure enough, when I looked in the next issue of the *Voice*, there was an ad for a GLF meeting, which had moved to the Church of the Holy Apostles on West Twenty-eighth Street. I decided that it was time to return to the GLF.

༄   ༄   ༄

At the end of June 1994 I went to a Gay Liberation Front reunion in Greenwich Village. It was Stonewall 25, and the city was bursting with a dizzying array of events, ranging from the Gay Games to museum exhibits. As we sipped our wine and munched on the hors d'oeuvres, I knew we had all changed.

We tried to recognize one another after a quarter century of separation. I had a much easier time than most. Having been active in the movement as a writer for all the years in between, I had often crossed paths with many of those in attendance.

After a while the room became crowded, and almost all the women slipped out the back door into a garden. "Look's like nothing's changed," I quipped to a friend. "Here we women are, still in the back of the bus."

A lot had changed, however. As we stood in the garden and swapped stories, I realized that most of the women were not simply older versions of our radical selves, though a few still adhered closely to their post-Stonewall politics. At least two of the women were now married to men. Many of the rest were in committed relationships with other women. Once-dreaded and -denounced monogamy was now the fashion. So, too, were the gender identities we had camouflaged with our androgynous flannel shirts. Maybe for many our political actions had been simply the fashion of 1969.

The attendees represented only a small fraction of the original GLF membership. Unfortunately, we had lost far too many activists along the way, not just from AIDS, but also from cancer, heart failure, and other diseases. A few had committed suicide, and at least two, including Marsha P. Johnson, had been murdered. N. A. (Nikos) Diaman, an early member of GLF, had collected the names of about thirty deceased members of early GLF groups around the country, including Lois Hart and Marty Stephan. Shortly after the reunion Craig Rodwell died of stomach cancer and Foster Gunnison dropped dead from a heart attack. Perhaps many of us had simply hit middle age and its attendant diseases, but AIDS and our skepticism about patriarchal medicine inflated the numbers.

The names of these pioneers—both living and dead—exist on some Web sites and in a few history texts, but there's no monument to commemorate their contributions to gay liberation. For the dwindling number of GLF veterans, our dead comrades live on only in our memories of them and of the actions they took to liberate all of us. Sadly, except for six-column-inch obituaries in gay community newspapers and footnotes in historical accounts, most GLFers have already been forgotten.

As I looked around the reunion, hugging people whose names I've long forgotten myself, I wondered whether I've inadvertently recapitulated the very problem I set out to solve. To recount the exploits of every hero would need the skill of Homer. By focusing on those I knew best, have I erased those I do not name? I know that history could not have been made without all those nameless faces in the room, the ones who never sang their own song.

uild the kind of family I had never had but still yearned for. I was
attracted to the idea of working politically with other groups,
gh as a feminist I thought that we first had to be clear and unified
it our needs and goals as women and homosexuals before we made
nces. Otherwise, we would be subsumed into other, larger groups
later oppressed by them. Cuba, I thought, was a case in point.
ugh many gays had supported Fidel Castro's revolution, the Com-
ist government later categorized all gays as decadent members of
bourgeoisie and tossed them into "reeducation camps," a eu-
mism for concentration camps. Many of the GLF radicals felt that as
ileged Americans we should refrain from judging the history and
oms of Third World countries such as Cuba, but others believed that
ural practices must be limited by other people's freedom. How could
condemn the incarceration of homosexuals by Hitler and overlook
imprisonment of gays by Castro? This contradiction defied even my
ble vision.

ut on issues closer to home, we could reach agreement more read-
One action that many of us enthusiastically took part in was the "lib-
ion" of gay and lesbian bars. After some Sunday meetings two or
e dozen of us would pile into cars or the subway or walk to a local
Since gay bars were divided along gender lines, our very solidarity
a political statement. Finding courage in our numbers, we would
p past the startled bouncers. Then we would hijack the dance floor
swirl around in a huge throbbing circle to the tunes of the rowdi-
rock music on the juke boxes.

ur main goal in these actions was to alert people to GLF's existence,
we wanted to support our brothers and sisters in the bars as well.
ce, we piled into Gianni's, a new women's bar on West Nineteenth
et, to protest the failure of the bar's owners and bouncers to protect
customers inside. The weekend before a group of straight men had
red the bar and had slugged several women. In response, the women
chased the men outside and pursued them down the street. Marc
s, a fabulously gynandrous butch who attended GLF meetings and
worked as a bartender when she wasn't typesetting, somehow got
ad of the pack. The men turned on her, beat her up, and ripped off

6

Houses of Fun, Prison of Pain

During the fall of 1969 my life became a whirlwind of activity.
Weekdays I worked a full-time job at Collier's; two evenings per week
I attended graduate classes. I was still involved in my Redstockings consciousness-raising group, which continued to meet weekly. Then, as if I
didn't have enough to do, I joined the Gay Liberation Front.

My initial contact with the GLF over the summer had made me increasingly dissatisfied with Redstockings in general and my C-R group
in particular. Rage is supposed to be a natural consequence of political
enlightenment, but not all my anger was directed at our proclaimed
enemy, men. I had started to develop a troubling double vision: I could
see that some of my college-educated Redstockings sisters were in fact
better off than some of the street people I met at the GLF. Redstockings' assertion that women are a "class" didn't allow for exceptions: We
were always directed to focus on how men were our oppressors, not on
how they might also be victims of discrimination because of race or
sexual orientation. It also seemed that this group of feminists, allegedly
on my side, was oppressing *me*—sometimes consciously, sometimes
not—by erasing the basic issue of heterosexism.

In addition to work, Redstockings, and GLF meetings, I attended a
meeting or two of the Daughters of Bilitis. I had become friendly with

two DOB members, Gail and Rosie, after they had given me my second cat, Pooh. Both women encouraged me to join. Although Martha Shelley had at one point been president of DOB and there were some younger women present, Gail and Rosie introduced me to their circle of friends, who, like themselves, were all fifteen to twenty years older than I was. At a time when I thought twenty-five was ancient, these women seemed Jurassic, and I unkindly nicknamed the group the "Daughters of Bursitis." They were equally wary of my youth, and a few of them openly referred to me as "jailbait," though I wasn't. They invited me to a couple of parties, where I was the only woman under thirty. I was attracted to older women, but my yearning wasn't reciprocated. Moreover, either Rosie was jealous or else she had some old-fashioned notion of trying to "protect" me from a lifestyle she wasn't entirely comfortable with herself. At meetings she would hover nearby and interrupt whenever I started a conversation with someone my own age.

After Samuel showed me notices for a GLF meeting, I decided to return there. During the six weeks I had been gone, attendance had mushroomed. Most importantly for me, many more women were present. I sat quietly through a few meetings to get a better sense of what the group was about. As I started to recognize more and more speakers, the proceedings seemed much less chaotic. I could now clearly identify people as belonging to certain factions and, after a few meetings, could usually predict a person's position on any given issue. I also became increasingly excited by the revolutionary politics of the GLF, and before I knew it, I was a convert, with all the ecstatic transfiguration of a (Jewish) saint. This group was the only place where I was apt to be accepted as both a lesbian and a feminist and where I could find a lover who shared both my political beliefs and my sexual orientation. I loved the fact that, despite disagreements on what demonstrations, dances, and even words meant, we went out into the world and acted, even if our analysis wasn't down pat, even if we weren't exactly sure what we were doing or why. It all seemed a wonderful antidote to Redstockings' endless processing.

Within the GLF there were two primary factions, which Toby Marotta aptly designated the "cultural reformers" and the "political ac-

tivists" in his 1981 book *The Politics of Homosexuality*.

[re]formers stressed that meaningful change stemmed from consciousness, which could come about only if there [was a vi]brant gay culture with which people could identify. T[hey] urged us to focus our energies on building a gay coun[try com]plete with dances, gay-run newspapers, a community [center] house, and other self-help activities. And they pressed fo[r people] to come out and accept themselves as homosexuals. If ev[ery les]bian person in the United States could be persuaded t[o . . . their] lives would be different because heterosexuals would ha[ve seen] how very many of us there were and grant us our right[s. This] view may seem a bit naive, it is depressing to realize th[at we have] not even begun to achieve this rudimentary goal: Far m[ore visible] today, but visible queers represent only a fraction of gay, [bi]sexual Americans. Consequently, it is still possible to [view us as a] much smaller and less powerful group than we actually [are. Re]formers did believe in some political engagement—p[olice] harassment, for example—but not so much with the g[oal of] political change as of broadcasting the acceptability of a [gay life.]

The political activist faction, meanwhile, believed in [changing the] system through political demonstrations. These activis[ts agreed with] Redstockings that power is never voluntarily relinquishe[d but must be] seized from the oppressor. They focused on forging a pol[itical agenda to] obtain our rights. They advocated alliances with other [oppressed] groups, such as the Black Panthers and the Young Lords[, their] Puerto Rican counterparts.

Ironically, both factions often agreed on a course o[f action even] though their goals were diametrically opposed. In the c[ase of dances,] Aquarians viewed them as fund-raisers as well as a fund[amental part] of the creation of a dynamic counterculture. Radicals th[ought—erro]neously it turned out—that dances were opportunities t[o recruit new] members.

The distinctions between political and cultural activis[m were not al]ways clear or compelling for all of us. I could often see [the merits of] both arguments. I was drawn to the cultural reformers, [. . .]

her wig—revealing a bald scalp. The bar owners gladly took our money, but the goons failed to protect us when we needed them. We wanted to show the women in Gianni's that we cared and that we thought something positive should be done. During the dance-in, some of us tried to talk to the bar's regular customers about the assault on Marc and others the previous week. They were indeed still outraged about that incident—word of it had spread throughout every gay and lesbian bar in town. They agreed that more should be done to protect us, but some of them saw our invasion of the bar as another assault on their space. They hated straight men, but they were also none too happy about androgynous kiki lesbians and "fags" invading Gianni's. Where would the habitués of the bar have gone, I now wonder, had we succeeded in closing down such venues? Not everyone would feel comfortable at our dances or our meetings; even I didn't at times.

Our answer to the bars consisted of the gay-run dances we held at the Alternate U, and I quickly volunteered to work on them. My favorite job was collecting contributions at the door, where I could size up every woman for attractiveness and availability as she arrived. Since most of the single women traveled in groups of two to four, it wasn't easy to figure out who was with whom. I knew three roommates who were inseparable; I never could figure out whether two of them were a couple or whether they were all three involved in some complicated relationship.

It helped to scrutinize people as they came through the door because it was almost impossible to find someone later on in the dense crowd unless I had zeroed in on some identifying piece of clothing. Since the vast majority of dancers were men, and since they were generally taller than the women, it was difficult to locate someone in the darkened, smoky room through the gyrating flesh. A few spotlights were trained on a large, faceted-mirror disco ball suspended from the ceiling. Patchy lights streamed over our bodies and the dance floor; everything was swirling and wavy. Colors were distorted by the party lights. As the room got hotter and hotter, the men would pull off their T-shirts and tie them around their waists or twirl them over their heads while the lesbians resentfully looked on. If we women took our tops off, we could be arrested. Moreover, we worried about getting harassed by men, even here.

Occasionally a few straight men came to our dances—there was no way to figure out who they were unless there had been previous complaints. These guys took advantage of the thick, fast-moving crowd to grope or harass some of the women. One time, I felt someone massaging my butt. Thinking it was a gay man mistaking me for another guy, I turned around and said, "Look, two earrings—it's a woman!" But that was exactly what he was looking for. He smirked; I scurried away.

These were by far the wildest parties I had ever been to. The music and the darkness made it a perfect venue for taking drugs. The room reeked of marijuana and amyl or butyl nitrate ("poppers"). The stench of the poppers, which smelled like dirty feet, was overpowering. Once Marsha Johnson put a dog-whistle-sized container of it right under my nose, and I inhaled some of the noxious substance. It made me feel dizzy and faint. Marsha may have dressed like a woman, but she was still turned on by boy drugs. Others downed "Black Beauties" or "Red Devils," two potent forms of speed. Many of the rest were on acid, mescaline, or other drugs. If the FBI and New York City's Red Squad had really been out to destroy gay liberation, they could have busted the entire organization in one evening. Since straight discos were also drug havens, the police probably felt it best to look the other way. Despite occasional harassment by men, the heavy drug scene, and the scarcity of available women, I felt more comfortable at our dances than I ever had at Kooky's.

I didn't meet any potential lovers during the first month or two, but I danced with women, men, drag queens, and, sometimes, myself. It was easy to move into the center of the crowd and let myself be pulled about by the thunderous maelstrom. I felt deliriously happy just to have a community where I fit. Meanwhile, I was making friends rapidly and learning who was who.

After the dances ended, usually around two or three in the morning, the cleanup contingent would try to put the Alternate U back into some semblance of order. The floor looked as if Wall Street had thrown a ticker-tape parade for hippies: It was littered with crushed cups and cans, cigarette butts and pot roaches, dropped capsules of speed, and odds and ends of clothing. The bathrooms were unspeakable. But somehow we would plow through the mess while Pat Maxwell, Marsha, or someone else gave a running and hilarious commentary on everyone at the dance.

"Did you get a load of her?" Marsha might start, referring to some ex who had dared to show up with another date on his arm. "I'm telling you that was one tired trick. She's a hundred if she's a day."

At first I had been put off by Pat's butchness and Marsha's drag. But they were both so earnest and fanciful that I was soon won over. One night, en route to liberating a bar, I wound up sitting on Marsha's lap in the back of a van. Suddenly, someone was feeling up my left breast. I squirmed around to confront her and noticed that she was feeling up her own left breast with her right hand. She wasn't being sexual—in fact, it was the least sexual grope I've ever experienced. Marsha was comparison shopping.

"What are you doing?" I demanded.

"It just ain't fair," she lamented. "I've had all these shots and thangs, and all I've got to show for it is these here lemons. And you ain't done no work, and you've got watermelons!" She gave me one of her sassy looks. What could I do but laugh?

"So do you really work as a hooker? And do the johns think those are real lemons or what?" With that, I gave her right breast a tentative feel. Both she and Sylvia Rivera were fiercely strong drag queens, and I didn't want to be tossed unceremoniously out of the back of the van. She was right, however: She had lemons, small and hard.

"I don't know what they think because I don't tell them. It's just like a grocery store; you either shop or you don't shop. If they want to go up my dress, why, honey, they pay extra, and so long as they pay up front, I don't give a shit what they think."

After that, although she knew I had mixed feelings about transvestism, we became fast friends. After all, who could help but like her or admire her unwavering nerve? I realized how much danger she had to face every day. Having been a victim of male violence myself, I admired her courage in going out on the streets night after night for a few dollars a trick. Many years later I learned from friends that she had indeed been found dead in the Hudson River.

When I completed my stint cleaning up after a dance, Marsha would take me to private after-hours clubs. I would crawl home at eight the next morning, hung over and exhausted. I noticed that I was losing a lot of the weight I had gained from breaking my back. I was literally dancing it off.

Perhaps due to my trimmer body, I suddenly began collecting female lovers like a pot of honey drawing bears. I had more offers than I could handle. I went to bed with some butch women, some femme women, some gynandrous women, political women, halves of couples, one-third of a lovely trio. If I had died and found lesbian heaven, this was it. One day I made love with two different women, one in the morning, one at night. The sex was much more satisfying than my affairs with straight women in the Women's Liberation Movement, who were constrained by panic and politics. Like a sailor who had been marooned for months in a lifeboat, my thirst was unquenchable. I feared I would open my eyes and all these fabulous lesbians would vanish, leaving me as lonely as before.

My sexually active life did not diminish my participation in GLF meetings. In fact, the sexual intrigue gave me all the more reason to attend. And the GLF was never boring—in fact, it was getting more complex and interesting all the time. I noticed that subgroups were forming within the groups, each like moths clustering around a lightbulb, only minimally interacting with the other groups.

The rhetoric within the GLF started to change as well. There was definitely more discussion about the connections between homophobia and sexism, and at least some of the men could see that they were oppressed as homosexuals because they were perceived by straight society to be acting like women. Most nongay men derided so-called passive Greek and active French sex partners who were penetrated during anal sex and who performed oral sex as "traitors" who played a "feminine role." Everyone from the media to schoolyard bullies picked on "sissies."

In November I thought it was time to introduce C-R groups as a way for people to discuss sexism further. I thought the group could learn a lot from the C-R process—in all the time I had attended the GLF meetings, people tended to talk *at* each other without listening very well. By this time, I felt that people from all factions would trust me if I introduced something new because I was generally well liked. I brought some others, including Michela Griffo, from my C-R group with me, and we broke up the meeting into several small units of about a dozen members each. Since friends tended to sit next to one another, I divided people arbitrarily by lots until everyone was in a group containing both women and men. Whereas some people felt that I was "imposing feminism" on the group, others were glad for the chance to talk—or cruise—in a more intimate setting.

The small groups were a great success, and several of them continued to meet on a regular basis. The groups were especially useful for helping us women better understand some of the men and where they were coming from. Whereas the women tended to talk about politics in a more personal way, leftist men hid behind their rhetoric. I, for one, often had no concept of what people were really like. In smaller groups people started to talk to one another as individuals, not political positions. Some of the more vocal men also discovered that the silent men and women had interesting points to make. People still disagreed, but some became more understanding of others and more willing to make space for others to speak.

Though I often felt during the fall that my education was the last thing on my mind, I was taking a brilliant course in modernism taught by Albert Sonnenfeld, a visiting professor of romance languages from Princeton University, who took an extraordinary interest in his students. The chair of the Comparative Literature Department threw an annual fall party at his country house for the graduate students, but Bert Sonnenfeld regularly invited us out for drinks after class and treated us as his peers. One day he invited the entire class to a party at his home in Princeton.

After I had boarded a bus at the Port Authority for the trip to Princeton, Terry, a fellow student, sauntered on and sat down next to me. A high-cheek-boned, stylish, and gaunt young man, Terry was a dead ringer for Audrey Hepburn, except for his handlebar mustache. His brunette locks flowed down the back of his cape, an item of clothing I considered an affectation. What good is a coat without sleeves? I would have described him as effeminate, and I assumed that he was gay, although we had never spoken. When we started to chat, I was a bit taken aback. This man, who was fluent in four or five languages, filled almost all of his sentences with interrupters. We discussed our modernism class a bit, and finally he got to the point.

"You know, I think, for sure, or maybe for sure I'm homosexual."

"No kidding, for sure," I thought, then added aloud, "That's cool with me."

"Do you think, like maybe, it's like a disease?"

"Like nah, dude." I was going to have to restrain myself as his speech pattern was obviously contagious. I could just envision myself making one of my rare visits home and sounding like a cross between Terry and Marsha. Wouldn't Mom be thrilled? I could just hear her say, "I didn't send you to Barnard so you'd end up sounding like someone from the Bronx!" Although Brooklynese was mocked throughout the English-speaking world, to Brooklynites, a Bronx accent was the nadir of inelegance.

When Terry and I reached the party, Terry went into a homosexual panic. He started to pursue a beautiful older blond woman around the house. Too shy to introduce himself, he asked Bert who she was.

"Hey," Terry pointed at her, "who is that? She is, for sure, like *the* most beautiful chick I've ever seen. Gotta meet her, for sure!"

Bert flicked some ash off his cigar, and without missing a beat, he replied, "That 'chick' is my wife."

Terry was mortified and stayed away from both of them for the rest of the afternoon.

"I think, for sure, I sank my grade. She's his old lady, are you ready?" Terry tacked the last phrase onto many sentences in the way some French people added *n'est-ce pas* to just about anything.

I assured him that Bert would probably be flattered that Terry found his wife so alluring. Bert didn't seem the vengeful type. I hoped not, since I had glued a sticker proclaiming, "This Oppresses Women!" onto the frame of a painting of a nude woman. As I was increasingly singled out as "the feminist" in most of my classes and addressed in the plural about "our position" on various works of literature or on the lives of certain authors, Bert wouldn't have to be Sherlock Holmes to figure out which student had come armed with political stickers.

Rebuffed on one front, Terry tried to assert his heterosexuality by asking me out. I suggested that we go dancing two weeks from Sunday in the late afternoon, but when he turned up at my apartment, I told him that I had had a change of plans and took him to a GLF meeting. He loved it.

Terry immediately became my closest friend and best ally in class. He, too, had suffered from sexism. Gender bending seemed his birthright. From the back people often mistook the shapely brunette for a woman. One time he had gone into a notions store in search of brass buttons. The saleslady tapped him on his back. "Miss, can I help you?"

When Terry turned around, she shrieked, "Omigod, it's a bearded lady!"

Our sense of difference—of being "queer" in many ways beyond our sexuality—and our many similar interests bonded us together. We loved the same rock bands; we adored the same actresses; we swapped macrobiotic recipes—he was also a devout vegetarian. He was smart and funny. Had he been a woman, I could have fallen in love with him.

Before I knew it, he had moved in with me.

I didn't think cohabiting with a gay man was going to be easy to explain to my parents, my feminist friends, or Mike. But Mike took the news that Terry was moving in with surprising equanimity. As a gay man, Terry posed no threat to Mike's relationship with me. Mike and I still had an easy sexual connection, though we had never shared other interests. During that fall he was living and working in Bergen County, New Jersey, and so I saw him less frequently than ever. Whenever Mike did come over, he seemed genuinely pleased to see Terry. I would often study alone in the bedroom while they rolled joint after joint, listened to music, and shared their stoned fantasies.

Terry became a clever and convenient cover for my lesbian activities. Terry was such a good and ardent dancer that Mike readily accepted the fact that one Saturday night per month Terry and I went out to disco without him. (Mike could barely get his boots on or off, let alone move his feet to a fast beat.) Terry and I would go off together to the monthly gay dance, where none of Mike's pals was likely to run into us. And no matter how stoned Terry got, he was always discreet about my "other life."

But one night the inevitable happened. Around 5:00 A.M. someone in the lobby rang our buzzer. It was Jasmine, one of the many women I had recently slept with. She was having a bad acid trip and begged to come up to our apartment right away. Mike was sleeping in the bedroom, and the buzzer hadn't even awakened him. It seemed wiser to let her upstairs than to have her lean on the buzzer some more. I was angry, since Jasmine had lots of other sex partners. Why was she bringing her bad trip over to my house? When I opened the door, however, I could see that she was really freaked out. Terry made her some herb tea, and we both sat down next to her on the edge of his bed, held her hands, massaged her back, and talked softly and reassuringly to her. Our LSD 101 techniques had no calming effects whatsoever. So much for the popular wisdom of magazines like *High Times*. Before we could stop her, Jasmine was dashing around the living room pulling off her clothes, which she tossed at the startled cats and at us. In the blink of an eye she was stark naked and still running in circles. I'm sure our downstairs neighbors were as delighted as we were.

There seemed to be only one solution. We yanked her into Terry's narrow bed and sandwiched her between him and me. Though I feared I'd wind up with permanent scratch marks from Jasmine's nails, she soon calmed down. Finally, we all fell asleep in a huge mound of human and feline flesh.

The next morning Mike emerged from the bedroom. Jasmine and I weren't exactly in flagrante, and the irony of it all was that of all the women I was having sex with, I wasn't having any with Jasmine that night. Mike didn't say a word, but I knew from the hurt anger in his eyes that he had inferred that Jasmine wasn't Terry's play pal. He didn't ask for or even give me time for an explanation. He threw on most of his clothes, lit a Camel, and headed out the front door without even tucking in his shirt or tying the laces on his work boots. However melodramatically, our relationship was over. Its collapse came as somewhat of a relief; things were far too complicated for the moment. It never occurred to me then that he was the last man I would sleep with.

In the wake of Mike's dramatic exit, Terry and I decided that we would be totally out of the closet and refuse to engage in heterosexual charades. My parents were the one exception. By 1969 I had been living away from home for almost five years. Though I had become a lot more understanding of my parents, I rarely visited them, in part because I was too busy but also because my mother could fly into a rage over almost anything—what I was wearing, how much I weighed, anything I inadvertently said. My parents telephoned frequently, but it was easy to distract them from my personal life with tales of graduate school and work. My mother had decided that I was in mourning for Trent: She had met him once when I was a sophomore. After that I never provided details about my dates, and I had not even bothered to mention Mike to my mother.

Now I feared a hugely negative reaction to my living with a man, even if my parents were told he wasn't a boyfriend. If I mentioned Terry, my mother would surely conclude that he, like any other man, would try to have sex with a woman. She had been raised never to have sex before marriage and to have as little as possible afterward. As a first step I informed my father about Terry's presence. My father refused to believe that Terry was a man and kept referring to him as "she." My father was (a) very hip about gay slang, (b) feared my mother's reactions and so pretended he had heard a female pronoun, (c) feared his own reaction and so altered his hearing, or (d) all of the above.

It never occurred to me to inform my parents that I was bisexual or lesbian. Though later on I spent years on the road telling people that coming out was always worse in imagination than in reality, at that time I suffered the same pangs of dread as everyone else. I could envision my mother's slit wrists accompanied by a massive dose of barbiturates and a de rigueur suicide note.

I suspect the notion that two women could be sexual together never crossed her mind. In fact, once she and I went to see a film about Lenny Bruce, whose wife, Honey, was bisexual. In one scene Honey was slowly tracing the outlines of her lover's breasts with her well-manicured nails.

"Oh my, look at that!" my mother exclaimed. I held my breath, waiting to hear her reaction to what was obviously a lesbian sex scene.

After a few seconds my mother continued in a tone loud enough to reach everyone in the theater. "They aren't wearing that shade of nail polish anymore." I guffawed: The film was in black and white.

A few years later, in 1976, I was scheduled to appear on Tom Snyder's *Tomorrow Show*. Certain that one of my relatives would see me, I wrote a letter to my father in which I informed him of my lesbianism. He was profoundly unhappy about it, but he agreed to make sure that the television was tuned to another channel in the bedroom. My mother could not sleep unless the television was on, and I feared she would recognize my voice and wake up.

My instincts were right. My gleefully vicious Aunt Claire telephoned my mother at 1:30 A.M.

"Your daughter's on television, and she's a queeah." She managed to drawl the last word into three syllables; moving to Florida hadn't been a total waste for her.

"Butch," my mother yelled to my father, who embarrassingly enough bore that nickname. He was secretly watching me on the television in the living room. "Karla's on the *Tomorrow Show*, and she says she's a lesbian. What is that?"

Her only experience with queers (or so she thought—no one had ever informed her that my favorite aunt, Queenie, had been bisexual) was with Mr. Bruce, her faithful and long-suffering hairdresser. My mother had always believed that homosexuality was a disease that male hairdressers somehow "caught," perhaps from some degenerative ingredient in the hairspray. My father supplied a definition. The following day she checked into a mental hospital. My instinct about not telling my mother the truth had been on target.

As for my C-R group, it wasn't thrilled that I was living with a gay man, whom I obviously adored. This wasn't exactly the engagement with the enemy that group members had envisioned. But I just didn't see Terry as the enemy and told them that in some ways Terry was oppressed because his appearance was so feminine. But to my Redstockings' sisters, Terry was a man—period.

I decided to ignore the complaints of my C-R group, and Terry and I continued to have great fun. I convinced him to shave off his mustache; his resemblance to Audrey Hepburn became more striking. We both thought he was more alluring as well. Indeed, he was—men started to pursue him in droves. He was also mistaken much more frequently for a woman, especially when he wore his wide-brimmed hat and cape—his "Holly Golightly" outfit, I dubbed it. All he needed was to put his hair in a bun and purchase a cigarette holder, and Truman Capote would be eating out of his hand—or crotch.

But Terry's effete charm attracted unwanted attention, too. Sometimes as we traveled to work together in the morning, people in the crowded subway car gave him startled looks if his deep voice disrupted their presumption that he was a woman. We both worked in the East Fifties, and he would come over to the Collier's cafeteria to join me for lunch. We no longer dined in restaurants because no food was pure enough for us, but also because we couldn't afford to eat out, pay the rent, *and* attend graduate school. Besides, ninety percent of our macrobiotic diet consisted of whole grains. At the time we were both surviving on an unleavened rice bread made by an organic restaurant in the East Village called the Paradox. One small slice sufficed for breakfast, and a peanut butter sandwich with rice bread was probably dense enough to sink the *Titanic*. Magically, the more we ate of it, the more weight we lost. ("Are you ready?" Terry hopped on our bathroom scale. "The more you eat, the more you shit! We're, like, disappearing, for sure!")

As Terry sauntered past several tables to our usual spot in Collier's cafeteria, I saw a secretary seated near me nudge another and stage whisper in a thick Bronx accent, "Here come dat strange boy with dat strange bread." These women always reminded me that I hadn't discovered until the fifth grade that there's a *th* sound in the English language. When Sammy from the indexing department joined us for lunch, we would all retaliate with a loud discussion of the carcinogens in the secretaries' hamburgers.

The more feminine looking Terry allowed himself to appear, the worse he was treated by strangers. His androgyny was a threat to many and an irresistible attraction to a few. Late one night Terry burst into my room in tears.

"What's wrong?"

"I've . . . I've been oppressed as a woman!"

"So what else is new? What happened exactly?" I wasn't prepared for the stammering torrent of words and tears that followed.

"Can you dig it? I was, like, riding home in the subway, and this man was staring at me. So I changed cars, but he changed cars, too. So I thought, 'Wow, he thinks I'm a woman, so I'll take off my hat, and then he'll know.' But, KJ, he was, like, clueless. I even puffed up my shoulders and went to, like, *another* car. He followed me again, are you ready? So I get off the train at Cathedral Parkway, and he follows. We're the only two on the platform, wouldn't ya know? After the train pulls out, he shoves me up against the wall and starts ripping my clothes off. So I yell at him, 'Hey, dude, you're making a mistake—I'm a MAN!' and he says, 'I don't care anymore; I want you.'"

"Oh, not cool. Look what he did to your shirt!" Shards of Terry's T-shirt were dangling from his shoulder. "So then what happened?"

By now Terry was crying hysterically. "I, like, knew he was going to *rape* me, so I pulled away from him and ran—all the way back. I can't believe it, you know? I was SO oppressed!"

"Welcome, Brother Teresa, to the sisterhood of pain and oppression." We both dissolved into hysterical laughter.

Nevertheless, it did sound pretty awful. In contrast, the members of my C-R group felt that the attempted rape of Terry didn't stack up to the victimization that women faced. His experience was an aberration because of a mistake—women were raped because of who we were. I could understand their point, but it didn't make Terry's suffering any less painful.

Despite my unwillingness to accept their rigid ideas about relations between men and women, I tried to stay committed to the women in Redstockings. After all we had processed in our C-R group, they were like members of an extended family. I knew more about their friends, relatives, spouses, jobs, educations, and childhoods than I knew about most of my other friends or my relatives. I regularly socialized with a few women, especially Elsie and Michela, outside the group, and most of us participated in actions organized by Redstockings and other feminist groups.

On Christmas Eve, for example, several feminist groups all converged for a demonstration in front of the Women's House of Detention. "The House of D," as it was unaffectionately nicknamed, stood on a triangular block in the heart of Greenwich Village. Amazingly enough, six streets—Greenwich Avenue, the Avenue of the Americas, West Eighth and Ninth Streets, Christopher Street, and Patchin Place—all intersected at the House of D, and I liked to think of them as accusatory fingers aimed at the evil culprit in our midst. The hulking mass might have be mistaken for a hideous apartment building were it not for the bars on the windows and the peculiar clotted color of the bricks, which looked as if they had been stained through the years with the blood of the inmates. The wretched institution cast a long, gloomy shadow over lively Greenwich Avenue, in marked contrast to the expensive boutiques over which it towered.

Tales of the deplorable conditions within the House of D were well known in the women's movement. Before the place was finally shut down, a number of famous women, including Grace Paley, Barbara Deming, Andrea Dworkin, Judith Molina, Valerie Solanas, and Dorothy Day, had been imprisoned there. Later on some of these women became our heroes. The filthy jail was crawling with rats and roaches, and the food was inedible. The women were routinely subjected to degrading strip searches, which included invasive and unsanitary "searches" of "body cavities," including vaginas and rectums, for possible contraband.

Though many American prisons humiliated prisoners in ways that would make our Puritan forefathers proud, the House of D had additional tortures all its own. Some of the cells faced Sutter's, a fancy French bakery on West Ninth Street: The smell of the baking cakes and bread was agony for the women who had to inhale its smells while swallowing prison grub. Day and night friends, lovers, children, husbands, parents, siblings, and even pimps shouted up advice, messages, words of comfort, and questions to the inmates. From within the hellish depths of the House of D, hollow voices echoed back—answering, crying for help, whimpering hopelessly. The prisoners were almost perpetually in their cells, and except for a bit of space on the roof, there were few recreational facilities, not even a yard. They were the forgotten women of our society, but I could never put their presence totally out of mind. I was certain that one day I would find myself within the building's cold cells, just like Valerie Solanas. For months the prior year, she had stood, a solitary, bedraggled figure in dirty and baggy clothes, right across the street selling a mimeo version of her *SCUM [Society for Cutting Up Men] Manifesto*. Suddenly, after her failed attempt to assassinate artist Andy Warhol, she was swallowed by the House of D until the authorities decided she was crazy and shipped her off to Creedmore, a mental institution with a wing for the criminally insane, a place even more hellish than the House of D. After all, it was much more frightening to imagine that a sane woman might choose to maim the oppressor than to declare that this was just a deranged act.

Feminists were outraged by the treatment of Valerie and other feminist prisoners. After the start of women's liberation, the House of D became a rallying point. From Christmas Eve 1969 through New Year's Day, men and women, including myself, kept a vigil in front of it night and day. We rallied, spoke, marched around the House of D, and sang Christmas carols to the prisoners. The prisoners responded by shouting, "Power to the People!" They burned matchbooks and pieces of paper and sent them sailing out the windows to the people below, whom they had no other way to touch. Some even set fire to their mattresses. We could see the prisoners darkly outlined against the flames as they jumped up and down shouting. Heedless of the heat, they screamed at us to free them. Helplessly, we sang on, choking back tears, unable to match their courage.

On New Years Eve Terry and Samuel joined me on the sidewalk across from the House of D. At the stroke of midnight we held our candles aloft and sang, "Auld Lang Syne" along with the women within, who lit matches in response to our candles. Somehow, it seemed fitting for me to end 1969 in this way, singing off-key to a bunch of prisoners I had never met and then going off with Terry for a night of revelry with our GLF cohorts. As we entered a new decade, the hope of change and the threat of defeat loomed before us, but we sure as hell were going to dance and sing, not just before the revolution, but until the very end as well.

CRL   CRL   CRL

Amid continued protest, the House of D transferred the last of its female inmates to Riker's Island in 1971. It wasn't clear whether conditions for the women were any better in the new location, but once the women were out of sight, they quickly disappeared from the public conscience. Until 1973 the empty hull, occupied only by rodents and roaches, remained, while the community debated heatedly about what to do with the site. Eventually, it was turned into a community garden of sorts. When I walked by the site recently, I noted that the beautiful flowers and shrubs are now kept away from the public by a wrought iron fence, while the descendants of the original rats continue to scurry about freely on their ancestral turf.

7

Zapping *Rat*
and the *Ladies' Home Journal*

The beginning of 1970 brought two additional roommates in quick succession to my Upper West Side apartment. One day, shortly after Terry had moved in with me, he nudged me in class and pointed out John Knoebel, a slightly built young man with horn-rimmed glasses and thinning brown hair.

"Get a load of him!" he whispered urgently.

"Which one?"

"The guy in the glasses—the one who looks like a grub. He's like gay. I'm sure."

"Well, I'm not so sure." All the men in the Comparative Literature Program looked gay to me. "You can't just assume everyone's gay because even the sun goes down." We snorted conspiratorially.

"Takes one to know one," he, who had been out all of ten minutes, announced authoritatively.

"Suit yourself. He's all yours."

"He's not my type, for sure. I just wanna know, okay?"

He started chatting up John but balked at asking him such a direct question. Then, as luck would have it, we saw John that very Sunday at a GLF meeting. Sure enough, John was homosexual, and he had come to New York after graduating from the University of Wisconsin to become involved with a gay community.

So now we had netted another ally in class. John and Terry became friends, and Terry soon convinced John to come out to his roommate, a naive suggestion. Though the roommate was yet another man in our program who looked gay, he said he wasn't and told John to move out. Of course, John moved in with us.

We added another phone line and another bed in the living room. Shortly after that Terry became infatuated with Jude Bartlett, a lanky dancer with a thick curly brown Afro. Jude had recently moved from Massachusetts to New York City to study modern dance with Martha Graham. When he discovered that his lover had a venereal disease, he was anxious to move out, and he wound up "staying with us" for a while as well. He and Terry were briefly lovers, but when that didn't last, the four of us cohabited simply as friends in a tightly packed two-room apartment.

I decided that Jude and John would have to move out in a few months, but for the moment we focused on the joys of paying less than $50 a month each, including utilities, and tried to coexist peacefully in our cramped space. For the most part things operated smoothly. We set up a morning schedule that somehow managed to get everyone to work clean and on time. Luckily, we had already discarded modesty. Several of us would cram into the tiny bathroom at once for a Three Stooges version of showering, shaving, and urinating before a bemused audience of cats.

The worst moments came during the weekends. We agreed that the best policy was for everyone to try to sleep over at lovers' houses as much as possible. Of course, this plan often didn't work out. I, for one, had just started dating Becky, a woman in her late teens who lived at home with her parents. I was her first lesbian lover, and she wasn't ready to bring me home just yet.

One Saturday night each of us brought someone home, and I woke up the next morning to discover six people ahead of Becky and me in line for the bathroom. Just when it was my turn for a shower, the doorbell rang. Since I was still wearing pajamas and the others were naked,

I went to open the front door. There stood Gay Liberation Front member Diana Davies, who lived around the corner.

"Hi, there," she beamed, clutching a bottle of Prell and a towel. "The hot water in my building isn't working. D'ya mind if I use your shower?"

"If you want a shower," I yelped, yanking her by her towel into the hall outside the bathroom, "take a number!"

"Oh, my, I see the problem," she looked around. There was more naked male flesh scampering about than in a YMCA locker room. "Okay, I can wait." She sat down and talked to Becky and Terry. It was a long morning.

All things considered, our lives ran remarkably well, in part because we spent so much time at work, meetings, classes, parties, and dances. Some nights Terry, John, and I studied in the tiny bedroom while Jude practiced his modern dance techniques in the living room.

Somehow on top of everything, I managed to add another commitment—writing and editing for *Rat Subterranean News*. Everyone I knew in the feminist, gay, and antiwar movements read *Rat,* a radical bimonthly that had begun publishing in fall 1969 out of a seedy loft on East Fourteenth Street, near Second Avenue, on the very northern fringes of the East Village. In many ways *Rat* was an important forum that helped bind together what were often otherwise separate social movements. The paper covered the antiwar movement in detail. It printed pieces written by Black Panthers. Afeni Shakur (Joanne Chesimard), for instance, occasionally contributed essays written in her jail cell, where she was awaiting trial for the murder of a New Jersey State trooper. "We are the truth," she proclaimed, "and you can't control us." The paper devoutly followed every terrorist action of groups such as the Weathermen, which advocated the violent overthrow of the U.S. government and the bombing of corporations that supported the war effort or exploited Third World nations. *Rat* also provided advice for the aspiring do-it-yourself revolutionary, such as what kind of helmet to wear during a demonstration or where to buy walkie talkies, hand grenades, chemical weapons, and even helicopters (a shopping tip clearly intended for those who had first robbed a bank). The paper once published a recipe for Molotov cocktails, noting that each one "yields at least one pig car in flames."

But if in some ways *Rat* reflected and helped create a community of radical activists, it nevertheless perpetuated some of the same injustices many of us were fighting. Even though *Rat* covered some feminist and gay events, the male leadership had very little consciousness about sexism, especially their own. Women were often relegated to cleaning up the office, while the men wrote. Finally, the women involved with the paper decided to take action.

On January 24, 1970, feminists, led by women who worked on the staff, seized the offices of *Rat*. In the following issue, under a cartoon of an armed and angry female rat, the new staff explained the takeover. "The blatant sexism of RAT in the past is only part of what made it necessary. . . . Can we still be under the delusion that the cultural revolution, in this time of heavy repression, of mounting police power and courtroom insanity, is going to pull down the state with its dope, music, and so-called liberated sex?" The editors went on to note that the office was "yielded to an all-women collective," and, indeed, the transfer of power appears to have been a peaceful one. At the time, however, wild stories circulated that several women had gone into the offices armed with shotguns and had driven the men out. In any event Jeff Shero, the editor in chief, and the other male staff members could hardly complain to the police, whose violent removal they advocated twice a month.

After the takeover the new feminist collective members, including Martha Shelley, who had previously written poetry and essays for *Rat*, recruited new staff members. Martha approached Rita Mae Brown and me about joining the collective, in part because she didn't want to be the token lesbian on the staff. Martha knew Rita from the student homophile movement, and I had met Martha at the Gay Liberation Front. It seemed a dream come true to be asked to work on a newspaper I read and admired. In high school I had yearned to be a writer, and when the school paper published a short story of mine written in the voice of an apple tree, I was sure I was on my way to a shining career. Most of my friends and teachers thought I would become an accomplished author of some sort. But when I realized in college that lesbianism was taboo, there was little I could write about without being damned for it. I couldn't forever disguise my feelings as those of a tree. And so, for the past six years, I had written nothing except term papers.

Now I had something to say, and I was no longer afraid to say it. I could feel the urge to write, so long suppressed, welling up. I headed over to the *Rat* offices, and there I became involved with a dangerously exciting group of women.

Rat's most notorious editor/writer was Jane Alpert, a radical who later pled guilty to acts of terrorism and fled underground. Her grandiose political ideology was a lot more militant and less pacifist than that of many of the other women on the new collective. "We [radicals] believed," she wrote later in *Growing Up Underground,* her 1981 memoir, "that the world could be cleansed of all domination and submission, that perception itself could be purified of the division into subject and object, that power playing between nations, sexes, races, ages, between animals and humans, individuals and groups, could be brought to an end." Jane believed that the status quo had to be derailed by violent acts that would put the government on notice that "business as usual" could no longer continue.

Many of us on the Left spoke frequently of the coming violent struggle, but in reality few of us were ready to take up arms, except in self-defense. Pacifists like myself balked even at that, and many of us hoped for a Gandhi-like figure who would transform our society nonviolently. However, Jane and her lover, Sam Melville, felt that acts of terrorism were intrinsically necessary parts of this revolution. During the half year before the women's takeover of *Rat,* Jane was busy putting her militant philosophy into practice. She, Sam, Nate Yarrow, and Patricia Swinton hijacked a truck carrying some explosives and used the dynamite on a number of targets, including a United Fruit Company warehouse, which they bombed on July 26, 1969, the anniversary of one of Castro's raids. Though United Fruit had been a notorious supporter of Fulgencio Batista's despotic rule in Cuba, the revolutionaries failed to note that the warehouse was currently rented out to another company, which was storing peat moss. Shortly thereafter Sam bombed a Marine Midland Bank branch in lower Manhattan, injuring about a dozen people, mostly low-level female clerks. Nate Yarrow bombed the Whitehall Induction

Center in October. On November 12, while planning to bomb a court-house, they were arrested by agents of the FBI.

Most members of *Rat* never suspected that one of the bombers they regularly wrote about was working on their staff, not that anyone would have informed on Jane even had they known. Sam and Jane had un-wisely become friends with "Crazy George" Demmerle, a founder of the San Francisco Crazies. George, "Prince of the Crazies," so embraced outlandish behavior, including wearing strange outfits and helmets, and called so many other people "pigs" that no one suspected he was an FBI informant.

By the time the women took over *Rat*, Jane had spent a few days in the Women's House of Detention on charges of terrorist conspiracy. Now out on bail awaiting trial, Jane helped us regroup and assemble a new collective. She recruited Robin Morgan, the charismatic cofounder of WITCH. Robin had recently had a baby, Blake, and she brought her son to editorial meetings, where he was the only male present. Another collective member was Sharon Krebs (who was arrested later that same year for a bank-bombing plot). Other regulars at the meetings included Lucy, a Yippie wannabe, and Carol (later Kali) Grosberg, who had been a member of the Bread and Puppet Theater group. Though Jane Alpert later depicted herself in her memoir first as a victim of Sam Melville (who "made" her get involved in the bombings through his irrational behavior and other forms of manipulation) and later as a victim of Robin (who somehow forced her to become a radical feminist), I recall her as someone who spoke up, not all that frequently, but with a defi-nite viewpoint. She was no one's puppet. In fact, as a terrorist out on bail and as one of the few members of the original *Rat* staff, she wielded a lot of power and got a lot of respect.

After the women's takeover, *Rat* became militantly feminist. We con-tinued to publish *Rat*'s usual fare of news about revolutionary groups and Third World countries, but we gave a lot more attention to issues such as free abortion on demand, the plight of Third World women, feminist actions, and gay-related material. Robin's classic essay "Good-bye to All That," which appeared in the first women's issue, warned left-ist men of the ilk who had run or read the old *Rat* that we were leaving

them behind: "The hell with the simplistic notion that automatic freedom for women—or non-white peoples—will come about ZAP! with
the advent of a socialist revolution. Bullshit. . . . Women were the first
property." She proclaimed that we were going to be "bitchy, catty, dykey,
frustrated, crazy, Solanisque, nutty, frigid, ridiculous, bitter, embarrassing,
man-hating, libelous, pure, unfair, envious, intuitive, low-down, stupid,
petty, liberating. WE ARE THE WOMEN THAT MEN HAVE
WARNED US ABOUT."

We edited all of the pieces collectively. We would each read copies of
the articles submitted for publication, and then we would jointly cri-
tique them. During this tedious and sometimes very painful process,
writers would be called to task for their perceived classism, racism, or
internalized self-hatred. I was once criticized for a piece I had written
about the attack that had fractured my spine the previous year. Several
women told me I was racist for mentioning that my assailants were His-
panic. But the detailed editing process also allowed for positive feedback, and I recall that Martha, Robin, and others were particularly
supportive of publishing young activists like me.

The first piece I ever published in *Rat* was about a feminist sit-in at the
Ladies' Home Journal, an action in which I was intimately involved. Early
in 1970 Susan Brownmiller and other members of a group called Media
Women, including writer Sally Kempton, spread word through Women's
Liberation Movement groups that they were looking for participants in
an action to draw attention to the deplorable content of women's magazines. I thought seizing the magazine was a wonderful idea—how could
these sexist magazines be the only ones out there for women? Glossies
such as *Vogue, Redbook, McCall's,* and *Cosmopolitan* were high on fashion
tips but low on feminist consciousness. As I noted in my *Rat* news piece,
"The *Ladies' Home Journal* consumer columns advise women to buy, buy,
buy—especially the products advertised in the *Journal.* The magazine
should in fact be telling their consumers how detergents pollute water."
Most of the articles and short stories in these magazines were penned by
men, some of whom used women's pseudonyms.

Media Women meetings usually took place in Susan Brownmiller's
Greenwich Village apartment. Susan was a thirty-something, accom-

plished, ambitious, and successful journalist and aspiring screenwriter. She possessed a certain savvy and polish that stood out in our circles. She had been published in a number of major newspapers and magazines. A meticulous researcher, she later became world-renowned for her 1975 pioneering work on rape, *Against Our Will*. We would show up with food, but Susan could actually produce enough matching coffee cups for everyone in the meeting—usually about a dozen women—and she didn't rely on old clamshells for ashtrays.

Over cups of coffee and countless cigarettes, women from across the New York feminist community hatched a complicated and well-oiled plot to bring the revolution to the world of magazine publishing and to its readers. We quickly focused on the *Ladies' Home Journal* because it was the only major fashion magazine being edited by a man, John Mack Carter. We scoured back issues and compiled our grievances against the *Journal*. Among other things, the magazine, like many others of its type, focused (as so many magazines still do) on what we now call the "rich and famous," such women as Jacqueline Kennedy Onassis and Elizabeth Taylor. It was simply futile for the average American woman to emulate their standards of wealth, beauty, and success, but the magazine naturally never questioned whether these women should be worshiped. At the time Jackie O's claim to fame was marrying two rich and powerful men. Liz Taylor had wed several more, although at least she had acting skills.

The magazine featured advice columns, including one entitled "Can This Marriage Be Saved?" It was patently offensive: No matter how brutal or demeaning the circumstances a woman faced in her marriage, she was advised to stick with it, be more compliant, and become more caring. Sometimes the columnist proffered advice on making a woman's husband a bit nicer, but women were generally expected to make any necessary adjustments themselves. The obvious question "*Should* this marriage be saved?" was never raised. Finally, we agreed as we looked through those back issues that the advertising was thoroughly degrading to women. One of our favorites was an ad that said that even a woman who had no idea of what a vice president (implicitly male) did could make Jello tarts.

We formulated a long list of demands to present to the magazine: (1) John Mack Carter had to be replaced by a woman; (2) women would fill all positions as editors, staff people, and writers; (3) Black editorial workers had to be hired in proportion to the Black readership (no African American worked there at that time); (4) a day care center had to be established on the premises; (5) the magazine had to agree to eliminate degrading advertising and columns (columnists such as Bruno Bettelheim and Theodore Rubin, two sexist psychologists, had to be replaced); and (6) an entire issue of the magazine, to be renamed the *Women's Home Journal,* would be written and edited by Media Women.

We plotted every detail of the plan with the meticulousness of bank robbers. Each of us contacted feminists whom we thought might be interested in participating in the action. Susan arranged for contacts who worked at the *Journal* to give her a tour of the offices, after which she drew up and distributed an extensive floor plan. Michela produced one fabulous poster to make a great visual impact on the media: On the cover of a mock magazine entitled the *Ladies Liberated Journal* was a photograph of a pregnant woman with a caption that said, "Unpaid Labor."

A few days before the action, we called the women on our list and told them to meet us on March 18, at 8:45 A.M., in front of St. Peter's Church on Lexington Avenue at East Fifty-fourth Street. Everyone was requested to wear "proper business attire"—that is, a skirt or dress—so that we could enter the premises without attracting too much attention. Leaflets and flyers were hidden under coats or in capacious handbags. We also called in a few "friendly" members of the press, including Grace Lichtenstein of the *New York Times* and Marlene Sanders, a producer at WABC-TV. By then every activist knew that a rolling television camera was the best protection against being beaten up by the pigs.

A few weeks before the action, I asked Collier's for a "personal day" off for March 18. By March 17 I was wondering whether I would have a job to return to after the action. I was certain that this time I would be arrested. It was unlikely that Carter would give in to our demands; it seemed equally impossible for us to simply walk away after so much planning. My feelings about the action were further complicated by an article that Susan had published in the *New York Times Magazine* the previous Sunday (the Ides of March—she should have known better!). In her analysis of the Women's Liberation Movement, Susan dismissed lesbians as "lavender herrings," a designation that so infuriated Michela that she backed out of the takeover. Several other lesbians followed suit. I considered doing the same, but I felt that I had spent too much time and energy on this action to walk away from it now. We could deal with Susan's remarks later on.

After a sleepless night, I donned my "revolutionary disguise": a blouse and skirt, an outfit I no longer wore even to my own job (much to my employer's consternation). Terry and John gave me a big hug for good luck, and I headed to the East Fifties for our action. More than a hundred women showed up. We handed out floor plans and told each group of women where to go. Some of us headed to the editorial offices, while others were supposed to raise the consciousness of the secretarial pool, in part to let them know that this was a prowoman action that we hoped would benefit them and in part to ask them how they felt about doing the most menial jobs at the *Journal* for the worst pay. In the late 1960s the mean salary of a male college graduate was $7,500, whereas a female graduate earned only $4,500. Fashion magazines paid even less for entry-level jobs. Working with glamorous models and editing stories about famous people were supposedly reward enough. Consequently, most of the employees came from upper-middle-class homes and relied on regular allowances from their families in order to work for these magazines and dress appropriately for the job. The notion that working in publishing is a "privilege" helps to explain why even today there are so few minorities in the profession.

Some of the women, including Kathie Sarachild, Alix Kates Shulman, and some of the other Redstockings, remained in the lobby for about an hour until they were sure that police vans weren't going to pull up and arrest us all, as Kathie had been predicting for days. The rest of us rode up in the elevators to the fifth floor. Carter and his assistant, Lenore Hershey, were waiting for us. Carter seemed smaller than I had imagined after all the build-up. Like Lee Harvey Oswald, John Mack Carter was a man so ordinary looking that he simply wouldn't be noticed in a crowd. He was a trim man with short brown hair. He was wearing a gray pinstripe suit and a rep tie—he could have been any of a hundred men working at 641 Lexington Avenue. Lenore Hershey stood slightly behind him, her gray hair tucked neatly under a black hat, her body covered by a plain black suit. I wondered whether she always dressed like a professional Greek mourner. In contrast to Carter, who faded into the backdrop, she stood out sharply. Hershey had the sharp-eyed look of an aspiring executive willing to do whatever was necessary to get ahead—including undertaking the unpleasant firings, luring writers from the competition, doing whatever it took. I felt that if she were in charge, we would be in jail in an instant. For now she lurked a meaningful step behind Carter. After all, if we managed to force him out, she might get his job.

A huge group of us trailed after Carter to his office. Much to my horror, I noticed that a few of the women had brought along prewritten statements, which they were reading over. They were ready to address the cameras even if no one asked them to. I was starting to get a bad feeling about the action. Were these women really in it out of feminist commitment, or did they just want to be on TV?

Nevertheless, I was among those who crammed into Carter's office. He barricaded himself behind his huge mahogany desk. Hershey stationed herself at his right elbow. One woman read our demands. The cameras rolled. Carter lit a cigar and contemplated its growing ember as the list droned on and on. Carter repeatedly insisted that he would negotiate only with a maximum of twelve of us in a conference room on the second floor. We perceived this as a divide-and-conquer scheme and refused to follow him. I asked someone to paste a sign saying, "Conference Room" on his office door. Everyone laughed.

The hours crawled by, and we didn't seem to be getting anywhere. The women who had been delegated to do consciousness-raising with the secretaries began to accuse those of us who were in Carter's office of being elitist. They tried to cram into Carter's office, too. His office was now jammed with feminists; television, radio, and newspaper reporters; and assorted members of the *Ladies' Home Journal* staff. We heard rumors that police had been called so that the building would be cleared by five o'clock. The pressure was mounting. The TV reporters were becoming impatient; they needed to get good footage and leave in time to edit it for the six o'clock news.

When the cameras started to roll, Shulamith Firestone flew into action, egged on by Ti-Grace Atkinson. Shulie was a slight young woman with long brown hair and glasses. Of all the amazing women I met in the movement, she was one of the very few I would classify as a genius. Though she was a promising leader and theorist, there was also something askew about her. She was impulsive and erratic, breaking angrily first with New York Radical Women and then with Redstockings. Now she leapt up on Carter's huge desk and lunged violently at him, her arms stretched out stiffly in front of her. He was standing with his back to the plate-glass windows, and I feared that she intended to shove him though them. I visualized him plummeting five stories to the sidewalk below, after which Shulie would spend the rest of her life in prison.

I was standing to the left of Carter's desk. In an almost reflexive action, learned from many hours recently spent in judo class, I grabbed Shulie's right outstretched arm and used her forward momentum to flip her effortlessly over my left shoulder. The room was so tightly packed that she floated, face up, on the arms of the packed-in bystanders, like a 1990s crowd surfer in a mosh pit.

Shulie was so humiliated that she immediately left, and she never spoke to me again. She felt that I had defended Carter, when in reality I had intended to save her, not him. Yet Shulie's lunge and my reflexive response transformed the entire tenor of the sit-in. Carter turned the same color as the ash on his cigar. He suddenly agreed to negotiate: Contrasted with Shulie's behavior, our demands seemed reasonable. Everyone except twelve of us left the office. When we emerged at 8:00 P.M., almost twelve hours after the start of the action, Carter had agreed to pay us $10,000 for an eight-page supplement to the *Journal*, which we would collectively write and edit.

It was a huge victory, but at the time I felt that we had sold out for very little and that the action might do little more than advance the careers of a few more female college graduates. As I subsequently wrote in *Rat:*

Somewhere, all demands, save that of the alternate issue or supplement, were gone. Another woman and I demanded that we ask for more than a page in July and vague promises for an issue. What about child-care facilities for the workers? What about hiring Black employees? What about a training program for secretaries so that they too could share in the editorial control of the magazine? What about the minimum wage? What about an end to the ads in the *Journal* insulting women? Somewhere in the night, the action came down with a severe case of anemia.

We started more and more to appeal to his capitalist self-interest— how much money he would make on a women's liberation issue. We started to stand behind money instead of the rightness and inevitable power of our cause. We appealed to his bourgeois instincts instead of to our needs, demands, and revolutionary ideals.

The action highlighted some of the tensions and inconsistencies in the feminist community. In particular, it pointed to a potential conflict of interest for those who considered themselves both writers and feminists. Some, such as Redstocking Ros Baxandall, had genuine concerns about the "contradictions between their [the writing professionals'] personal goals and our radical socialist ideals." Ros had apparently spotted some "new career types, who came armed with their vitae. They didn't want to change *Ladies' Home Journal* in a major way; instead, they wanted to write feminist pieces for the magazine." Yet Alix Kates Shulman, who later complained about "writers coming in and ripping off the movement," was herself a novelist and a chronicler of the life and writings of Emma Goldman. She did not reject mainstream male-owned publishers for her own work. Others were angry about being left out of leadership roles. After the action, Ti-Grace, Shulie, Minda Bikman, and Anne Koedt were publicly bitter about it. Accustomed to being in charge, they were dismayed that those of us who had planned the action weren't about to step aside and beg them to be our spokeswomen when they hadn't been involved in the organizational work.

Despite our mixed feelings about the outcome of our protest, we followed through on our agreement with the *Ladies' Home Journal*. About a dozen of us met again with Carter and Hershey in the once-rejected second-floor conference room to hash out the content of the supplement. We decided to take on major issues such as work and education. I could see that sexuality, particularly lesbianism, was going to be ignored. I initially worked with one of the subgroups on an essay about education, but as the writing dragged on into May, I became involved in plans to head out to California and dropped out of the writing process. I had no illusions that a career at the *Journal* lay in my future.

Whatever the failures of the sit-in at the *Journal*, it was without a doubt the most successful one-day action taken by the Women's Liberation Movement. A few days later, on March 23, forty-six women at *Newsweek*, almost all of them editorial assistants, filed a sexual discrimination lawsuit against the magazine. Several months later Media Women set up a fund that distributed the entire $10,000 to women's causes, such as a revolving bail fund and a women's center.

I walked away with only one small memento: As I was about to leave the final editorial meeting, John Mack Carter shook my hand. "I don't know why you did what you did," he said, "but thanks." I didn't know what to say. Then he handed me a small, black jewelry box, inside of which was a gold heart engraved with the motto of the *Journal:* "Never Underestimate the Power of a Woman."

∂⃰   ∂⃰   ∂⃰

I rarely saw Shulie after that action, and when we did run into each other, she refused to speak with me. She had left, or perhaps had been asked to leave, New York Radical Feminists long before it folded in 1972. She started, but never completed, a second book, which dealt with women's images in advertising.

Years later I heard unsettling stories about her. At one point she returned to Orthodox Judaism and renounced feminism. I heard she accepted a speaking engagement at a college; of course, she was expected to talk about *The Dialectic of Sex.* The audience was stunned when she spoke about the Rosicrucians.

Susan Brownmiller told me that she had run into Shuli⟨⟩ New York Public Library and had at first mistaken her for a ba⟨⟩ "Look at me! Look at what I've become! You did it! You did it!" Shu⟨⟩ screamed at Susan, pointing an accusatory finger.

Perhaps we had all done it; certainly we didn't know how to take care of her as she slipped further and further into madness. Finally, in 1989 or 1990, her fellow tenants feared she was going to set her East Village apartment on fire. Shulie had failed to pay the electric bills and was using candles for light. Kathie Sarachild went to speak to her, but Shulie wouldn't let her in and made Kathie perch outside Shulie's window on the fire escape. Ti-Grace Atkinson, Kate Millett, Kathie Sarachild, and Phyllis Chesler, among others, heard about Shulie's plight and decided to help. Someone called me, but because of my unfortunate history with Shulie, I thought any involvement on my part would be counterproductive. Phyllis tried to find a suitable private feminist facility where Shulie might be rehabilitated at no charge. Because Kate had had such negative experiences at the hands of psychiatrists (which she wrote about in her 1990 autobiographical book *The Loony-Bin Trip*), she was opposed to any institutionalization. Finally, several women, including Kate and Kathie, became Shulie's legal guardians. After many difficult years Shulie has become productive again as an activist for and writer about mental illness.

Though some women who were at the *Ladies' Home Journal* sit-in, including Ros Baxandall, were sure that Shulie had no intention of harming Carter, I did see a murderous glint in her eye, and I was the one standing almost directly in front of her. Perhaps it was a glimmer of the madness to come, something we all should have paid more attention to then. But as Phyllis Chesler has so brilliantly pointed out, insanity is so often a charge used to control women that at the time we never would have labeled a sister in those terms. Back then Shulie was simply more radical or extreme than many of us and nothing more.

And it wasn't just Shulie. I can see now that there were many marginally sane people—both gay and straight—in the movement. Back then homosexuals and feminists were so angry at being judged by the patriarchy, by our parents, by our employers, by physicians, and by other

e refused to evaluate one another's mental status
have. Psychology was the patriarchal child of
no one trusted therapy until feminists later re-
ts. Perhaps we had been called "crazy queers" and
r so long that we believed society thought us all
Perhaps it was abnormal—or simply quixotic—to
imagine that ould overthrow the patriarchy and forge an equitable
society.

When viciousness erupted, as it did all too frequently at meetings or demonstrations, or when one person was angry that someone else was selected by the media as spokesperson of the moment, it was easy to hide envy and malice behind accusations of racism, classism, sexism, or "star-tripping." These were real issues, but the differences were often not as much about class or race as some historians have implied. Both the women's and gay movements were much more white and middle class than we would like to admit, even now.

One of the untold and unpleasant truths is that much of the internal animosity was fomented by people who were simply disruptive or wanted to be stars. In an era in which elitism was anathema, no one could admit to such evil ambitions, but it's clear to me now that many secretly hoped that they would become our acknowledged leaders. And when they didn't, they attacked and tried to tarnish anyone who shone. Just as importantly, many other individuals acted selflessly. They worked tirelessly for changes they might not live to see and for improvements for which they received no credit.

8

Guns, Bats, and Whistles

The *Ladies' Home Journal* action was an extremely liberating experience for me. I didn't get arrested; in fact, Media Women emerged victorious. But I did come to terms with the likelihood that I would spend some part of my life in prison; it seemed more a question of when, than if, the end of my days of freedom would come. But though I was terrified every time I thought the police were coming for me, I had lost most of my fear of the Women's House of Detention. The struggle for liberation was now more important to me than my personal well-being. As Gandhi had put it, to find something to live for, people have to find something they are willing to die for. I had found not just one, but two causes—women's liberation and gay liberation. I knew that the day I stopped organizing and protesting because I was afraid, I would already be admitting defeat.

I continued to attend GLF meetings and became more involved in the organization. It was easier to attend meetings now that I lived on the Upper West Side with three men also committed to the organization. On Sundays Terry, Jude, John, and I would meet up with our neighbor Diana Davies, and we would all head downtown to the GLF meeting at the Church of the Holy Apostles on West Twenty-eighth Street. Afterward we would swap views of the meetings and discuss what we thought of people's positions. Because the four of us were regular attendees, we became a force to be reckoned with. If any one of us attended a committee meeting, everyone in our apartment knew the outcome. Our information tended to be much more complete and focused than committee reports given at the GLF. Such knowledge was power. For one thing, few people took notes, for to do so would have made others think they were police informers. People rarely took photos either. Only Diana Davies, Ellen Shumsky, and a few others owned decent cameras, and when they wanted to snap photos, they had to obtain the verbal consent of anyone they wanted to include. As a result, only a few dozen people ever turned up in the group portraits, even though many additional people may have been present. I, for one, didn't want to make it easy for the police to identify me when they came to round us all up.

In January 1970, much to my surprise, my name was drawn out of a hat, and I became the chair of the organization for the month of February. I was the first woman chair, though Lois Hart had cochaired very early meetings. Once I had been named chair, I naturally became more public and outspoken (though I still avoided photos). I had to attend and run every general meeting. Trying to instill some order in the chaotic proceedings was a daunting task, but I was determined to use my tenure as chair to make some changes. Just being heard was the first problem. My voice carries well, but shouting has always given me laryngitis, and it's no accident that after years of movement work I have vocal chord nodules. What I really needed was a gavel to call the group to order in some way, but such an instrument was too "bourgeois."

I decided to bring my trusty softball bat to the meetings. I banged it gently on one of the poles that ran from floor to ceiling in the center of the room. The bat called the meeting to order and stopped people from shouting or talking out of turn. There was also another unexpected advantage: People gave me more space in the subway—they avoided a woman with a bat, especially as it was February and hardly baseball

weather. The bat was a great success; the meetings wer
Years later, if gay people from that era remember me f
for bringing that bat to GLF meetings.

I hoped that I could get the men to deal more with
Some guys were just starting to come to grips with their oppressive behavior, months after the first consciousness-raising groups had started to
meet. Some of them still cut in or didn't listen when women spoke.
Some men gave the impression that they didn't consider the women
(with a few exceptions) capable of running anything. They also didn't
want to deal with the fact that the women had different issues to con-
tend with, that we were doubly oppressed as both women and homosexuals. Some of the men argued that they were more oppressed because
women weren't busted in baths, under the highway, or in the Central
Park Rambles cruising area. They overlooked the fact that women didn't
usually have sex in the open, just as they discounted the benefits of
being white and male. The women conceded that sissies were beaten up
and stigmatized for their effeminate appearance, but in those days most
of us considered swishy mannerisms and campy diction to be learned
behavior, not biological destiny. So gay men were being oppressed for
what they did, we felt, whereas women were oppressed on the basis of
our biology. (Though academics like myself still believe that behavior is
socially constructed, most gay men and lesbians I've met in the last
decade are convinced that their sexual orientation is genetically determined.) In any case gay men, lesbians, bisexuals, and transsexuals were
not, we women asserted, a unified group just because society lumped us
together. Gay men, among others, had to acknowledge our differences
and our needs.

Along these very lines, one of the first issues we dealt with was the
harassment of women by both straight and gay men at the dances. In a
gesture of solidarity the men ceded us a back room at the Alternate U.
The space, dubbed the "make-out room," would not have been considered a prize in the real world. It was seedy and furnished with torn,
filthy couches; decrepit easy chairs; and a few folding metal chairs. Separated from the dance floor by a door, the room mostly served as a so-

izing and necking mecca. The women figured that the door could also be useful for keeping men out and creating a safe haven for women. Since this back area was one of the few places where people could sit down and hang out during a dance, many of the men objected to transforming it into a woman-only space.

I hoped that by becoming the chair of the GLF, I could shape the dialog so that there would be not just a room but also a women's dance. Many of the men resisted the idea of a separate event even more than they had resisted the idea of a woman-only space. They might have seen it as the first sign of our independence—a step that would inevitably lead to our forming an autonomous group. But how could they not see that denying us such a privilege would hasten the end of cooperative efforts? The arguments usually revolved around the treasury—that is, whether women had a right to use funds for an event to which men weren't invited. Since only about fifty to a hundred women ever showed up at the dances, which might attract as many as a thousand people in the course of an evening, some of the men claimed that a women's dance was a money-losing proposition that would further drain our meager financial resources. A few men groused that soon transvestites and people of color would demand their own events. ("What's wrong with that?" I wondered.) Radicals also objected to additional dances as a frivolous diversion from revolutionary politics. Instead of dancing, we should be dialoguing with the Black Panthers and Young Lords. They saw a women's dance as a divisive tactic. Many of the women—especially those of us with feminist leanings—felt the men were treating us as their wives: giving us the "pin money" they thought sufficient while failing to treat us as full and equal partners. (I doubt that lesbians receive an equal share of "gay money" even today.)

Even though I fought for instituting an all-women's event, I shared some of the men's reservations about the dances. I agreed with the radical faction that holding dances wasn't exactly furthering all our political aims. Instead of creating a new society, we were imitating the existing one, a subculture that circulated around alcohol and drugs. For some, the dances recapitulated the worst of high school proms, where people were marked as wallflowers or singled out as beautiful and popular. We were simply providing a cheaper alternative to the bar scene, one that mirrored its pitfalls exactly.

Dances highlighted "looksism"—that is, selecting or rejecting others on the basis of their physical appearance. In a noisy room where talking was impossible (unless people were deaf and used sign language), the only thing to go on was appearance. The consciousness-raising groups I had helped start in November had encouraged both men and women to consider others' feelings. A few took the concept rather too far and called those who rejected them "looksist." The other side of the issue was that everyone still had the right to decline sexual activity. But both Allen Young and Terry told me stories of unwanted advances that they felt unable to reject for fear of being labeled "looksist" or worse.

Even though I knew dances wouldn't solve all our problems, I felt I could use my temporary leadership to improve the position of GLF women within the group and foreground our needs—including our entitlement to a portion of the treasury money. Armed with my bat, I set about chairing discussions of the dance issue. Countless arguments later, we women got some money and the reluctant acquiescence of the majority of the men, though some gay brothers were strongly supportive of our needs. We chose April 3, 1970, and booked the Alternate U.

At first we were gleeful that we had finally won a tiresome battle. And then we panicked. What if we had a party and no one came? What if we couldn't attract more than the fifty or so regulars? Fearing failure, we turned to our heterosexual sisters in the women's movement. We asked them to come to the dance as an act of support. Many of the women I knew from Redstockings and *Rat* agreed to come. Just under the surface of solidarity, however, lurked tensions. When I mistakenly asked one woman twice, she accused me of trying to transform her into a lesbian.

Some of the women I asked refused to attend. Many of them objected to the very notion of dances for the same reasons I did. A few feminists had additional objections as well. One woman, writing for *Rat*, expressed a "fear of breaking down this political, nearly formal relationship with my sisters and sisters I would meet." Her phobia about "dancing with sisters because it means 'sexual'" was one I encountered often. It might have been difficult for straight women to appreciate just how political a women's dance was. In New York State it was illegal for two people of the same sex to dance together. Just by dancing, we were challenging a system that refused to let us be ourselves.

In addition to publicizing our dances in feminist circles, we also wanted to let the women in the bars know that we were creating an alternative scene. But how would we reach them? Aside from *Rat,* the *East Village Other,* and the *Village Voice* (which by this time would use the words *gay* and *homosexual,* but would they use *lesbian*?), there were no venues where we could advertise. A few of us stood outside Kooky's and Gianni's and passed out leaflets, but we were quickly chased away by the bouncers. One night a few of the very bravest made forays into Kooky's, but she spotted them after only a few minutes and had her goons toss them out into the snow. Kooky clearly wasn't big on First Amendment rights. She read the leaflet and threatened, "If you goils keep dis up, there ain't gonna be no gay lib!"

The *Ladies' Home Journal* action had helped me conquer my fear of arrest, but I was still terrified of Kooky and her cronies, who were commonly believed to be connected to the Mafia. For one thing, their marksmanship was much better than that of the military or the police, and they made fewer mistakes. How many times do you read in the paper that organized crime has wiped out the wrong group in a restaurant? How many times does the Mafia stuff the wrong body in a car trunk? The last thing I wanted to see was Kooky pointing her cigarette at me and saying to the goons, "Get *dat* one!"

In the end the dangers of the bars were themselves the most compelling reasons not to brook any intimidation by the likes of Kooky. In fact, on March 8, while we were in the midst of our leafleting campaign, the New York City Police Department raided the Snake Pit, a male after-hours club in the West Village. Among the 167 arrested was Diego Vinales, an immigrant from Argentina. Terrified that the publicity surrounding his arrest would lead to his deportation and notify his family of his sexual proclivities, he leaped out of the second floor window of the Village precinct house. He was impaled on six spikes of the wrought-iron fence below. Blowtorches were employed to extricate him, and he was taken, with a spike still sticking out of his gut, to the hospital. Later, according to the *New York Times,* everyone else was released, but when Vinales survived, he was booked for resisting arrest. Bars were clearly not a safe center for gay life.

When we finally held our first dance, it surpassed our expectations. The weather was cold but clear. The place was packed. We even attracted some media stars such as Jill Johnston, a columnist for the *Village Voice,* and noted essayist Susan Sontag. We were thrilled. My straight friends from Redstockings and *Rat* sat nervously on the make-out couches and hoped no one would ask them to dance. When no one did, some were insulted. Other straight women unabashedly danced with each other and with us. As one woman wrote in *Rat* afterward: "Dancing with women is something else again. It was one of the most beautiful experiences of my life—a total high. . . . I am learning to love women, and the dance was a first step." A few of the straight women went home together and brought each other out.

The GLF women had a fabulous time as we danced to our favorite music. We danced fast, we did some Greek and Jewish dances in groups and circles, and we even played some slow songs. It was the hip 1970s, and we rarely touched on the dance floor. Free drugs were easier to find than a slow tune. There were times at some GLF dances that I was definitely nostalgic for the bars. Those sexy bar butches, now reclassified as politically incorrect, held me tight when we danced.

We were ready to congratulate ourselves on our success. But one detail made us nervous: We sent a scout over to Kooky's and Gianni's, and she reported back that both bars were fairly empty. On a Saturday night, too! We tried not to worry and kept ourselves busy chipping ice, selling drinks for "donations," and dancing.

When the first women's dance came to a close at 3:00 A.M., we began the massive cleanup. We had made little progress sweeping up the cups and other debris when we saw several extremely large men in trench coats with guns in their belts filling up the door of the Alternate U. The men flashed something shiny and said they were the police. (Later, when we discussed this event, we realized that the so-called badges had gone by so quickly that no two women could even agree on their color.) I was skeptical as to whether any of these guys had ever fit into a police uniform; moreover, police officers don't wear their guns in their belts. Nevertheless, the very word "police" set off general pandemonium as some women stampeded to stash pot under the couches in the back room, while the less economically minded flushed pot, acid, and all sorts of other drugs down the overworked toilets.

We asked the largest "officer," who seemed to be in charge, whether we were under arrest and on what grounds. "Unlawful assembly," he replied. The guy behind him nudged him and whispered something in his ear. "I meant you're selling liquor without a license." We pointed out that we weren't selling anything but were giving the drinks away for a small donation. They didn't like this answer, so they started to shove and punch some of the butchier women.

Before the dance started, Florynce Kennedy, a radical African American lesbian lawyer, had given me her number and said to call her in case of trouble at the dance. I had inked her number on the back of my hand—the 1970s version of the electronic organizer. There were no pay phones in the Alternate U, and even if there were, calling for help would have got me reprocessed into Swiss cheese. Someone had to escape and contact Flo. Another woman and I headed for the back stairs—it was always good to know more than one way out. One of the guys saw us make a dash toward the fire exit, and he charged after us—actually, he lumbered. I ran down the stairs and heard a noise that I hoped was the metal door slamming behind me. I had never heard a gun fired, and I wasn't about to inquire now. Later that night two illegal Cuban immigrants who'd been at the dance were spirited down the same stairs, just in case these guys were really cops.

When we got into the cold night air, we ran to the closest pay phone in front of Kooky's bar, less than a block away. From there we called Flo, who told us she'd get the police (it wouldn't hurt to call more cops if the others were real) and call the press.

As we finished our business in the phone booth, two men emerged from Kooky's. They were not employees but drunks who had accidentally walked into a lesbian bar and been tossed out. They were enraged and looking for the first lesbians in sight to kill them. Conveniently, there we were in the phone booth. (In those days there were still self-contained phone booths, which doubled as urinals.). This was not our lucky night. They asked us whether we had been in the bar, and we told them no. They didn't believe us and showered us with a stream of abuse, calling us "pussy suckers" and other names. They threatened to kill us. When I insisted that we hadn't been in the bar, they asked us what we were doing in a phone booth at that hour of the night. "Fixing it, we're from the phone company," I replied nervously. I was so desperate that I ripped the receiver off its cable. "See, it's broken."

They had to agree and tottered down the street. Never underestimate the power of a woman in trouble.

When we returned to the loft, the fray was over. Somehow, Bob Kohler from the GLF showed up; he cleverly told the "police" he was the Alternate U manager. The media had come, the men had fled, and then the real police had arrived. The police denied that anyone from the vice squad or alcohol commission had been sent over. They left and never found the culprits. The media left, too, after receiving our thanks. Several women had been bullied and hit, but no one had been seriously injured.

Despite our close escape and the message those thugs tried to send us, we were not deterred. We started to have women's dances on a regular basis. Each dance drew more women. When the bars saw that they would not go out of business from an occasional dance, they stopped harassing us and even let us leaflet outside (some let us inside). Today we take the privilege of same-sex dances for granted, but in that winter of 1970 we were aware that we had broken new ground. We were proud and amazed at our daring.

Having again escaped from danger, I became further emboldened. I suppose I felt invulnerable, both to the police and the Mafia. Now that my term as chair was over and I was no longer concerned with my role in changing the workings of GLF, I turned my attention to other issues. That spring, for instance, the news ran several stories about a large-breasted woman who was hassled every day on her way to work in the financial district. Men waited for her outside the Wall Street subway station, and when she emerged, they tormented her with stares, wolf whistles, and rude comments about her anatomy.

Most women could identify with this kind of treatment. During my first semester in college, when I was still commuting from home, several times men rubbed their penises against my butt in the crowded subway car. I started carrying a dissection kit from zoology class and would pull out my scalpel as soon as a hand or hard cock started to touch me. The sight of a sharp, shiny blade brought a quick halt to their sexual interest. One time in the subway, I heard a woman shout: "Whose hand is this? I found this hand on my body, so someone must have lost it there!" In her iron grasp was the wrist of a very red-faced man. As I watched the news reports about the Wall Street woman, I realized that this sort of thing was still happening to me. I generally couldn't get from my apartment building to the subway station three blocks away without at least two men making catcalls or sucking noises at me. Being a woman on the streets of New York felt a lot like being a tormented animal in a zoo cage.

After I studied judo, I felt stronger about defending myself. If a man stared at my breasts, I would stop and stare at his genitals. Once when I was making a call to Terry in a telephone booth, the Times Square flasher that my mother had always warned me about made his appearance outside the booth, as if he had just walked out of some dreadful screenplay. There he stood in a long, tan trench coat, which he opened like bat wings in front of my booth so that only I could see his wonderful equipment. In consciousness–raising I had discovered how men like him got off on women's fear, so very calmly I told Terry: "Hold on a moment. I seem to have a flasher outside my booth." I put the phone down, carefully opened up the door, took a long look, and said, "My, my, that looks just like a penis—only smaller." He closed his trench coat faster than he had opened it and fled.

The Wall Street woman had made it into the news because she was being harassed by well-dressed white men; apparently, this was surprising to some. Feminists needed to proclaim publicly that what we now call harassment happened all the time. All sorts of men did it to all sorts of women. It seemed to me that it was high time to protest. In late

March, I decided to organize what I named "The First National Ogle-In." I contacted Marlene Sanders of WABC-TV and some other media contacts I had made from the *Ladies' Home Journal* action. I asked some friends from my Redstockings C-R group and from *Rat* to join me. Elsie agreed to go to WBAI (a somewhat radical radio station) and report on the event while it was happening. Alix Kates Shulman, Carol Grosberg, and Lucy were among those who participated.

We arrived at Wall Street before the stock exchanges and brokerage houses opened for business. We followed men as they emerged from the subway. I blew a metal whistle at them because I've never been able to create that kind of sound by myself. I made loud comments about their clothes, their looks, their legs, their butts, their hair or lack thereof. Lucy went so far as to put her arms around some of the men; she even hugged them against their will. The men were horrified. We were having fun, and in many of the clips I'm laughing (as usual) at my own jokes. Marlene Sanders captured several men on film with gaping jaws, too surprised to comment. Marlene asked Lucy whether love and sex were passé. "Unless men change very soon," Lucy replied, "it's going to be out."

Next we went to a construction site and hassled the workers. I had prescreened several sites and selected one where all the workers were white. Unfortunately, that wasn't difficult to do: Men of color and women were still having a hard time getting into the trades. Not surprisingly, the cameras and the press weren't interested in the construction workers.

Soon after the demonstration someone called me to inquire whether I would go on Barry Gray's radio show and discuss our action. Gray was a pioneer of talk radio, and his show was a lot tonier than most of what passes over the airwaves today. It was my first radio show, and Gray wasn't very profeminist, so I expected a hard time.

I feared Gray might call in a psychiatrist to tell us to accept our female role. I refused to appear alone, and Lucy agreed to accompany me. But as it turned out, he was not hostile, merely baffled. Lucy and I had a difficult time explaining to him the humiliations women suffered every day. A big sign in the studio warned us that certain words could not be used on the air, although many of these forbidden words described our plight perfectly. Since terms such as "sexual harassment" hadn't even been coined yet, we were at a loss for words. Gray looked bewildered. Finally, I gestured to the parts in question. Gray blushed and understood. He cleverly rephrased our points for the audience by using suggestive language without naming these organs.

I knew that the women who listened to the show didn't need a translation to understand exactly what we were talking about. They had experienced what we had, and they were thrilled that someone had got even a speck of revenge. During the next few weeks, I was deluged by letters from grateful female listeners. A few angry men who were offended by my behavior and some antifeminist women wrote as well. I felt like a minor celebrity.

꙳꙳꙳   ꙳꙳꙳   ꙳꙳꙳

At the Veteran Feminists of America awards dinner in December 1997, I ran into Alix Kates Shulman.

"Alix!" I gushed. "You won't believe this. I found Marlene Sanders's documentary of the first ogle-in I organized down on Wall Street. There you are along with Carol Grosberg and Lucy."

"Oh, yes," Alix chimed in. "I remember that woman they were tormenting as she came out of the subway. Why didn't you take me to see the footage? Where is it?"

"It's down in New Jersey at Rutgers University, and until I saw it, I didn't remember that you were at that particular action. But I'm going back to collect a still from it, and you can come with me."

"Okay, don't forget to call me."

We moved on to schmooze with other old friends.

Two hours later Alix was called up to the microphone to claim her Medal of Honor and to represent WITCH. Along with tales of hexing the bridal fair and the stock exchanges, Alix regaled the audience with the details of the ogle-in that I had just passed on to her, except that she claimed the event as a WITCH action.

After the dinner I bumped into Alix again.

"Alix! *I* organized that ogle-in! It wasn't a WITCH action, though it was certainly WITCH-like!"

"Why didn't you correct me?"

As if I could have just stood up and disrupted an entire evening of events where awards were timed to run five minutes each. As if I could ever be that rude to someone as fine as Alix.

Besides, there is a lesson in Alix's innocent slippage. If history can be altered somewhere between the cocktails and the desserts, what hope do I have of getting it right almost thirty years later?

9

The Lavender Menace

The Lavender Menace zap that took place on May 1, 1970, at the Second Congress to Unite Women remains for activists, for historians, and for those of us who participated in it the single most important action organized by lesbians who wanted the women's movement to acknowledge our presence and needs. That event completely reshaped the relationship of lesbians to feminism for years to come.

Lesbians whose only involvement was with the Women's Liberation Movement were generally no better off than those of us connected with the Gay Liberation Front. Most heterosexual feminists were no better at hearing us than gay men were. Conservative elements of the women's movement were openly hostile to lesbians. For instance, Betty Friedan had branded us a "lavender menace." Lesbians, she believed, would blight the reputation of the National Organization for Women if its members were labeled "man-haters" and "a bunch of dykes." The very threat of such appellations led NOW to deny the number of lesbians in its ranks. Lesbophobia was so virulent that NOW omitted the name of the New York chapter of the Daughters of Bilitis from the list of sponsors for the First Congress to Unite Women, a conference that NOW organized in November 1969 as a forum for New York area feminists. Rita Mae Brown was so incensed over this omission that she resigned her job in

January 1970, though she did so in part because NOW had eliminated her paid position as administrative coordinator in the national office. As Rita wrote in her final issue of the newsletter, she "decided to go down fighting." She told her readers that she was disgusted with the NOW leadership because of "its sexist, racist, and class-biased attitudes." "The leadership," she added, "consciously oppresses other women on the question of sexual preference. . . . Lesbian is the one word that can cause the Executive Committee a collective heart attack. This issue is dismissed as unimportant, too dangerous to contemplate, divisive or whatever excuse could be dredged up from their repression."

In some ways the stage was already set for a massive lesbian rebellion. Not all feminist groups, of course, were as homophobic as NOW, and a number of radical women were quietly experimenting with lesbianism. Redstockings' "prowoman line" publicly supported all women, including lesbians, even if many straight women privately considered our concerns less weighty than those of women who had to do battle every day in the master's bed. Ti-Grace Atkinson, who had broken from NOW in October 1969 and founded The Feminists, may have been the most pro-lesbian. The Feminists was the only group to limit the number of married women in its ranks. Ti-Grace preached abstinence (the Republicans today would adore her) but accepted lesbianism as an alternative form of sexuality, at least until the revolution had equalized power relations between the sexes. In *Amazon Odyssey*, a collection of her writings published in 1974, Ti-Grace wrote that "lesbianism has been a kind of code word for female resistance. Lesbianism is, in many ways, symbolic of feminism as a political movement." She admired lesbianism as a "full commitment" to other women that surpassed the part-time involvement of women who were married or living with a boyfriend. Of course, some heterosexual women, including Ti-Grace, were fully devoted to feminism, even though they had never engaged in lesbian sex.

But this provisional acceptance was an exception in a movement that was apologetic, dismissive, or even downright derisive about the presence of lesbians in its midst. Calls for attention to lesbian issues were attacked as divisive. Ironically, as the struggle for the right to have an all-women's dance demonstrates, many gay men thought along the same lines. But just as many of the GLF women believed that our liberation was intrinsically linked to that of gay men, lesbian/feminists felt a pressing need for the women's movement to recognize our oppression. As Sidney Abbott and Barbara Love later wrote in their 1972 book *Sappho Was a Right-On Woman:* "For Lesbians, Women's Liberation is not an intellectual or emotional luxury but a personal imperative. Living without the approval or support of men, Lesbians desperately need women's rights. For Lesbians, independence and responsibility for self are lifelong realities and not merely interim needs between support by father and support by husband."

By the spring of 1970 many lesbian/feminists were frustrated at feeling ignored by both the women's and gay movements. As a result, when Rita made her one appearance at the Gay Liberation Front that spring and announced the creation of separate consciousness-raising groups for lesbians, many of the women there were ready to heed her call. Several all-lesbian groups formed. Because Rita had wide-ranging contacts, she, Martha Shelley, Lois Hart, Sidney Abbott, Barbara Love, and other women, including me, who belonged to more than one organization were able to encourage lesbians from various activist groups to join.

In retrospect, I think that Rita, having fallen out first with NOW and then later with Redstockings, had decided that she could best form a power base with other lesbians. She had previously avoided any connection with the GLF women, whom she looked down on as a bunch of unliberated butches and femmes. "Many lesbians have no political consciousness of woman oppression," she later wrote in a 1972 essay in *Out of the Closets: Voices of Gay Liberation.* "One of the ways in which many lesbians have protected themselves from the pain of woman oppression is to refuse to see themselves as traditional women. Society encourages this view because if you are not a traditional woman, then you must be some kind of man. Some lesbians do assume a male role (become imitation men)."

But now, alienated from heterosexual feminists, Rita Mae Brown turned to the GLF women. Inviting us to her apartment on West Fifteenth Street for parties or for films, such as *Gold Diggers of 1933,* Rita cultivated her new social contacts. In addition, she carefully constructed a C-R group that contained many of the leading GLF women. Then she called a meeting at her apartment, where she and Martha Shelley divided up the women into C-R groups.

The groups had been meeting only several weeks when an essay by Susan Brownmiller entitled "'Sisterhood Is Powerful': A Member of the Women's Liberation Movement Explains What It's All About" appeared in the *New York Times Magazine* on March 15, 1970. Susan quoted Betty's remark about the "lavender menace" and retorted that we were "a lavender *herring* perhaps, but surely no clear and present danger." It was this essay, as it turned out, that finally pushed us into taking action and helped define our protest. Susan has recently explained to me that she felt that she was attempting to "disassociate from this [Betty's] position" by making what she thought was a humorous remark. But some lesbians, especially Michela Griffo, felt that representing lesbians as gay versions of "red herrings" was evidence of Susan's homophobia or closet homosexuality—that is, she was attempting to distance herself from lesbians by insulting us. Susan's detractors believed that her comments were even worse than Betty's: They were a dismissal of lesbians as totally unimportant, an unnecessary distraction from the real issues. Michela dropped out of the Media Women action at the *Ladies' Home Journal* after Susan's remarks appeared in the *Times,* and at our first lesbian dance she showed up in a pale purple T-shirt onto which she had defiantly hand-stenciled the words "lavender herring."

Rita Mae Brown suggested that we organize an action around the lavender herring comment. The Second Congress to Unite Women was scheduled for the beginning of May. We noted that not a single speaker, workshop, or plenary involved an open lesbian. It was time to tell the women's movement that we would not be ignored any longer.

A large group of us began to meet regularly—about forty women were involved in the Lavender Menace action, but only about half that number planned it. March Hoffman (later Artemis March), a recent Vassar graduate, along with Lois Hart, Rita Mae Brown, Ellen Shumsky, Cynthia Funk, and a few others set about crafting the now-famous manifesto called "The Woman-Identified Woman." The entire group read and edited several drafts, making the document truly a group effort, although some of those involved later tried to claim individual authorship. By the end of April we had honed "The Woman-Identified Woman" down to a ten-paragraph manifesto. It has become an oft-reprinted classic because it summed up so much of what we as radical lesbians thought about ourselves. It started by defining a lesbian as "the rage of all women condensed to the point of explosion." The true lesbian, we wrote, acted "in accordance with her inner compulsion to be a more complete and freer human being."

Though the manifesto was in some ways a daring and radical assertion of lesbian pride, in other ways it was cautious and conservative. Nowhere does the document discuss lesbianism in terms of sexual behavior. We chose to downplay our sexuality because our primary goal was to make a political point, and back then the vision of a lesbian in bed conjured up an image of perversion, not radicalism. We even eschewed the term "lesbian," with all its sexually loaded baggage, and called ourselves "woman-identified women"—that is, those who chose to work with and for others of our gender. It was a term even heterosexuals could feel comfortable claiming. At the same time, we separated ourselves from the category of "woman" by declaring that "self-hate and the lack of real self are rooted in our male-given identity; we must create a new sense of self."

In retrospect, I think our position was a tragic error. We should have taken a more blatantly sexual stance. Our "cop-out" on this issue allowed straight women to continue thinking that lesbians really didn't do much in the absence of a penis and let them assume that straight women, too, could be "political lesbians," since our definition didn't depend on sexual acts. Subsequent generations of lesbians, having read this, and only this, manifesto have incorrectly concluded that the Stonewall generation didn't have sex.

In addition to desexualizing lesbianism, the document declared that lesbianism is a socially constructed "category of behavior possible only in a sexist society characterized by rigid sex roles and dominated by male supremacy. . . . In a society in which men do not oppress women, and sexual expression is allowed to follow feelings, the categories of homosexuality and heterosexuality would disappear." This statement was not meant to be taken as a proclamation that sexual acts would disappear; rather, we believed people were forced to choose relationships with either men or women. Were gendered roles to disappear, we would each be free to relate to others as individuals. Every person would be a potential sex partner.

We did not equate this utopian ideal with bisexuality. In fact, radical lesbians considered bisexuals dangerous "fence sitters" who refused to commit to lesbianism because they wanted to hang onto their heterosexual privileges. A 1971 manifesto called "Realesbians and Politicalesbians," which grew out of a group called the Gay Revolution Party Women's Caucus, derided bisexuality as a "transitional stage, a middle ground, through which women pass from oppressive relationships to those of equality and mutuality. It is a struggle with privilege and fear, and not all women come through it to their sisters on the other side."

We summed up our manifesto by asserting that the mission of the women's movement was "the primacy of women relating to women, of women creating a new consciousness of and with each other which is at the heart of women's liberation, and the basis for the cultural revolution." Thus, we placed lesbians at the forefront of the struggle for women's liberation.

When we finished the manifesto, we had to decide what to call ourselves. We rejected lavender herring because we didn't want to denigrate ourselves, even in jest. We settled on Lavender Menace as a provisional name for the group.

I was part of the contingent that planned the logistics of the Lavender Menace action. Ironically, Michela and I had honed these organizational skills working with Susan Brownmiller on the *Ladies' Home Journal* action, and now here we were protesting something she had written. Several Menaces hand-dyed T-shirts in a bathtub. Then they silk-screened enough purple T-shirts with the words "Lavender Menace" for the entire group. No two shirts looked exactly alike; the color of each depended on how long it had been in the tub. All the shirts were the same size, however, since we could afford only one box. We also made up a number of placards. We decided to go for a humorous approach, since we knew some women were going to be shocked (or perhaps delighted) to discover themselves completely surrounded by lesbians, especially as we had just been dismissed as a minute faction of the movement. The posters, written in rose-colored ink, blared a variety of messages:

TAKE A LESBIAN TO LUNCH!
SUPERDYKE LOVES YOU!
WOMEN'S LIBERATION IS A LESBIAN PLOT.
WE ARE YOUR WORST NIGHTMARE,
YOUR BEST FANTASY.

Finally, we were ready. The Second Congress to Unite Women got under way on May 1 at 7:00 P.M. at Intermediate School 70 on West Seventeenth Street in Manhattan. About three hundred women filed into the school auditorium. Just as the first speaker came to the microphone, Jesse Falstein, a GLF member, and Michela switched off the lights and pulled the plug on the mike. (They had cased the place the previous day and knew exactly where the switches were and how to work them.) I was planted in the middle of the audience, and I could hear my coconspirators running down both aisles. Some were laughing, while others were emitting rebel yells. When Michela and Jesse flipped the lights back on, both aisles were lined with seventeen lesbians wearing their Lavender Menace T-shirts and holding the placards we had made. Some invited the audience to join them. I stood up and yelled, "Yes, yes, sisters! I'm tired of being in the closet because of the women's movement." Much to the horror of the audience, I unbuttoned the long-sleeved red blouse I was wearing and ripped it off. Underneath, I was wearing a Lavender Menace T-shirt. There were hoots of laughter as I joined the others in the aisles. Then Rita yelled to members of the audience, "Who wants to join us?"

"I do; I do," several replied.

Then Rita also pulled off her Lavender Menace T-shirt. Again, there were gasps, but underneath she had on another one. More laughter. The audience was on our side.

By the time the street theater portion of our action was over, about forty Menaces plus audience members who spontaneously joined the action were in the aisles. We passed out mimeographed copies of "The Woman-Identified Woman" and stormed onto the stage. Michela turned the microphone back on. We explained how angry we were to have been excluded from the planning and content of the conference. We wanted our issues and voices included in the congress.

At first one or two members of the planning committee tried to restore order and return to the original program. But not only were these women completely outnumbered by the forty or so members of our action, who now stood on the stage with our arms in solidarity around one another's shoulders, but also the audience was backing us. Audience members indicated via applause or boos that they wanted the lesbian issue to remain on the floor. Some of the straight women turned out to be very supportive. One stood up and said: "Wow, I really need to hear this tonight. I thought I could put off dealing with my feelings for a woman for at least two more years." That statement struck a chord with many of the other nonlesbians in the audience.

Since the panel scheduled for that evening was clearly not happening, women from the audience began to walk up to the microphone. They initiated a dialog with us and with other members of the audience. Pleased with this unexpected openness, we decided that the discussion should continue. When we spotted Marlene Sanders filming the zap for WABC-TV, a Menace stole her film. We wanted the exchange to be free and unfettered. At the end of the speak-out several members of the Lavender Menace, including me, agreed to run workshops the next day on the topic of heterosexism.

Although the Second Congress to Unite Women is best remembered for the Lavender Menace action, there were two other groups that joined us in expressing their dissatisfaction with the event. Black women and members of a class workshop used the stage and then workshops to address how the conference reflected racism and classism in the Women's Liberation Movement. An anonymous author wrote in *Rat* about the confusion of some audience members at the conference: "They were so used to dealing with women's liberation . . . from the shelter of their status as educated, secure, white privileged women. Suddenly, they had to consider why other women hadn't wanted to stay with them, hadn't wanted to play their game." So much discussion made me hopeful. For a short time after the congress, I was naive enough to believe that the middle-class, straight, white women might actually change.

For lesbians, the best thing that emerged from the Lavender Menace action was the group of protesters itself—the first post-Stonewall group to focus on lesbian issues. Only weeks earlier, we had been a random group of women associated primarily with gay liberation and women's liberation. For the moment at least, we emerged a victorious organization with a sense of solidarity, common purpose, and sisterhood. We knew we would no longer accept second-class status in the women's movement or the gay movement. We would be equal partners, or we would leave the straight women and gay men behind.

For a while we hotly debated what to call ourselves. At one point we even called ourselves Radical Radishes because so many of our members were red (Marxist) on the outside but white (capitalist) within. Pat Maxwell, who had been in the GLF, made a button featuring two intertwined radishes with women's symbols emerging from their root end. Eventually, we settled on the name "Radicalesbians" in one uninterrupted word that underscored our unity.

Our only regret about that weekend was that Betty Friedan and Susan Brownmiller, the two women whose words had spurred us to action, were not present. We knew, however, that in a movement as small as ours word of the Lavender Menace would reach them in a matter of hours. We felt as well that the zap was only the first of many actions to come and that lesbian liberation was suddenly and unstoppably on the rise.

એક્ષ્,   એક્ષ્,   એક્ષ્

Although it seems like a long time ago, mainstream feminists still remember the Lavender Menace action. In 1987 I was invited to an awards ceremony at which Adrienne Rich was presented with the Brandeis University Creative Arts medal for poetry. Afterward, in the lobby,

I found myself standing next to Betty Friedan. I was certain that she wouldn't recognize me—it had been more than a decade since she had last seen me. But she hadn't changed much, so perhaps I looked more like my old self than I thought. Betty scowled at me. She shifted her drink to her left hand and crooked a gnarled finger in my direction.

"You! You!" she squealed. "You caused me so much trouble!"

I laughed, even though I didn't think she intended to be funny. "No, Betty," I replied, "you caused yourself trouble. Get over it." And I walked away.

10

Triple Trouble

Despite our optimism, the euphoria of the Lavender Menace action faded within a week. A growing paranoia about "infiltrators" and "government agents" in the women's and gay movements was, for the first time, becoming seriously demoralizing. Nevertheless, just because activists seemed paranoid doesn't mean that they weren't being followed—I discovered, much to my horror, that I really was being spied on by the government.

In a way it all began with Jane Alpert. Jane was one of the people most concerned about government agents, and she certainly had reason to be because she and her coconspirators Sam Melville, Nate Yarrow, and Patricia Swinton had been the dupes of an agent provocateur named George Demmerle. It was not considered entrapment then for government infiltrators to suggest a bombing and even supply the guns, dynamite, or technology. Jane had learned this ruse the hard way from Demmerle, who had seemed too crazy to be a plant.

Certainly, there were police informers and agents provocateurs in groups; not all the talk of watching out for them was paranoia. Released FBI memos that I've heard about over the years indicate that gay movement leaders were spied on from 1953 to 1975—Del Martin and Phyllis Lyon were among those being watched for organizing the Daughters of Bilitis. In the early 1970s the FBI spied on twenty-five chapters of the Gay Liberation Front. In the early 1980s I participated in the "Red Squad Case," a lawsuit against the City of New York. A wide-ranging coalition of individuals and organizations banded together to obtain the files the intelligence unit of the New York City Police Department (an oxymoron if there ever was one) had collected on us for over two decades. Redstockings was just one of many groups on the list. By the time the lawsuit began, Ronald W. Reagan was president, and I thought we had better start fighting harder against a police state, or we'd all finally be rounded up for those dreaded detention camps we had so long imagined. I discovered, however, that I was one of a mishmash of plaintiffs who had nothing in common except that we had all been labeled "extremists" and put on a watch list by some bureaucrat. Those spied upon included neo-Nazis, anarchists, leftists, artists, feminists, and so forth.

Not much useful information came from our suit and from individual efforts to obtain files from the FBI. For one thing, government agencies blacked out most of the material that was eventually released. For another, most of the files appeared to have been compiled by semiliterate agents, whose listening and writing skills would not have advanced them in any other career. Bertha Harris told me that her FBI files said about ten times that she went to "feminisems" and "talked about lesbunisems." She is still annoyed that these morons make more money than she, a brilliant novelist, does. Other information was just wrong. I might say that it was hilariously inaccurate, except that people's lives and freedom often hinged on these documents. The Central Intelligence Agency labeled Allen Young "an infamous homosexual," which pleased him, but the agency also noted that he was fluent in Italian, of which he speaks not a word.

We hoped, probably foolishly, that the lawsuit would force the government to curtail such illegal intrusion into our lives in the future. Government espionage was both a colossal waste of money and an invasion of the privacy of groups that for the most part hadn't broken any laws. It wasn't illegal, surely, for homosexuals to meet and talk about our rights and to picket or sit in to get them. Some of those involved in the

Red Squad Case claimed that in the early 1970s there were more agents in some branches of the Socialist Workers Party than real members.

However, if government espionage was damaging because it was a real threat, it was equally dangerous as an imagined one. For every real agent, another person, probably an innocent one, came under suspicion. Radicals circulated "profiles" of agent behavior to keep an eye out for. First, we were all wary about people who urged others to commit illegal activities, especially violent acts, against the government or private corporations. Second, in an era in which few of us had meaningful employment and the rest of us were downwardly mobile, we suspiciously eyed people who seemed to have free-flowing cash but no job, inheritance, or other explanation for their financial resources. We radicals were certain that such people were being funded by the government so that they could attend meetings full-time. Suspicion, for example, swirled around the head of Jim Fouratt. He was flamboyant, unemployed, and connected with such stars as CBS president Clive Davis and pop artist Andy Warhol. As Martin Duberman wondered in *Stonewall*, "How could someone who never seemed to have much money or, until the CBS job, any visible means of support, manage to fly off, at the drop of a hat, for mysterious meetings in distant parts?" It is possible, as Jim has pointed out, that the FBI itself spread such rumors about him to cause dissension in the movement, but since Jim's colorful—some might say, "ostentatious"—demeanor and garb must have made him some enemies, one of his adversaries might have tried to ruin his standing by spreading suspicion. Many activists, including me, never believed these allegations—had Jim been an agent, he would have received his government pension a decade ago.

After the exposure of "Crazy George" Demmerle, activists began to worry about people who were weird or somehow didn't fit in with an organization. On the one hand, behavior that might seem crazy today was accepted because we honored individuals who rebelled against the rule of the patriarchy. Many of the people who had started gay liberation, including those at the Stonewall uprisings, had already been marginalized by society because of their sexual preference. On the other hand, some people were simply odd. For example, the late Warren Johannson, a regular at early GLF meetings, claimed to read and speak a dozen languages but looked as if he had been dressed in the wardrobe department of a bizarre television sitcom: His tie, tweed jacket, and unkempt beard recorded recent meals like a food diary, but his black shoes were relatively shiny and reminded me of those worn by police officers. Warren was an academic of sorts but had no doctorate, no paid institutional affiliation, and no real job. It turned out years later that he probably crashed at various people's houses and may have been homeless in between. Wildly peculiar, he was equally harmless, but he was exactly the kind of misfit who must have been searched every time he went through an airport. He raised eyebrows (and turned noses) at every meeting he went to. Once, years later, Warren was even accused of molesting women in the Columbia University library stacks. "Oh, no," protested Gene Rice, a history professor who quixotically rushed to Warren's defense. "Warren is perhaps capable of many things, but I assure you he would never molest a *woman.*"

In the post-Demmerle period we all began to wonder, when someone like Warren was especially bizarre, whether this wasn't just a very good cover. We all developed personal guidelines to help us sort the pigs from the genuine lunatics. I recall being particularly on the alert for activists whose stories about their pasts didn't match the person I saw in front of me. Very often people claimed that they came from impoverished childhoods, yet they had fancy middle-class dentistry such as caps and porcelain crowns. The really poor people I knew either had naturally good teeth or a mouth full of metal. But it was more difficult for me to go around suspecting everyone than to eschew violence and hope for the best. Aside from frequent lesbian sex, political demonstrations, and occasional tokes of marijuana, I was practically a model citizen anyway, right? Well, maybe not, but striving for liberation for all people was certainly in the spirit of the Declaration of Independence.

Doubtlessly, the fact that so many activists used marijuana, LSD, and other hallucinogens heightened the general level of paranoia. Behavior that might appear harmless under ordinary circumstances took on ominous overtones under the influence of drugs. In the mid-1970s, after eating a pot brownie, Allen Young, one of the men in the Gay Liberation Front I became friendly with, became convinced that two men visiting his farm were government agents. He felt it was urgent that the other men who lived with him recognize this fact and ask the two visitors to leave immediately.

"Calm down, Allen," said one of his friends. "You can't seriously believe that government agents are going to come two hundred miles from New York City to bake bread for you and give you a massage just to extract information."

"You don't understand," Allen insisted. "They're trained to bake bread and give massages just so we'll think they're like us."

To his credit, Allen never ate another pot brownie after this incident.

One rumor circulating that spring until it gained the status of truth was that undercover agents, if asked, had to admit who they were, or all the information they had gathered would be thrown out in court. The first time I heard this "fact" was at a Redstockings central meeting in the East Village, at which one or two people from each C-R group were present. I could hardly contain my skepticism. An agent would have to be crazy to admit she was a pig in a radical group where someone might be armed. I couldn't imagine the government passing such a law or the courts upholding it. I figured that some Redstockings had this nonsense mixed up with the Miranda warning (the reading of a person's rights after an arrest, made mandatory by law in 1966). At the time I said nothing: Redstockings' "leaderless leaders" were not women who took contradiction lightly. As it turned out, an undercover agent *was* present at many of those meetings, and I was flabbergasted when some government documents published in *Majority Report,* a feminist newspaper, made clear that someone was in the room with us at those small meetings, not simply listening in on a recording device. For a while I replayed the meetings over and over again in my head, trying to figure out which one of the seven or eight women present was the informant.

Shortly after this Redstockings meeting, at the first lesbian dance, Irene Peslikis, Kathie Sarachild, and I were sitting on one of the infamous make-out couches. Forgetting that I had been present at the Redstockings meeting where the topic of agents had first been raised, Irene casually asked me whether I was an undercover agent. Resisting the temptation to roll my eyes in disbelief, I replied in a deadpan manner: "Sure I am. How astute of you to ask."

Irene's jaw dropped. Kathie's did, too. Then I laughed. "Actually, I'm not, but clearly you've forgotten that I was at that meeting where you said that agents have to identify themselves."

"But why did you just say that you're an agent?"

"Just to show you how stupid you're being."

It was foolish of me to make such a joke in front of humorless politicos, but I've never been able to resist the temptation to play a practical joke. In the end it didn't hurt me, but they could have spread a rumor about my so-called confession all over the movement.

Others were not so lucky. In April 1970 I got wind of a *Rat* collective meeting at which Lucy was going to be confronted for her alleged activities as an agent provocateur. Lucy liked to shoplift—an activity that most of the people I knew participated in (for some it was a major survival skill as purloined food was a basic dietary supplement). She apparently egged on anyone who was with her to shoplift, too, and some members of the collective decided that she was simply trying to get the goods on everyone else. Another "proof" of her government paycheck was the fact that she had nice clothes. None of this "evidence" seemed particularly damning to me. I knew of several women, including Rita Mae Brown and Ti-Grace Atkinson, who would have chosen a stylish outfit over a decent meal any day.

The evidence was enough for the collective to drum Lucy out of *Rat*. It seemed to me that once a person fell under suspicion, it really didn't matter whether she was guilty: She could never undo the rumors flying around her. And so, like many other members of the movement, Lucy simply dropped out of sight and stopped working for a cause that decided to label her its enemy.

Though I was not particularly close to Lucy, I felt she had been treated unjustly, much like the medieval witches these so-called feminists pretended to revere. They turned on one woman after another and demanded that each pass impossible tests to prove her innocence. After all, how could a person prove she *wasn't* an agent? As a result, after I wrote about the Lavender Menace action at the Second Congress to Unite Women for the June issue of *Rat,* I left the collective.

Even after I stopped working for *Rat,* I couldn't extricate myself from all the intrigue. On May 4 Jane Alpert, Sam Melville, and Nate Yarrow pled guilty to various charges related to their terrorist acts. Then Jane jumped bail while awaiting sentencing and disappeared. This was not entirely a surprise. On March 5 a Greenwich Village townhouse had burned down when the dynamite from antipersonnel pipe bombs the Weathermen were preparing unexpectedly exploded. Afterward, the Weathermen "went underground"—that is, they disappeared and hid in large cities and in rural communes throughout the United States. This tactic had been part of their plans for a long time; they hoped to remain safe and wage war from the heart of America. The sudden spotlight of media around the country on the townhouse explosion merely hastened their inevitable flight.

After Jane's disappearance, a swarm of local and federal police descended on everyone who had known or who had worked with Jane. Carol Grosberg, a member of the *Rat* collective, looked out her window one morning and spotted a man in a trench coat standing across the street from her building. When she looked again hours later, he was still there. She decided to confront him. She went right up to him and asked him whether he was with the FBI.

"Sort of," he replied.

"Well, then," she said over her shoulder as she walked away, "I have nothing more to say to you."

While Carol was keeping track of her trackers, I began noticing that my telephone sounded even stranger than usual. For the past few months there had been a lot of clicking on the phone. One day I came home from work and started to catch up on a backlog of telephone calls. I made one call, depressed the receiver button, and began to make the next one. Before touch tone, there was a very brief pause between the time the phone was picked up and the dial tone kicked in. This time, much to my shock and horror, instead of the dial tone, I heard two men discussing my previous call.

"What d'ya think she meant by that?" the first one asked his partner.

"I dunno, but it didn't sound all that important to me."

Clearly there was a "loop" on my phone. I had always assumed my phone might be tapped, and I never used it for anything even vaguely illegal. Most of my calls were as ordinary as anyone else's, but I pitied the agent who had to listen to my conversations with my mother and make sense out of them—even I couldn't.

"I made some chicken soup for you, Karla," she might say.

"Ma, I'm a vegetarian."

"Don't worry, dear, I took the chicken out after."

But a romantic notion that I was important enough for the government to be taking a personal interest in my activities was one thing; to hear actual agents on my line was quite another. I was quietly appalled and didn't know what to do.

I discussed the situation with my roommates, John, Jude, and Terry. We didn't know whether the phone had been bugged because of Jane's disappearance or whether we had been watched all along. We decided that the best course of action was to continue with our political activity as if nothing unusual had occurred. We agreed that everyone had to be very careful about phone conversations. Calls about demonstrations where we didn't want a police presence should be made from a phone booth. We had a depressing sense that the government was closing in on us, but we were committed to fighting for our liberation, no matter what the cost.

That same spring I developed romantic fantasies about travel in general and about the golden sunshine of Southern California in particular. In the summer of 1968 I had had a roommate from Los Angeles named B. Meredith Burke. When she moved back there, she invited me to visit her and stay in her apartment for as long as I wanted.

The prospect of living as far away as possible from my family had become increasingly compelling. During that spring my mother's mental illness worsened considerably, and I began to face pressure from relatives to return home to become my mother's caretaker. My mother's mental decline had accelerated when I left home in 1965. Now her grasp on reality was slowly evaporating, like air leaking from a threadbare tire. Sometimes she telephoned and in the middle of the conversation forgot who I was. At other times, it was obvious that she had taken too many tranquilizers. She spoke slowly and incoherently, slurring her words like a drunk. Once, halfway through an incoherent monologue about ending her life, she dropped the handset and then crashed to the linoleum floor in the kitchen. Waiting for her to get back on the line, I could feel my own heart trying to make up the beats she might be missing. Breathing felt like drinking pea soup through a straw. But after an eternity during which my gasped pleas for her to get back on the phone went unanswered, I hung up and dialed 911.

"She's taken a lot of barbiturates, and I don't think she's conscious," I stammered to the operator. "She said she's alone in the house, so I don't know how you'll get in."

I gave them my number and waited. Soon my father called back, in a fury. He had been somewhere in the apartment, probably asleep in his easy chair. He had turned the police away, saying that my mother was merely asleep and I had misunderstood.

"Why the hell did you call the police?" he shrieked, brushing aside my explanations. "Goddamnit! I told you—never, NEVER get anyone else involved."

"But I thought she was dying. What else could I have done?"

"You should've let her die."

That would have been an easy solution, one I had sometimes shamefully imagined after she would humiliate me in front of other people. But it was one thing for her to float quietly away on a raft of Elavil. It was quite another to hear her talk about dying—however incoherently—and then drop the phone. Though I had become increasingly sympathetic to her plight and less so to my father's, she sure didn't make it easy to like her, let alone spend my life taking care of her.

Her increasingly irrational and violent behavior had finally made my father realize that he couldn't keep his vow, if indeed there had been one, not to commit her to an institution. With my brother working in Manhattan and me living there, she was alone in the Brooklyn apartment most of the time. She was certainly now more a danger to herself than to anyone else. Overdoses of barbiturates brought her closer and closer to death. From about 1967 on she began to spend short periods of time in different private institutions, none of which seemed to improve her life or her mental outlook. In the spring of 1970, in the wake of the 911 debacle, she wound up in the locked ward of a voluntary hospital, which happened to be just across the park from my Upper West Side apartment. Too close, alas.

I dutifully visited her daily on my way home from work, but she no longer recognized me. On the rare occasions that she spoke to me at all, she assumed I was a nurse or an orderly. The fact that she recognized my father and brother made this all the more painful, as if her amnesia had singled me out, as if her real problem was an attempt to erase my existence, pill by pill. I felt doubly invisible—both as her daughter and as a lesbian. I had hoped she would never discover the latter; now she had forgotten the former.

Most of the time she sat silently, staring at some blank spot on the wall. The thorazine and shock treatments had temporarily dispersed the ghosts of the relatives with whom she communed at home. Without their company, she fell into a heavy silence. Sometimes I thought she was about to speak, but it was only a Lifesaver rattling against her teeth. The medication had turned her tongue to dust. While I sat with her, I would read from the Pléaides edition of Proust that I carried everywhere. Like my book in its plastic jacket, each of us was encased in our own private language. I hoped that my company had some value. A reminder that I had not completely abandoned her. Penance for my failing to save her from this circle of hell. The dead, tight air of the windowless room was crammed with the smoke of her Larks. Sometimes she kept two or three of them burning at once in a plastic ashtray. The attendants had confiscated her matches, and she was terrified her cigarettes would go out. It was too much for me: I was just a casual smoker. I felt as if someone was using a wrench to ratchet down my bronchial tubes, the air squeaking as it crept in, even though I would toke on some asthma spray before entering the hospital. My dry eyes burned constantly. Weeping would have been a relief, but I had long since learned to swallow my emotions along with my mother's smoke.

It was exhaling—letting go in any sense—that was dangerous. The best way to deal with my mother was not to react to her.

Finally, one day she recognized me. A fierce yellow light glowed from her pale olive green eyes.

"You! Are you Karla?"

"Yeah, I'm your daughter. Remember?"

Cursing and shrieking, she picked up everything within reach—magazines, paper slippers, the plastic ashtray, the crumpled and empty packs of Larks—and hurled them at me. She was so frail that they never reached me. My boots were littered with ashes and filters. The trash filled the small space between us like a metaphor for our relationship. The attendants, hearing the racket, rushed in with a straitjacket and a needle.

"Don't go, don't go!" she was crying and pleading, but I couldn't bear to watch them truss her up like a capon. I left the hospital, crossed Fifth Avenue, and sat for a long time on a cold dark bench outside the park. I felt empty and dead. I went home and didn't go back to the hospital again.

After my mother was released—in a more sedated but no more tranquil state—her cousin Emma telephoned and tried to pressure me to move back home. Cousin Emma had cared for her own mother so well at home that, though my great aunt Mollie had all the mental agility of a zucchini, she lived (much to my horror) in a semicatatonic state well into her nineties.

Time to go. I felt a bit like a rat abandoning a sinking ship, but I also believed I was entitled to enjoy my life. The only way to do that was to travel beyond the reach of a local telephone call. Perhaps I could outrun the guilt I felt.

The final event that whirled me to California was my acquiring a set of broken ribs. One Sunday afternoon in late March 1970, I was headed to the weekly Gay Liberation Front meeting with my neighbor Diana Davies and my roommate, Terry. As usual, the downtown train was crowded. The three of us stood clinging to one pole in the center of the car and compared our weekends. I had a hacking cough, the result of ignoring a bad cold that had turned into a mild case of pneumonia and then into persistent bronchitis. I had breathed steam, taken purifying herbs such as red clover, and cut back on smoking, but nothing cured it. Now one sudden cough sent a sharp blade of pain into my back. It was so excruciating that I couldn't breathe.

"What's the matter?" Diana asked, peering into my face with concern.

"I don't know. I think I'm having the worst case of gas ever."

Diana patted me gently on the shoulder. "It sure must be bad; you're turning blue."

"Blue's not your color," Terry chimed in. "Must be, like, too many aduki beans."

We got off at the West Twenty-eighth Street stop and headed for the Church of the Holy Apostles for the GLF meeting, but I could barely make it up the stairs. Every breath was a sword running through my back. Beans had never been *this* lethal. Diana and Terry packed me back into my coat and took me to the emergency room at St. Vincent's Hospital in Greenwich Village. There I was placed in an examination room with a young woman who was under arrest for drug possession. The two cops who were guarding her looked at her and then at me. One muttered insults under his breath about "damn hippies" to no one in particular. All I wanted was to get out of there before they mistook her for me or vice versa.

I was X-rayed and then sat in the examining room awaiting the results while Diana and Terry hung out in the waiting room. They weren't allowed in with me because they weren't "family." Finally, the attending physician called one of the officers out into the hall. A few minutes later the doctor returned with the cop, Terry, and Diana in tow.

"You have three broken ribs," the doctor announced. "Two on the left where it hurts, but there's a tiny fracture on the other side as well." He tacked the X rays on the screen and pointed to the faint lines running through my ribs like tiny tree branches. The left lung, like a helium balloon from last week's party, was only half inflated. "This just doesn't happen from a cough, so tell this officer which one of these two did this to you." He pointed his beefy right index finger at Terry and Diana, who shrank back from the accusation. I wondered whether they would believe that Terry could beat me up. Terry knew what I was thinking and shook his head back and forth, mouthing, "NO, NO."

"All I did was cough. That's how it happened."

"Impossible."

"Okay." My mother was ample proof that the truth is no defense against illusion. "I forgot. I got thrown in judo last week. Twice. That must be it." I had actually been hurled into the mat during a match with a vicious opponent, but at the time it hadn't hurt very much.

"Oh, judo, yeah. You didn't mention *that*." The doctor nodded encouragement as he latched onto a diagnosis that conformed with his medical training. Terry exhaled audibly. When my color returned to normal, the doctor taped my ribs and sent me on my way. I went home and removed the tape, which made my skin itch and gave me the sensation that I couldn't breathe.

I realized, suddenly, that I was sick and exhausted. I was literally falling apart from endless meetings, dances, consciousness-raising groups, political actions, and my mother. I worried that something was wrong with my bones—first my spine had been fractured, now this. If only I had liked milk when I was a child! Maybe I needed to take a pause from work and the movement. I filed for disability and left my job at Colliers.

A few weeks later my ribs still hurt. Every time I took a drag on a cigarette, I coughed and my ribs felt as if they were splintering. Though I had unsuccessfully tried to quit smoking a few times before, it became more painful to smoke than not to. I checked the New York University bulletin boards for a ride to share to California. I had never learned how to drive. My father had once been a truck driver, and he was very proud that he still retained a "chauffeur's license," a classification that allowed him to drive everything except a bus. But even though he had taught my brother to drive, he didn't even offer to help me get a learner's permit.

A fellow student at New York University agreed to drive me to California. He said he'd be leaving New York around May 10. Terry, Jude, and John agreed to cat-sit for Ringo and Pooh and find someone to sublet my room for the summer.

Of course, there's always at least one hitch. Mine was getting hitched right before I left. At the end of April, just before I was scheduled to leave town, I went to a GLF dance, which I looked upon as a sort of going-away party. It was my last chance to see some of my friends for a while. I was schmoozing with a small group in the make-out room when my ex-lover Becky walked in with a woman. Samuel, the indexer from Collier's, was behind them. What was *he* doing at a gay dance? He was decidedly straight.

Samuel had told me that he was in love with an unnamed woman who had moved to Amsterdam, and Becky had told me about a woman named June who had refused to sleep with her and then had moved to Amsterdam. "That's cool," I had replied. "Everyone's gone to Amsterdam. Must be the hash." How could I possibly suspect that they were enamored of the same woman? But the instant they walked in the door with her, I guessed what was going on.

"This is my friend June," said Becky. "She's just back from Amsterdam."

"That's groovy," I gave a cheesy smile. "Gotta go dance." I was certain there was going to be bloodshed any second.

From time to time I glanced back into the make-out room and could see June looking my way, Becky looking wistfully at June, and standing behind them just outside the women-only space, Samuel, smoldering like a cigar butt. Time to leave.

The following Friday there was a May Day antiwar march. It turned out to be small—fewer than a thousand people. We trailed down Broadway to Union Square, where speakers at a rally assailed Nixon and demanded the liberation of imprisoned members of the Black Panther Party. Members of the neo-Nazi National Renaissance Party taunted us from the sidelines. Samuel had brought June with him, and we started to talk. She was really sweet, and very cute, too, with a short Dutch-boy haircut, her straight dark hair framing a round face and green eyes. She told me she was a Taurus, a good sign for me. She asked whether we could get together.

"It has to be soon. I'm splitting town in two weeks!"

We agreed to go dancing at Kooky's a few nights later. June picked me up in her car. I was impressed, even though it was only an old Ford Falcon.

June showed up wearing a butch outfit—a man-tailored shirt with a scarf tie pulled through two brass rings—a popular lesbian accessory. On the way to Kooky's she told me about Amsterdam, where she had worked for an English-language publisher as a copyeditor.

"But why Amsterdam?"

"Oh, I wasn't getting through college, and I needed a change of scene."

"So why did you come back?"

There was rather too long a pause. "Well, it was hard to make a living there. I studied Dutch but never got a chance to practice it. Every time I opened my mouth, someone would reply in English. Everyone there speaks English."

"Maybe I should go there. How's the cheese?"

"Great."

I pondered whether Gouda and Edam were yin or yang. When we got to the door, she paid my entrance fee and bought me a drink. Was she butch or what? I knew she wasn't going to ask me the "butch or femme" question. She had already decided I was femme. Keeping an eye out for the Illustrated Woman I had ditched the previous year, I followed June on to the dance floor. I was anxious to see what it would feel like to dance with her. For lesbians, dancing isn't just like sex; it often is sex. When lesbians grind on each other's thighs, orgasmic energy flies around the room. Some delicious sex hormone fills the room like the smell of buttered popcorn. If your bones start humming together during the slow tunes, things usually work out fine later on. At the moment we were being symphonic.

Since I was leaving New York so soon, there was no time to waste. I invited June back to my place. Her performance on the dance floor had been no false advertisement. She was much butcher than I had hoped for. From my point of view, receiving is often better than giving. She managed to cover very inch of my anatomy like an expert cartographer.

I turned to her in surprise. "I thought Becky said you had slept with only a few women."

"It's true."

"You could've fooled me! But she also said that you wouldn't bring her out because you weren't in love with her. So why would you want to sleep with me?"

Instead of answering, she rolled over to go to sleep.

After that night we were practically inseparable for the time I remained in New York. She even got along with Ringo, whose jealous tantrums had sent more than one sex partner screaming into the night. But unlike the proverbial lesbian who pulls up to her second date in her U-Haul containing all her worldly belongings, I was heading in the opposite direction. Despite my instant sexual and emotional attachment to June, I had no thoughts of inviting her to accompany me. I wanted to be free of everyone and at any cost. I had no intention of winding up half of a monogamous couple—either hetero or homo—for fear of ending up like my parents, married and trapped. Despite my new romantic interest, I packed up and headed West.

꙰   ꙰   ꙰

"Whatever made you think Angela was an agent?" I asked Michela one night in 1997 while we were having dinner in a Chelsea coffee shop. We were discussing a member of Radicalesbians who, during the summer of 1970, had been kidnapped and taken to a farm in Upstate New York, where a few Radicalesbians interrogated her about her role as an "infiltrator." One or two underground newspapers then printed "Wanted Posters," alerting others about Angela's alleged government activities. I was only mildly surprised that Angela hadn't pressed charges against her kidnappers or sued the newspapers because back then many lesbians preferred kidnapping over telling the cops that they were gay. Michela and I had no part in the kidnapping, but she firmly believed, even now, that Angela had been an agent.

"Nobody knew where she came from," Michela explained. "She didn't go out with anyone. . . . I'm Italian. . . . We call it *sangue, simpatico.*"

"Huh?" I knew she was referring to the fact that Angela was also Italian American, but I still didn't get what she meant.

"When I meet another Italian woman, I connect with her in a very visceral way. I felt nothing, nothing, no passion, no concern, no nothing. I always said she was the first Italian woman I ever met who didn't have any juice inside her."

We laughed, but I wondered whether I could condemn a woman for lack of "juice." For some, it was simple then, and it's simple now. You're either an agent, or you're not.

For me, such things were never this easy. I generally saw the good as well as the evil in people. Unlike my radical friends, I found it impossible to see the world in black and white. Friends, other activists, men, and even my parents all had redeeming features I sometimes wished I could ignore. People were too complex and nuanced to cast out without a second thought. In the end I never did follow the family physician's orders not to look back.

Perhaps, back then, if only things had seemed less complicated to me, I might have been a great revolutionary. I could have led a charge to the barricade and then ordered heads to roll with the sangfroid of Madame Defarge. But I always felt sorry for the oddballs like Lucy and Angela. Perhaps they were only misguided or needed help, rather like my mother.

Ironically, my mother, a total misanthrope, taught me tolerance for eccentricity. I found it impossible to write off people as irredeemable. And so, despite leaving my mother in the Hades of the hospital, I returned to her again and again—trying to find some way in which we were *sangue, simpatico.*

From finishing school...

...to perfectly queer.

My parents (far right) late 1940s, around the time of my birth. The last time they were seen touching.

Summer camp, 1956. Even then they knew. Everyone called me "Billy."

From college proms…

…to funky gay dances.

Sidney Abbott, Ellen Broidy, and Michela Griffo check ice supplies for the first women's dance.

Two Fliers Advertising Dances

When we weren't zapping our oppressors, we were making fun of them

Gay liberationists considered psychiatry an oppressor of homosexuals. Until 1973, the medical establishment labeled homosexuality a "mental illness."

Attacking Sexism in the Media

In March 1970, feminists "liberated" the *Ladies' Home Journal* in New York City and confronted its editor, John Mack Carter (in suit) and his assistant, Lenore Hershey (far right). Dressed to kill, I'm at the left in a headband.

Fighting Homophobia:
"Take a Lesbian to Lunch!"

Moments before zapping New York's Second Congress to Unite Women in May 1970. From left to right: Rita Mae Brown, me in hat, Arlene Kisner, Lois Hart, and Martha Shelley. We're all wearing Lavender Menace T-shirts under our clothes and carrying the "Woman-Identified Woman" manifesto.

A tender moment…

…with three complete strangers. This photo was rejected for a Los Angeles Gay-In III poster because it looked "too heterosexual." The photo that was accepted appears on the cover of this book. That's me in the Lavender Menace T-shirt.

Allen Young and I thought this American Gothic take-off would make an eye-catching publicity photo for *Out of the Closets*, 1972. What were we thinking?

Neither rain, nor sleet, nor snow kept me from marching for human liberation. Lunch bag in hand, my arm around June, we take on Albany, New York in March 1971 to demand civil rights for gay men and lesbians.

11

Sunny Days, Hazy Nights

In late May 1970 I arrived in Los Angeles. I discovered that my friend B. Meredith Burke lived in the "Miracle Mile" district, a section of town near the museums and the famous (and odiferous) La Brea Tar Pits. It was so smoggy there that the only "miracle" was being able to breathe.

At the time, the La Brea area was a nondescript lower-middle-class neighborhood. Meredith's studio apartment, for which she paid only $85 a month, came with a Murphy bed and a small separate kitchen. Its major attraction was being near Wilshire Boulevard, a main venue with lots of buses running on it. It was also close to the La Brea entrance to the Santa Monica Freeway, a major east-west interstate. Having no car or license turned out to be a major handicap. Omigoddess, there was no subway system! The buses came infrequently and rarely connected conveniently with other bus lines. Perhaps I was simply being paranoid, but the routes seemed to be primarily organized to transport Mexican household help to and fro. (Now there's a tram to get the help to their chores even faster.) Taxis were expensive. How did Angeleans survive?

Meredith was generous about helping me out when she could. A native Angelean, she knew her way around well, and about once a week we piled into her scorching Rambler to go shopping, not at our neighborhood supermarket but at one run by the same chain over in Beverly

Hills. She had cleverly discovered that not only was produce fresher in the zip codes of the rich and famous, but also it was cheaper. (This is probably a national pattern.)

Living on small amounts of money was an art I had long since mastered. Chipping in for gas on Meredith's car was painless: Because of a price war, gasoline cost less than a quarter a gallon. Since I was on a macrobiotic diet, I ate the same meal once or twice a day—brown rice smothered with squash and carrots that had been sautéed in garlic, onions, and soy sauce. For breakfast, I ate left-over rice or whole-grain bread. I even got Meredith to eat some rice, not a grain she adored. (She still mentions the inspirational five-pound bag I left behind.) I could eat for pennies a day, and Meredith, who had a visiting instructorship in demography, refused to charge me any rent.

In addition to copping rides with Meredith, I quickly mastered the art of hitchhiking, which got me pretty much anywhere. I guess I was lucky or smart or both, but I never had a problem. Los Angeles wasn't very dangerous then, except for a few areas such as Watts, where race riots had taken place in 1965. Most people understood how hard it was to get around without a car and were sympathetic. I would never get into a car that had more than one man in it, and if the guy started to make suggestive remarks, I would tell him that I was a minor. Back then molesting a minor in California was a major felony; today it's a national sport. If I told a driver I was a minor, he would usually pull over and let me right out. Women often stopped to pick me up. Though sometimes they would lecture me about the dangers of hitchhiking, they took me where I wanted to go.

My first weekend in town I went to a lesbian bar someone had told me about over on Melrose. There I met Micki and Anita, two women as lanky and pale as the Kansas wheat fields they had left behind. Micki, hiding her face under a thatch of dark hair, seemed shy, so at first I struck up a conversation with Anita, who was taking courses every day at the Church of Scientology, which I had never heard of. Los Angeles had just the right sort of doomsday mentality for a cult, as it was called back then, that swore a person had lived through many lifetimes and had accumulated a lot of bad karma. L. Ron Hubbard, the science fiction writer who founded the church in 1954, promised to bring that person back—again and again—in order for her to get rid of past-life injuries and keep paying her debt to his "church."

Anita, like others, had signed a "billion-year contract" with the church. It was probably going to take her that amount of time to pay for her courses. Though Anita was supposedly almost "clear," as Scientologists call those at the apex of spiritual achievement, when she came to Los Angeles, she had nevertheless borrowed and spent thousands of dollars on church-run counseling sessions. She was now broke and still had hang-ups. I tried to act surprised. During her time off, Anita was usually hooked up to an "E-meter," a crude lie detector. Anita and Micki took me back to their tiny, dilapidated room and showed me the machine. It looked like the tin-can telephones my friends and I used to make when we were children. Anita claimed the machine told her where her hang-ups were. I could have told her where they were for free.

Anita's preoccupation left Micki with a lot of time on her hands—and with Anita's car. Micki and I decided we would have some fun together, go to a gay beach and a few bars, and then catch a local Gay Liberation Front meeting. Like magic, I was set.

I let myself sink into the hedonistic pleasures of sun and sand. I had spent so much time working for two movements and earning a living that I had almost forgotten how to relax.

Micki and I quickly settled into a routine. Micki would pick me up at noon; then we would head west on the Santa Monica Freeway to the gay part of Venice Beach, near the Venice Pier (which has since been torn down). Los Angeles basked in at least four months of continuous sunshine from May through September, so almost every day was perfect for a trip to the beach. (Only occasionally would we arrive in Venice to find it swathed in fog.) We would sun for a few hours, before heading for the "Happy Hour" at a nearby dingy gay bar on Lincoln Boulevard, one of the main thoroughfares. Micki had black hair, but her pale, freckled skin burned and peeled instead of tanning. She didn't know how to swim either—it was a useless skill on the dry Kansas plains. As a result, she didn't much like the beach. I didn't like smoky bars anymore, so the suffering evened out. She would pay for the gas, and I would pay for the beer, which was a quarter for a Hamm's on draft, about the same price as a gallon of gas. I didn't like beer, but it was by far the cheapest thing to drink—about half the price of a Pepsi, for instance. It was so hot and dry on the beach that I would find myself glugging about half a pint down before I recoiled at the sour taste. Micki would finish her beer and then polish off mine.

Life on the beach was relaxed; even illegal activities were laid back. The young white lesbians on the gay beach all seemed to be employed selling pot, primarily sensemilla, an extremely potent and virtually seedless variety. Sometimes our entire section of the beach was covered by a fragrant smoky haze. Most of the dykes wore Band-Aids over their nipples at the beginning of the summer. Since topless bathing was illegal, they thought they could escape prosecution via this extremely minimal coverage. In mid-June, fearing an uneven tan more than prison, they discarded the plastic strips as well and donned muscle T-shirts for swimming and surfboarding. The beach was wondrously wide, maybe a half mile or so from the boardwalk to the water (though it has since eroded dreadfully).

Although the cops patrolled the boardwalk, they rarely ventured onto the hot sand in their shiny black shoes. When they did, we could spot them from a great distance away and toss on some clothes in plenty of time. The cops had a hard time arresting people in Venice anyway, even when crimes were committed right in front of them on the boardwalk. The benches were frequented by elderly Jewish women, most of whom had an amicable relationship with the local hippies. They protected us as if they were our grandmothers. They would surround the cops and shout: "Gestapo! Gestapo! This is Auschwitz, you think! Aren't you ashamed to be bothering such a nice girl?" The pigs would beat a hasty retreat.

Much more of a nuisance were curious men who would camp out nearby and ogle us. These surfer girls weren't political, at least not in the New York feminist sense I was used to, but they were tough. If anyone tried to take a photo, they would kick sand into the camera lens or brazenly seize the man's camera, open it, and dump the film (and sometimes the man as well) into the sand.

Most of the time, however, we were left in peace to our own pleasures: napping, partying, gossiping, flirting, swimming, and chomping on the endless munchies that the pot smokers always had with them. I never ate any of their fruit, however. Early on Tima, the leader of the group, counseled me that oranges were almost always injected with LSD ("orange sunshine") and watermelons could be—and generally were—spiked with anything,

Despite the name, the Pacific Ocean was much rougher than the Far Rockaway surf in Queens where I had summered during my early childhood. Tima taught me how to bodysurf, as I was afraid of reinjuring my ribs on her surfboard. I enjoyed letting the waves pull me out and then float me effortlessly back to shore. Even that, unfortunately, turned out not to be completely safe. One day a violent undertow smacked me into the craggy bottom, recracking one rib. Peaches, one of the regulars, led me back to her house for the night, and Micki stayed, too. It was the first time Micki and I had slept in any proximity, and Micki used the opportunity to make a pass at me. Though I was in some pain, it wasn't nearly so bad as the original break. Besides, nothing would ever be so painful as those three fractured vertebrae. The next thing I knew we were having sex.

I wasn't very attracted to Micki, but I had grown totally dependent on her goodwill. I lay there and let her suck my breasts and then lick my clitoris slowly until I came. Her technique was pleasant but a bit languid. I grabbed her torso and pulled her cunt over my face. I used one hand to massage her clitoris while my tongue explored her vagina. Then I used the other hand to finger-fuck her vigorously from behind until she came, quietly emitting a sigh as if sex were a small relief rather than a pulsating pleasure. My technique seemed to be a real thrill for her, and I thought I spotted one of those loving looks that's quickly followed by a discussion of an apartment suitable for two. I was already slightly bored. Micki and I didn't have sex very often after that, as neither of us had a room of our own. Anyway, Micki was drunk so often that she spent more time passing out than making out. However, Micki was a safe alternative to the Venice beach dykes. Though I was certain that Tima—or any of her pals for that matter—would have been a lot more fun in bed, I didn't want to get involved with anyone who sold or was hooked on drugs.

Though I missed June and wrote to her regularly, I had not promised her I would remain monogamous, which I regarded as a dubious capitalistic method of transforming a romantic attachment into personal property. The politics du jour fit my thirst for sex and adventure. I couldn't fathom how a woman could promise not to be attracted to anyone else for the rest of her life—or refrain from acting on that attraction. June was just the opposite. Monogamous by nature, she focused on one individual at a time until that relationship was over, and then she moved on to her next exclusive and eternal love. But despite the fact that I cared about her, I wanted to explore the lesbian scene in LA.

On Friday and Saturday nights Micki and I would remain in Venice to hang out at a lesbian bar named Brothers, on West Washington Boulevard. In a city where almost everyone drove and seemed to detest walking (except on the boardwalk or beach), no one parked in front of Brothers, which I thought was peculiar. The customers were much more boisterous than the denizens of Kooky's. People were generally friendlier, too. That seemed part of the Venice scene in general. A waitperson, for example, would be as likely to sit down at my table to chat as to take my order.

I found the crowd harder to read than the women in Kooky's or Gianni's in terms of gender identity. Unlike the short, slicked hair and men's shirts favored by butches on the East Coast, some of the tougher natives like Tima were just as likely to wear their hair long and bleached. Accessories included dangling silver earrings and tong sandals. In short, here a butch could look exactly like me. The one sure way to decode the butches was to watch who engaged in fights over other women, and after a few weeks I could set my watch by the 1:00 A.M. brawl. All the bars closed at 2:00 A.M., and as a result, the partying—and drinking—started fairly early. About an hour after midnight some of the women were tanked and ready to spar over lost lovers or sunken eight balls. Almost all of the fights involved only two participants. The rest of us would form a circle and watch, but the combatants generally wound up outside because either the fight or the bouncer spun them in that direction. If a car was parked directly in front of Brothers, someone was inevitably tossed into its doors, or worse yet, over the windshield. Weapons were a rarity, but occasionally pool cues were used, which could mean a smashed car window or mirror, chalked and dented sides, scratched bumpers—and bruised lesbians. No wonder no one parked there!

I was amazed by how rarely anyone intervened in a fight. Most watched, sipping their beer with studied apathy, but I would look the other way and pray no flying object was about to sail into the back of my head. The first time I witnessed such a fight, the pacifist in me was frantic to see it stop, but my martial arts instincts told me there was no safe way to stop these women. Micki, who came from a Quaker family, was equally distraught and picked up on my agitated despair. During the first fight she witnessed, she stepped in between the two women and pleaded with them to stop. Steeped in her own alcoholic haze, she failed to notice that the combatants were too drunk to hear her, and the next thing I knew they had both belted her, thinking that they had hit each other. I grabbed her arm and yanked her away from them, and then tried to wipe away some of the blood dribbling down from the right corner of her mouth. I started to muse nostalgically about the Illustrated Woman.

I also began to miss politics. Political radicalism was in the air that spring more than ever. On May 4, 1970, students protesting the war in Vietnam and some by-standers were shot by the National Guard on the campus of Kent State University in Ohio. The violence fueled, rather than quelled, antiwar organizing by reminding us that the government was waging an undeclared war against radical students, the Black Panthers, the Weathermen, and other New Left groups. I longed for the solidarity of a consciousness-raising group and for the drama of political action. I wanted to seize a building, just for the fun of it.

I had some contacts with some local women from NOW, and I agreed to help them start up a C-R group. I traveled over to one woman's house in Brentwood and persuaded Meredith to accompany me. I thought she'd enjoy it. In hindsight, I should have told her at some point that I was a lesbian, but since it had never come up when we shared my New York apartment in 1968, I found it a hard topic to bring up now. In fact, coming out to people who had always presumed I was straight was much more stressful than simply informing new acquaintances that I was a lesbian. Even though I had never said I *wasn't* a lesbian, I still felt as if I had been lying to old friends every time I let an opening pass. And now Meredith and I were living together for a second time, and Meredith still wasn't catching on. It's not that Meredith was stupid, not even slightly. But beneath a breadth of knowledge and an erudite vocabulary was a sweet innocence that just didn't notice things like homosexuality, even when it was right there in front of her. Once, she unexpectedly entered the apartment and caught Micki and me making out on the couch. Meredith said nothing about the incident. I figured she had to know but didn't want to broach the subject. After all, we were sharing a tiny studio apartment, and my lesbianism might make it seem even smaller than it was.

Unfortunately, after a few initial meetings the C-R group settled on the topic of relating to men. Of course, of course. As one woman across the room from me started her narrative, I took in the architecture of the Brentwood mansion in which we were seated. I was mesmerized by the solid oak front doors, which were about twenty feet high. The rugs and couch were white, a color scheme no sane New Yorker would contemplate. And these throw pillows we were all leaning against—were they, eek!, real zebra? Perhaps I could divert attention from my own lesbianism by a tirade on the destruction of wildlife, though I wasn't quite sure whether zebras were an endangered species.

In the end I was so intimidated by the palatial environment that I simply fessed up. For one thing, I was hoping they wouldn't invite me back. Would people who thought zebras made lovely pillow covers find Jews like me suitable lamp shade material?

"Uh, I can't relate to this topic," I started, when my turn came. "For one thing, I'm a lesbian, so I don't deal with men in the way that you mean."

"That's cool," one woman said, and everyone except Meredith nodded enthusiastically.

Meredith's head seemed to spin in my direction, and her mouth dropped slightly open. She said nothing. I hoped I wasn't going to find myself sleeping under the Venice Pier that night. The narratives plodded on for two agonizing hours. Hadn't I heard these same stories several times before in my Redstockings group? I felt jaded and anxious.

Back in the Rambler, Meredith broached the topic.

"I had no idea you're a lesbian. Why didn't you tell me?"

"I thought you knew. What did you think was happening when you walked in and saw me holding Micki?"

"I thought you were comforting her."

We both guffawed. It didn't seem to be an issue for Meredith. She had trouble finding men who were her intellectual equals. The interesting men often turned out to be gay or divorced and claiming to support five children. She probably would have considered a lesbian option if she'd had any homosexual inclinations. Moreover, Meredith was unwilling to "settle" for just any man, as all too many of her acquaintances had. She had a definite type in mind: She preferred tall, slender men with long bony fingers. They had to be smart and hospitable and have a sense of humor. The last was a particularly crucial attribute as she thought of herself as a small brown bear trapped in a person's body. At Christmas she would let out her inner bear and lap eggnog from a bowl on the floor. I didn't find this too unusual—compared to my parents, Meredith was downright normal—until one day she brought home a very promising young man who fit all the requirements, or so I thought, especially when he announced that he was really an adolescent panda.

"Cool! A match made in heaven!" I clapped my hands in appreciation.

"You don't understand. It just won't work," Meredith frowned at my ignorance. "He's a panda—*Ailuropoda melanoleuca*. I'm a brown bear—*Ursus arctos*. It would be a mixed marriage!"

I didn't think her prospects looked too bright.

After it became clear that the NOW C-R group was going to re-hash all the material I had already gone over in Redstockings, I per-suaded Micki to drive me over to a local GLF meeting. The history of the LA GLF was similar to that of its New York counterpart. The Los Angeles branch had been founded in December 1969, and by the time I arrived between fifty and seventy people, most of them men, were at-tending the meetings.

The group convened at a bar named Satan's, which was located on Sunset Boulevard in the Silver Lake area of town. (Conservative Chris-tians would find the name of the bar all too apt for a gay group.) I found this choice odd because in New York so much of the thrust of the movement was to get gay men and lesbians *out* of bars. But here clubs seemed to be owned by ordinary straights or gays, and the Mafia didn't seem to profit from them.

I found the seating arrangement in the bar problematic. Every New York group I had attended made a point of placing chairs in a circle so as to suggest that everyone was equal, but at the LA GLF there was no pretense of equality. Satan's had one large table—which one friend dubbed "the dais"—at which all the "leaders" presided, while the less important people were relegated to the smaller tables. This arrangement made me uncomfortable, reminding me of large gatherings of relatives at my paternal grandmother's house where I had been restricted, along with all the cousins of my generation, to the "children's table."

Among the local stars at the big table that first night was Morris Kight, a fifty-something, silver-haired denizen of the local political scene. As an antiwar activist, he had been involved in, among other things, boycotts of Dow Chemical, maker of napalm. Now he collected and sold antiques. As one of the founders of the group, he was, of course, seated at the big people's table. He spoke with elaborate elocution, a charming vestige of his East Texas childhood. Behind his back those who didn't like him referred to him as "the pope" and complained, ac-cording to the *Los Angeles Times,* that he took "undue credit for other people's work." Despite his high status, he was certainly no dapper Dan. He favored outfits that didn't quite fit him, and I wondered whether he had purchased them during slimmer days or whether he hoped that by buying smaller clothes, his apple-shaped body would grow—or rather, shrink—into them. Though he often wore khaki pants and knitted shirts with his sandals and even owned some suit jackets, he was just as likely to be seen in "hot pants," as we called them, with his stomach bulging out of his too small T-shirt above and his thighs stretching the shorts beyond the limit. He always seemed to have a retinue of followers that included a young minion, over whose shoulder Morris would drape a friendly and paternal arm.

Morris was a bigwig, but if there had been a local charisma award, it probably would have gone to Troy Perry, a Pentecostal minister, originally from Tallahassee. In 1968 he had founded the Metropolitan Community Church (MCC), an Evangelical Christian church for homosexuals—a concept I found oxymoronic. However, the nondenominational group drew dozens of gay men and lesbians who wanted to practice their Christian faith but no longer felt welcomed by their original denominations. They certainly couldn't show up back then arm-in-arm with a lover at any mainstream church or synagogue. By 1970, 2 more MCC churches had opened in San Francisco and San Diego. (By 1998 there were approximately 230 congregations, making MCC the largest gay group in the world.) Troy was darkly handsome in a way reminiscent of Elvis Presley, with thick black wavy hair that ended in sideburns pointing the way to a Crest-white smile. He attended LA GLF meetings erratically, often being busy elsewhere with his congregation, but his voice still carried a lot of weight. The fact that he headed a patriarchal Christian church also seemed of little concern to most LA GLF members. On June 12 Troy performed the first lesbian—but nonlegal—marriage, between Neva Joy Heckman and Judith Ann Belew, at a time when most gay liberationists favored nonmonogamy and were questioning the structure and intent of the nuclear family in the hopes of formulating alternatives. Troy would not have gone over well in New York.

Jim Kepner, an unobtrusive man in his forties, was another of the "big table" leaders. Originally from Texas, he had once been a shipyard worker in San Francisco and later wrote pieces for the Communist Party's *Daily Worker*, until the organization expelled him for his homosexuality. He was a relatively quiet man whom I didn't notice at first, but when I got to talking to him, I could see he was probably the smartest person there. He knew something about every gay topic. At GLF meetings he sat where he could watch everyone from under his wiry eyebrows while he quietly took minutes. In retrospect, I'm amazed that he wasn't tossed out under suspicion of being some sort of police operative. But he performed a lot of the hard organizational work, and people were familiar with his articles on gay history that had appeared in *The Advocate* and other publications. The other occupants of the dais varied, but they included, from time to time, Harry Hay, one of the founders of Mattachine; Don Slater, who had broken from the One Institute (which had in turn broken away from Mattachine); and Don Kilhefner, a bearded, bespectacled graduate student who had recently returned from living in Ethiopia.

I naturally found myself drawn to the more radical members of the group, although there were some characters who proved too difficult for me. There was one radical transvestite/preoperative transsexual, Angela (Douglas) Key, who wrote for the Los Angeles *Free Press*. In a "Letter to the Editor" of the *Free Press*, Marcus Magnus Overseth accused Angela of "constantly disrupting GLF meetings and social events." When Angela told me that she wanted to become a lesbian and that it was my political duty to help her with her sexual transformation, our friendship came to an abrupt end.

As in New York, relatively few people of color were present—I recall only four or so Black men and a few Latinos. I don't recall any women of color in the group. Greg Byrd, an African-American man, was one of the first cochairs of the group, and Bill Beasley, who was later active in San Francisco Pride activities, was also an active member.

Sandy Blixton, an organizer for the Peace and Freedom Party (PFP) and a vocal advocate in the gay community for the Black Panthers, became my best friend. A Harvard graduate, he was better read in Marx, Trotsky, and Lenin than in the fare usually taught at Ivy League colleges. Though he was in his late thirties, he looked a decade younger. His lean body was always tanned, and his hair was freshly streaked by the sun and peroxide. The way he gesticulated emphatically with his hands and rolled his eyes when he spoke made him seem familiarly ethnic to me: He was a fellow Jew in a group where we seemed much scarcer than in New York, for reasons that are still unclear to me, since Los Angeles had a large Jewish community. I suppose that to Sandy's enemies the same qualities contributed to the impression that he was too radical and maybe "flaky." At one meeting he pulled a pistol from his pocket and shot a bullet into the ceiling. Morris claimed that Sandy tried to kill him, but Sandy said that was the only way to get a word in edgewise. Sandy used the stunned silence to make his point. Who was going to interrupt a revolutionary waving a smoking gun? (Why hadn't I thought of that when I ran the NY GLF with a mere softball bat?)

Perhaps because the men were so clearly and firmly in charge, there were a lot fewer women at this GLF meeting than on the East Coast. One regular was Del Whan, a graduate student at UCLA, who was a few years older than me. Del gave out contradictory signals: She appeared to be shyly hiding beneath a mop of frosted blond hair and oversized glasses, but her flashing smile and sharp laugh often accompanied biting comments. Later on a tall, rangy teenager named Virginia Hoeffding, who was an undergraduate at an Oregon college, became another regular. Soon the two of them started going out. Shortly after I arrived, Cherie Matisse, an artist as well as a descendent of the great French Impressionist, also joined the group. But even with a few more of us, we were still, as Del once wrote, "lost in a sea of men." Although the LA GLF elected leaders, Morris and Troy (and later Don Kilhefner) simply assumed that they were the official spokespeople rather than opening up this possibility to the entire group by lot, by rotation, or by some other means. I recall no move to give women equal representation in any sense.

In a way it was surprising that any of us women remained with this group. On paper the goals of the Los Angeles GLF sounded almost identical to those of its New York brothers and sisters. The official group manifesto even demanded "an end to sexism," but this was mostly lip service. Underneath the radical rhetoric I didn't notice much discussion that took into consideration either women or feminist ideals, and except for Del, I don't think any of the other women who attended the earliest meetings would have identified themselves as feminists. Among the men, Sandy was the loudest in support of his "sisters," and that was one reason I bonded with him. Jim Kepner's minutes for the May 7 meeting note a planned "rap session" with women's liberation, but it's not clear whom the organizers had in mind or whether the event ever took place. After I arrived, I addressed the group and reported on the politics and actions of the New York group, including the Lavender Menace zap. I hoped to make a point about the danger of ignoring lesbians, but I doubted the members were going to listen and understand. Later on I arranged for some C-R groups. My efforts seemed pretty useless. The chauvinistic attitudes persisted, but I had no genuine alternatives. Here in Los Angeles there was no radical, all-lesbian group to turn to. The feminists I had met lived on a different economic and political plane, where zebra pillows were acceptable. The beach dykes were potheads. The GLF was the best alternative, whatever its limitations. Moreover, since I was planning to return to New York in the fall, I felt I was simply a tourist of sorts.

Actions of the LA group paralleled those in New York, although there was almost an exclusive focus on men's issues. In February and March the group had repeatedly picketed Barney's Beanery, a Hollywood café that posted a handwritten cardboard sign warning, "Fagots stay out." It was hard to imagine that such a sign could survive at all in a city as liberal as Los Angeles, but according to Angela Key, in an article for the *Free Press,* when a protester tried to draw an analogy between the sign and one that might read, "Niggers keep out," a fight erupted between this man and a Black patron of Barney's over the use of the word "nigger." When the Black patron realized that he was scorning the protesters in the same way that whites had reviled Blacks during sit-ins at Woolworth counters in the South, he reportedly sat down on the curb and wept. After another protester threw beer on the sign, the owner called the police, who determined that the poorly spelled item was worth about a dime. The owner then sold the sign to Morris, who stepped forward to offer $2.50. If any women attended these early demonstrations, the press took no note of them.

Many of the demonstrations and actions targeted the Los Angeles Police Department, which actively and frequently entrapped gay men in cruising areas such as Hollywood Boulevard and Griffith Park. GLF members posted hard-to-remove stickers in toilets and other cruising areas to warn gay men about recent police activity. One Day-Glow orange sticker featured a circle around a pig's head that was crossed through to read, "No Pigs." Borrowing from a wallet-sized card, called something like "Ten Things to Do in Case of Arrest," that the Peace and Freedom Party had developed after a beach party was busted in Venice, the GLF Gay Survival Committee developed a similar fold-over, miniature handout that GLFers distributed in gay male bars and cruising areas. It featured the LA GLF motto, "None of us are free until all of us are free," and it provided a number to call for advice on draft counseling, venereal disease, personal problems, and job help. It dispensed the rather standard legal advice about an arrest: Don't resist, but note the name of the officer and his badge number (whether or not you are arrested). Finally, it summarized relevant penal codes. The print was so small that far-sighted individuals probably had to carry a magnifying glass. As usual, the leaflet and the action ignored the realities of lesbian life, since we were unlikely to be busted in toilets or to have problems with either the draft or venereal disease. The LA GLF hardly seemed to notice that lesbians had lifestyles and issues distinct from those of gay men.

Just as the NY GLF had done earlier in regard to the *Village Voice,* the LA GLF tried to make the media more responsive to gay concerns. In April the LA GLF had successfully pressured the *Los Angeles Times* into removing its ban on the use of the word "homosexual" in advertisements. In addition, the group wanted *The Advocate* (which was then a newspaper published in Los Angeles) to cover more GLF activities. There was even some talk of forming a gay liberation press service.

There was also a lighter, and more inclusive, side to Los Angeles gay liberation. The GLF sponsored several "gay-ins," huge love fests in Griffith Park. The first one, held in early April, attracted about two thousand revelers. I attended the second one, which took place on Memorial Day with a much smaller crowd of about five hundred. Christopher Isherwood showed up around noon. "I just came here because I'm with you and wanted to show it," he announced. We cheered and whooped. He was the biggest name to date to endorse the gay movement.

We set up some stands with information about the GLF. Sandy Blixton and Don Kilhefner were working a voter registration table for the Peace and Freedom Party. I volunteered to woman the kissing booth for a while, and a few lesbians paid for my services. A couple of straight guys were also ready to ante up for a lip-to-lip alliance with a lesbian. Perhaps they had illusions that they could convert me that way, but I told them what they should kiss instead. There was also some guerrilla theater, and five couples were "married" by Morris, including two men wearing mu-mus.

It wasn't long, however, before trouble broke out. Shortly after noon the Park Rangers complained to the Los Angeles Police Department that an unlawful gathering was taking place. The cops asked Morris to cease and desist from taking donations, and they also asked us to remove our huge lavender and orange GLF banner. I was among those who felt that we should have the right to leave it up. Wasn't our free speech protected by the Constitution? Were the police going to claim in court that the banner, strung between two trees, was damaging the environment? Morris, who always pushed for peaceful resolution, agreed to take the signs down, except at the PFP table, where the guys refused to remove their posters. They were not arrested.

In fact, there was something comical about the police presence. According to *The Advocate*, "One GLF member was warned to stop pointing out the plainclothesmen [from the LAPD], or he would be arrested and face a $650 fine." Maybe this fellow should have been fined for stupidity, for in a crowd of long-haired, topless, and shoeless men and midriffed women, most covered with body paint and looking cheerfully glazed from their spiked oranges, the guys with crewcuts, patent-leather shoes, and vests layered over shirts to "hide" their guns might as well have been wearing a sign saying: "Hi, I'm a pig. What's your name and address?"

Despite the Rangers calling the cops on us, we thought the event was a great success and immediately began planning a third gay-in. Lee Mason, a professional photographer who lived on La Brea not far from me, picked me up in his car one day and drove me to Griffith Park, where I decked myself out in my Lavender Menace T-shirt and met up with four other GLF members: Cherie Matisse, Howard Fox, Randy Shrader, and someone I remember only as Chuck. We posed for a photo that became a poster to advertise Gay-In III, scheduled for the first week in September. Lee had all five of us hold hands, run, and leap through a field. I was still a bit overweight from the days of my broken back, and it seemed that the only part of me flying into the air in most photos was my long hair. He did get one shot he liked, with all five of us smiling and charging forward in unison. Though we were all young and white, the odd number meant no one would mistake us for couples, and the photo captured the *jouissance* that had so marked the gay-ins. It misrepresented the proportion of lesbians involved in the movement, but I hoped it would encourage more women to join.

After dozens of copies of the poster were printed up, I started to see it in the bars I frequented. Every time I closed a bathroom stall in a gay establishment, there I was on the back of the door watching myself urinate. It was not a wonderful sensation. Nevertheless, the photo gained the same sort of iconic status on the West Coast as Peter Hujar's photo featuring a larger group of smiling gay men and lesbians running down a New York street with arms flung around one another and fists heaved defiantly in the air, a montage that first appeared in *Come Out!*, a GLF newspaper on the East Coast. I don't think one photographer consciously copied from the other—in those days we all seemed to be cheerfully racing toward the revolution.

In addition to the gay-ins, the GLF sponsored a number of dances, most of which were held at Satan's or Troupers Hall, a former Hollywood theater, on North La Brea. As in New York, the dances were supposed to boost the treasury, which had slightly over $100 in all, and get people involved in movement politics. This tactic was no more successful here, so far as I could tell, even though the inducements to attend the dance were much greater. For a quarter sometimes revelers could eat all the spaghetti and cold cuts they wanted, providing they arrived early enough to get any at all. Beer and soft drinks were usually included in the nominal cover charge.

One difference from the New York dances was the restrooms. In New York the bathrooms at the Alternate U were "singles," but at Troupers

Hall there were larger men's rooms and women's rooms. I had learned from my earliest days at Kooky's to get in line for the bathroom *before* I had to go as the wait could be painfully long. But what I hadn't counted on at Troupers Hall was the queue hardly moving at all. We crept along, and only one out of the four cubicle doors would ever open. A half hour later, as I neared the front of the line, I bent down and peered under the doors to see whether anyone was in them—sometimes people assume a closed door means a toilet is occupied when it isn't. The stalled stalls in question were indeed occupied, each by two people busily engaged in what appeared to be sex acts.

As I supposed that "tearoom sex" in toilets was something only men engaged in, I assumed that some guys were in there blowing each other because the men's room was occupied. Moreover, the women's toilets would probably be a place male undercover agents would avoid. I was furious, not because they were having sex in public, but because they were taking up almost all the stalls and my eyeballs were starting to turn yellow from too much Pepsi.

"Hey!" I yelled. "Have some respect and get the hell outta there! Some of us gotta go!"

When no one responded, another woman and I started banging on the doors of the stalls. If there had been a romantic mood to start with (though I highly doubted that), our vociferous complaints quelled it in a hurry. Suddenly two or three doors opened almost simultaneously, and I was gobsmacked to see six women scurrying out. I recognized one of them as an occasional visitor to Venice Beach. But I wasn't so shocked that I didn't rush to claim a stall, safely locking myself away from the ire of the interrupted, one of whom had inked a mustache on my poster self on her way out.

၈၃   ၈၃   ၈၃

Sadly, both Lee Mason and Peter Hujar are dead, Lee having died in the early 1970s in a motorcycle accident, Peter in the 1980s of AIDS. I hardly knew Peter, but Lee would have been pleased, in his own modest way, to see his poster grace the cover of this book rather than the back of a bathroom stall.

Some of Lee's work would have been lost to us had Jim Kepner not been such a professional pack rat, saving every flyer, leaflet, and newspaper clipping that crossed his path. Before he died in 1997, Jim had one of the largest gay and lesbian collections in the world. He turned it into the Barney/Carpenter Library, which eventually merged with the One Institute to become the prestigious One Institute International Gay and Lesbian Archives in affiliation with the University of Southern California.

In the archives I came upon some of Jim's meticulous notes of LA GLF meetings. Some were scrawled on a pad only two inches long. As I pored over his Lilliputian notes, I thought about how many large items I had misplaced or lost over the years. History is so precarious—it could hinge on one careless trip to the laundry without first checking the contents of the pants pockets.

12

Stepping Out, Sitting In

In the late spring of 1970 much of the energy of the Los Angeles Gay Liberation Front went into planning a march on June 28, the last Sunday of the month, to commemorate the one-year anniversary of the Stonewall riots. Since a similar march was to take place in New York City, we decided to call ours the Christopher Street West Parade. We had raised enough money from the dances to cover our basic expenses, and a local group offered to put up $1,000 in bail money, enough to free about ten demonstrators should they get arrested. No major event in Hollywood, of course, would be complete without floats. Several were proposed, one featuring two guys making out on a mattress (voted down), another with gay men and lesbians coming out of a closet (over and over, I presume), like an endless parade of clowns from a tiny car.

Our plans collapsed on June 10 when police chief Edward M. Davis refused to give us the necessary permits, demanding an impossible $15,000 from the LA GLF for police overtime and insisting that we take out a policy for more than $1 million in liability insurance and indemnity for protection against counterprotesters. He made things worse by telling the press that he would just as soon "discommode the people" by permitting a parade of "thieves and burglars." We didn't take kindly to the comparison.

At the last minute the American Civil Liberties Union managed to overturn the restrictions, and we were permitted to march in the streets. We pulled the event quickly back together. Groups scrambled to create floats, which were more spontaneous and much bolder than we had originally planned. One sported a huge jar of Vaseline; another displayed a Christ-like figure tied to a cross with a sign that said, "In memory of those killed by the pigs." A hastily written flyer made the event sound like a hippie festival. We urged people to bring incense and musical instruments and to wear "Colorful Attire, Costumes, Flowers and Perfumes." Some people read the message as an invitation to a Halloween party or a drag ball. Men showed up in frilly dresses, clown suits, and fairy outfits that allowed the participants to seem both hip and outrageous while protecting them from being recognized by friends, colleagues at work, neighbors, and their relatives. On the morning of the event one fellow handed out pansies. At least one man wore an American flag (for which he could have been arrested). One gay man draped a seven-foot python around his muscular neck; an Amazonian lesbian rode a gigantic palomino.

We expected violence, and we felt that Chief Davis's linking us to common criminals might incite bystanders to attack us and even to feel justified about it. Most of us believed that, no matter how badly we were provoked, we should not respond in kind. Davis and his men were just looking for an excuse to beat or bust us. Others encouraged us to come armed. One cross-dresser told me he planned to carry a rifle under his skirt, making me think of the Mae West line, "Is that a pistol in your pocket, or are you just happy to see me?" (In this case, make that *extremely* happy.) I didn't think guns were the right solution, and in fact I had never touched one.

On the evening of the march we lined up at six in the evening on the corner of Hawthorn and McCadden Place in the Hollywood area. It was eighty degrees and smoggy, as usual. I can't recall why we didn't march earlier in the day. Maybe no one wanted to forfeit another good beach day; it was a challenge to be political and to stay tan, too. As we milled around waiting for the march to begin, we kissed and hugged one another. Here it was at last—our big moment! I knew we were making history, for never had such a large group of homosexuals taken to the streets. We passed out our GLF buttons, banners, and placards, printed with slogans addressing the evils of the church, the state, and Ed Davis. A common theme (at a time when many of us referred derogatorily to heterosexuals as "breeders") was that homosexuality acted as a form of birth control. "More Deviation, Less Population" was a popular slogan before the lesbian baby boom. At seven sharp, straight people's time, we began marching east along Hollywood Boulevard toward Vine, singing songs about how if it was good enough for Sappho, it was good enough for us. "Two, four, six, eight, how do you know your grandma's straight?" we chanted. We called out, "Give me a G, give me an *A,* give me a *Y,*" . . . until we were hoarse from spelling out and shouting, "Gay Power!" over and over. The MCC choir sang, "Onward Christian Soldiers."

I started out in the front, carrying one pole of a GLF banner. I wasn't afraid of newsreels and photographs of the event reaching my family. I figured, correctly, that the march in New York would grab all the attention in the east. Still, I had an overwhelming sense of being watched and recorded. Police cameramen lined the sides and photographed everyone they could. Newspaper photographers sought out colorful clusters. There were over 1,000 marchers—someone with a mechanical counter clocked exactly 1,169 people. Later I learned that the New York march had included between 3,000 and 5,000 participants, with some estimates even higher. I wished I could have been at both events at once.

Spectators lined the sidewalks. At some places the crowd was ten deep. Most of the people cheered us on, and we responded by yelling: "Join us! Join us! Off the sidewalks and into the streets!" Not all of the onlookers were friendly—some were there to jeer and curse us. One thing I had learned early on was to stay in the center of the crowd, as the people on the edges were most likely to get hit with flying debris— or to get shot. There were humorous moments as well. When a group from conservative Orange County carried a banner supporting Ronald W. Reagan, one woman in the crowd screamed that she didn't mind people being gay, but supporting Reagan was going too far!

The march seemed to go on for an eternity, although it couldn't have taken us more than an hour or two to traverse the mile-long route. We did have to stop regularly to allow cross-traffic through, and many of the native Angeleans were handicapped by never having walked a whole mile in their entire lives. After the parade was over, we were rather at a loss as to what to do. Because of the legal bickering, we had had no time to plan a street party. The dance at Satan's we'd planned wouldn't start for another two hours.

Unlike the rest of us, Reverend Troy Perry was never at a loss for something to do. Like Morris Kight, he was a master at grabbing attention. Troy was still seething over Chief Davis's insulting remarks. Many whispered that Troy aspired to be our Martin Luther Queen. Davis presented him with an opening to launch the type of protest that that other martyred minister had made famous and vice versa. What Troy didn't recognize was that part of King's strength was his originality. Troy was a poor imitation.

On June 14, according to *The Advocate*, Troy, "with tears running down his cheeks," had told his congregation that he would begin a fast on the day of the march that would last until he had a pledge from public officials that they would work to get "these laws changed that discriminate against the homosexual in America." A man of his word, Troy traveled the parade route in a limousine and then returned to the intersection of Hollywood Boulevard and Las Palmas, which was near the beginning of the march route, and sat down on a blanket on the sidewalk. (It was one thing to risk arrest, but getting his pants dirty was out of the question.) He was joined in his action by two women—Carol Shepherd, who was the president of the local Daughters of Bilitis chapter, and Kelly Weiser, who represented a group called Homophile Effort for Legal Protection. By fasting, Troy was either making a grandiose gesture or planning on entering the *Guinness Book of Records* as the world's thinnest man.

Because of the dense crowds, no one spotted the three figures sitting on the curb as we danced by, even though Troy's black clerical garb stood out in the sea of tie-dyed T-shirts. After the crowds had passed, all three were arrested for "malicious obstruction," a legal term that for me conjured up images of clogged bowels.

Most of us didn't realize anyone had been arrested until Morris arrived at the GLF dance that evening at Satan's. In his officious manner he ordered that the music be stopped so he could make an announcement. "Party pooper!" someone yelled out. Morris grabbed the mike and moved it to a central location. With his grandiloquent flair, Morris told us of Troy's arrest. I don't recall that he mentioned the women at all. The crowd quickly got worked up, and many of us, including Jim Kepner, Sandy Blixton, and me, starting making noises about driving to the Wilcox Avenue police station and staging a protest. After so many months of hard work, tedious planning, and legal wrangles, how could we do nothing about such a travesty of justice? Sandy, frustrated at failing to get a word in edgewise once again, shook his bottle of beer and sprayed it all over Morris. "Morris," Sandy announced, "you're all washed up."

Despite Sandy's dramatic interruption, the voices of moderation reigned. Several participants vowed to join Troy in his fast. A few people went to post bail for the three protesters. The two women accepted the quick release, but Troy refused and was kept in a cell overnight. According to his memoir, he spent the night alone, until he was joined by a drunk at 4:00 A.M. His clerical collar probably protected him from being thrown into the tank.

Meanwhile, not to be outdone, a group of us went home, gathered our sleeping bags (every bona fide radical owned one) and some food, and returned to the same corner where the trio had been arrested. We were left undisturbed. Two men decided to stay the night, but after a while the rest of us went home. The next day, after Troy was released on his own recognizance, he took his sit-in equipment—an air mattress, a blanket, water, and a Bible—to the steps of the federal building, which had already been the scene of other left-wing demonstrations. The change in venue was agreed upon as we would now be situated on land belonging to the federal government, where we believed we would be immune to arrest by Chief Davis's storm troopers. Some hoped that moving onto federal property would propel our actions into the national limelight and that, after the sit-in, the media would regard Los Angeles, not New York, as the happening scene of gay liberation. In short, Troy and some of the others hoped the Federal Plaza would be our Selma.

The Federal Plaza was in a downtown area nicknamed the "spaghetti bowl" because four or five huge interstate highways all crisscrossed there. One wrong lane and a driver might find herself discovering beautiful downtown Fresno. In those days no federal building had the familiar, decorative concrete planters that today serve to stop terrorists' bomb-laden trucks from barreling into the front lobby. There were simply a few concrete steps and a wide red brick plaza, on which we set up camp. After a few hours it looked like a tent city for homosexual hoboes.

GLF members took three different positions regarding the sit-in. One faction, including Ralph S. Schaffer, the current GLF chair, joined the fast. A second faction, including me, joined the sit-in but not the fast. Fasting belonged to the realm of Buddhist meditative practices; the Federal Plaza seemed to me more suited for eating glazed donuts. A third group—the majority, in fact—felt that Troy was "grandstanding" or had simply taken a "no-win" stance. The action, this group believed, could end only in arrest or surrender—in short, defeat.

The vigil on the steps of the federal building managed to be both riveting and dull at the same time. It was suspenseful because we had no idea what might happen at any moment, dull because nothing did happen. The federal workers, for the most part, kept as far away from us as possible, averting their eyes. On some level I felt as if I were in some encampment for the homeless, part of a community of societal pariahs people would rather not see. Generally, we were left alone, and U.S. marshall Gaylord L. Campbell (who had the most perfect name for the event—how many men can claim both "gay" and "camp" as a family tradition?) told the press he had no intention of doing anything about our protest so long as it remained peaceful.

As a result, most of the time things were dull. Cameras appeared only when Troy called a press conference. He had already issued a press release about his arrest, complete with a handsome black-and-white photo of himself in clerical garb standing against a brick wall. The press statement linked all the injustices that had been perpetrated on the local gay community: "Purposes of the fast are to esculate [sic] the removal of puritanica [sic] and repressive laws against sexual freedom; to protest the enticement and entrapment procedure of the police; to call attention to the tragic misunderstanding of homosexuals; and to ask that the community search its conscience in total reevaluation of its attitudes and ideas." The manifesto went on, somewhat illogically, to suggest that the action had some cataclysmic purpose—that is, in Troy's words, "to save the world from total destruction." I did have to wonder whether Troy's seminary taught spelling; more seriously, I thought that pressing the issues beyond common reason wouldn't advance our cause.

The sit-in dragged on. About once a day Troy called a press conference to refresh the memories of the fickle public, which was getting ready to flee to the beaches and hills for the Fourth of July weekend. Except for Troy, who went home to shower, usually more than once a day, the fasters were looking a lot grungier. They all looked thinner, especially Ralph, who was scrawny to begin with. About two days into the fast some rumors began to fly around the plaza that Troy was eating on the sly during his trips home. Angered, a few participants abandoned their fasts.

Most of the time those who were fasting and those who were just hanging out and supporting the action, like myself, sat on the plaza and tried to amuse ourselves. We didn't have any portable radios; this was before the era of Walkmans and boom boxes. We got to know each other really well by exchanging coming out stories, tales about where we had grown up, and anecdotes about our best and worst dates. One man read Tarot cards for everyone. I wasn't sure I wanted to know my immediate future, which probably involved bologna sandwiches on white bread and the manufacture of license plates. Occasionally, people came by with food, flowers, candles, or batteries for our flashlights.

I didn't do very well sleeping outdoors on the ground. My back was beginning to hurt a lot, and I longed for my own humble cooking. One evening Micki came by the Federal Plaza to visit, and I decided it was time to take a shower and have some sex, in that order. I was starting to feel—and smell—like aged cheese. Back at Meredith's, I knew I couldn't return to the federal building to sleep. It was like breaking a spell or a fast; once I'd undone it, I couldn't imagine willfully torturing my body again.

On July 7 Troy publicly broke his fast, which had lasted ten days. By this time he and other fasters looked terrible. Ralph looked as if he were about to disappear. Troy called a press conference and announced that he had received a "meaningful response from someone in authority interested in changing the laws that discriminate against homosexuals." Since Troy refused to name anyone and his statement was vague, I took this maneuver as his way of saving face. After all, it would take the entire legislature of almost every city and state to change the oppression his fast was intended to challenge. Moreover, Troy's actions were unpopular, even among many of his own parishioners. According to Jim Kepner, "Perry's fast on the Federal Building steps looked to conservative parishioners like a filthy hippie encampment." However, even though Troy had given up his fight in the face of waning public interest and the defection of some of the fasters—in the end only about seven were left—he did manage to hold out until people had come back from their holiday weekend.

Troy refused to admit defeat. He was determined to be acknowledged as our sacrificial lamb and earnest shepherd: In a carefully crafted scene worthy of Hollywood, he led a group of his supporters—mostly parishioners—back to the corner of Las Palmas and Hollywood Boulevard. Micki and I arrived just as Troy started passing around pieces of bread and then a cup of grape juice. Then everyone sang, "We Shall Overcome." If he had added even a touch of camp, I might have been able to get into it. I thought gay people should be a little more original.

I turned to Micki. "You know," I draped my arm around her shoulder, "tell Anita that Scientology is looking better every day. Let's go to the beach, get fried, and then get wasted." And we did.

Troy Perry was tried on August 12, 1970, and was convicted of malicious obstruction. He received a suspended sentence of ninety days in jail and a fine of $50. The appellate court overturned the decision on June 28, 1971. Troy was retried and acquitted in April 1971.

Now Troy is again trying to lead queer nation. Troy's MCC, along with the gay Human Rights Campaign (HRC), is organizing a "Millennium March on Washington for Equality for Lesbians, Gays, Bisexuals, and Transsexuals," which will take place on April 30, 2000. Though a March 1998 press release suggests that the event will generate "excess revenue," the last queer march on Washington produced more than $100,000 worth of still-unpaid debt. Furthermore, according to *Sojourner,* the Federation of Statewide Lesbian, Gay, Bisexual, and Transgendered (LGBT) Organizations had already started organizing for "LGBT actions coordinated across all 50 states, scheduled for March 21 to 27, 1999," with the theme of "Equality Begins at Home." Troy's Washington march could split the efforts and resources of the North American lesbigay movement.

The MCC and HRC organizers hope 1 million queers will show up. I love huge crowds of gay people, but I've already marched to the Washington Mall many times for other events. The AIDS Quilt was the loudest statement we could ever make about the price some have paid for the indifference and injustice of others. Moreover, I'm concerned that Troy has gone from copying the Reverend Martin Luther King's sit-ins to imitating the Reverend Louis Farrakhan's Million Man March.

Troy has many devoted followers, but I don't expect to dust off my Lavender Menace T-shirt for this event. One of Troy's open letters that starts "Dear Saints" (clearly not addressed to me) advises people that they "will have the opportunity to hear and embrace the Gospel of Jesus Christ through our participation." As a Jew, this isn't my idea of a good time or of an event that embraces all. It isn't my millennium, either. The themes of faith and family remind me, as they do *Sojourner* essayist Stephanie Poggi, of the Promise Keepers. And what exactly does Troy mean by "family?" On his Web site, according to Stephanie, Troy allegedly complains that "we pay more taxes than anybody else! We pay to send everybody else's kids to school!" He seems out of touch with the fact that gay people actually earn *less* than our nongay peers. And some of those school kids have gay moms and dads. Troy may have a huge moment in the spotlight, but I doubt that outmoded strategies and misleading rhetoric will win us our rights in the next century.

13

"Marry Me and Help Us Sue"

For a few weeks after the sit-in at the federal building, all I wanted to do was lie on the beach. I soaked up and enjoyed what was equally and freely given to all—the sun, the sand, the ocean. Choosing between the struggle for equality and the call to pleasure would always remain a basic conflict for me. At the moment it seemed to me that I needed a break from the movement, so I headed north.

During the gay pride march in Los Angeles, I had met a gentle-looking young man, with a slight build, long dark hair, and a black beard. He told me, with a perfectly serious face, that his name was John Jefferson Fuck Poland. His name was surpassed only by his attire—he was wearing nothing but a lacy pair of red underpants.

In 1967, at the age of twenty-five, Jeff had added "Fuck" to his name during the Free Speech Movement at Berkeley so that he could say the word as much as he liked, though he said the bank got a bit testy when he tried to put his new name on his checks. Despite his reason for acquiring this hilarious name, his diction was not peppered with foul language. He told me that he was the minister (presumably of the mail-order variety) of the Psychedelic Venus Church (PVC), where sex and drugs were the order of the day. Making the PVC a religion probably protected the gatherings from police raids and the group's income from the Internal Revenue Service; calling the PVC a "religion" entitled group members to constitutional privileges—and deductions. After the march Jeff invited me to visit him, and I agreed to keep in touch.

After Troy's fast ended on July 7, I joined three friends from Venice on a camping trip north. Our little band consisted of two fortyish heterosexual women, Trisha and Cindy, and Nick, a gay man who owned the old blue Volvo wagon in which we were all crammed. We took a leisurely trip up Pacific Route 1. And I do mean "trip." As we rode in the car, we munched on a tray of brownies laced with pot Cindy had grown in her garden, which was conveniently located behind the Venice police station. Cindy had her own dynamite recipe, part of which entailed spraying the drying marijuana with gin. Alice B. Toklas would have given Cindy the keys to her kitchen. After ingesting one brownie, my head was spinning for the rest of the day, so I decided to chew my fingernails instead of having another brownie.

During the day we stopped at every cove and beach, where we examined tide pools, small pieces of jade and agate, jagged shells, and other items interesting only to the totally stoned. As a result of our condition and the winding road, it took us four days to make the one-day drive from Los Angeles to the Bay Area. As we had almost no money among us, we snuck into state parks at night and camped illegally.

By the time we reached the Bay Area, the Volvo seemed uncomfortably smaller, and my back was stiff from sleeping on the ground. Jeff's Psychedelic Venus Church was located in a second-story loft in a rundown area of Oakland on Market Street. Though it was meant to be commercial space, Jeff had clearly been living there for a while, even though the furnishings consisted of nothing but old mattresses, stained gym mats, and worn sleeping bags.

We all stayed with Jeff for one night. He decided that Cindy and Trisha were a lesbian couple. Like so many other men, he read my dangling earrings and long hair as hippie bisexuality. He propositioned me while warning me that he really wasn't much of a "fucker" despite his name. Since I had met him during the gay pride march, I had assumed he was a gay man. We laughed at our mistaken assumptions, and then he suggested that I make love with one of his girlfriends. "She should have a lesbian experience," he confided. How could I not agree on a philosophical level? I had, however, long ago sworn off bringing out straight women. Instead of having sex, Jeff and I curled up in sleeping bags and went to sleep.

I decided to stay on with Jeff. Trish, Cindy, and Nick continued their camping trip in Mendocino County and up and down the Russian River. They borrowed my sleeping bag and agreed to pick me up on their way back in a couple of weeks.

Jeff turned out to be an agreeable host. He cooked vegetarian meals on a hot plate as he talked passionately against the war in Vietnam and for any form of sex. It would have been easy to dismiss Jeff as a horny guy who had figured out a clever way to have sex with as many women as possible, but in his own way he was seriously committed to his beliefs in sexual liberation and equality. He had a long history of activism that included registering Black voters in Louisiana and helping to form the Sexual Freedom League (SFL; at first called the League for Sexual Freedom) in New York in 1963. According to Linda Grant's 1993 history of the sexual liberation movement, *Sexing the Millennium*, early members of that group included Beat poets Diane Di Prima and Allen Ginsberg, Julian Beck of the Living Theater, Yippie Paul Krassner, and Mattachine activist Franklin Kameny. The group, originally a civil libertarian effort to get the government out of people's sex lives, attracted both heterosexual and homosexual liberals. When Jeff returned to Berkeley a couple of years later, the SFL began to specialize in "adult parties," or orgies. The year before I met him, he had grown disenchanted with the SFL, which (in his opinion) had become too bourgeois; as a result, he had formed the more countercultural and revolutionary PVC.

Jeff and I often debated the meaning of sexual consent. As a feminist I believed that it was a tricky matter and that men often read assent where none was implied. I saw many limits to consent in terms of age, pain, and power, to name but a few. Had slaves, for instance, ever really "consented" to sex with their masters? Did women sold into marriage "consent" to have sex with their husbands? Could children ever "consent" to sex with adults? I thought not. Jeff saw no limits to consent and viewed intergenerational sex as liberating.

Much of Jeff's time went to organizing "parties," mostly for the PVC. Basically, he had to spread the word to potential "guests." Coded messages about the parties were placed in local papers such as the *Berkeley Barb,* a small underground newspaper; in addition, both the SFL and the PVC had memberships that were kept apprised of events by phone and mail. The first party I went to was in someone's private home. Jeff, some of his friends, and I carted over the mats from his church for the event. We spread them in the bedrooms. Then we unloaded about one hundred brown paper bags from the local supermarket. Along with a few other people, I took turns working what we still called the "coat check," except in this case *all* clothing was parked in the bags at the door. The only personal items besides cigarettes or pot that people took into the house were items of jewelry, mainly necklaces. Since Jeff feared that rings and earrings could become sharp hazards in sexual encounters, he advised me to leave these at his place. Now, of course, an extra ring in a pierced navel, tongue, or labia has become a common sexual accessory in some circles.

Guests arrived, disrobed, and placed their clothing in one of the paper bags. Working the door at the PVC party, I could guess people's sexual preference by the way they undressed. The gay men were very neat, folding their pressed jeans carefully on the bottom of their bags and stacking their T-shirts on top. Straight guys practically jumped out of their clothes in their rush not to miss any action. Straight women undressed slowly as if they were performing a striptease. They also tended to bring handbags with makeup and sometimes diaphragms. The lesbians favored checked flannel shirts, jeans, and work boots or sandals. They used their shoes as weights at the top of their bags. All too often the shoes toppled out and were impossible to tell apart from the other size seven brown Frye boots or Birkenstocks when it was time to get dressed again. Each guest wrote his or her name on the bag with a marker, and soon the front room looked like a government surplus food store.

antly felt guilty for excluding him from my pleasure. "No" was a sa-
ed word at play parties, one that had to be given more weight than
es." Anyone who didn't respect another person's wishes was uncere-
oniously ejected.

My remorse lasted three seconds, after which I went down on Pam
hile Rocky kissed her, and then we took care of Rocky. Or rather
ocky took care of herself by squeezing herself so hard against Pam's
igh that I thought it would break off like a ripe banana.

We all lay on our backs on the mats like wrestlers after a tournament.
ould see a guy sitting cross-legged, watching us from the shadows. Was
Jeff? Could I, for that matter, tell Pam and Rocky apart if it weren't
Pam's sweet scent and Rocky's muscular arms? We were all engulfed
the sulfurous lights and the foggy smoke from cigarettes and pot in
room. Rocky pulled me down for a gleeful Round Two. Well, if this
s hell, count me in.

Before we left, Pam asked whether I would like to see them again for
ner and maybe something else. So thoughtful! I still believe the epit-
e of good manners is to (1) give your name first and (2) ask your sex-
partner how she likes her eggs in the morning. Pam had Jeff's
mber, so I took hers, kissed both women good night, and napped on
at (I considered taping a big "NO" sign on my butt) until Jeff was
dy to take me back to his place.

woke up with an incredible hangover, not from the wine but from
smoke-filled rooms and too much of a good thing. All my brain cells
st have orgasmed. Maybe that's what "fucking your brains out" means.
y in one of Jeff's sleeping bags and prayed for a cup of coffee. If Jeff
been sly, I might have even slept with him for a cup—I was that des-
te. If I ever go to prison, it will probably be for looting for lattes.

ly eyes finally peeled open to a sunny Saturday, one of those rare
mer mornings in the Bay Area not covered by haze. Jeff and I de-
d to go up to Baker Beach, a private nude beach slightly north of
Francisco. Jeff was a dedicated naturist. In August 1965 he had been
sted with two other sex radicals for swimming nude, except for the
ers he wore behind his ears.

Not allowing anyone in with clothes had the practical effect of dis-
couraging undercover police officers from trying to infiltrate the group.
There was no place for them to hide their badges and guns. And how
would it look in court when we all identified the officers by their gen-
italia? Another way the cops were kept out was by strictly limiting the
admission of lone men. Heterosexual men generally had to be accompanied by a woman, and the gay men, a distinct minority, were generally known by someone present. Letting in too many unaccompanied
men, even if they weren't cops, would have thrown off the gender bal-
ance. The PVC was apparently more tolerant of male homosexuality
than the SFL, where the sex was almost exclusively heterosexual, with
some occasional lesbianism, but both groups felt that gender parity
made for a better party.

Since I was new, Jeff soon released me from coat check duty and sent
me off to join the party. The living room was already crowded, and the
prize seats against the windows and walls—perches from which the
scene could be surveyed without craning one's neck—had long been
claimed. I grabbed a glass of white wine and carefully sipped it. I imagined that the hot black coffee available could be a real hazard in the buff:
If I burned my tongue, my fingers, or my crotch, I'd be a pariah in this
crowd. Despite my initial self-consciousness, I found that sitting in
someone's living room wearing only a necklace and a glass of wine is a
wonderful way to cut through bullshit. Somehow, the usual Bay Area
conversation complaining about the summer fog and the drought would
have seemed inane in these circumstances. "Do you come here often?"
had another meaning in this group. It was pretty clear that everyone
wanted one thing only, even if that one thing was voyeurism. Some people never had sex but loved to watch. So long as they didn't offer a running commentary on other people's techniques and body parts, they
were completely welcome.

I sat on the rug for a while talking awkwardly to an attractive blond
woman who chain-smoked cigarettes. At that moment I regretted having quit smoking: The anxiety was making me drink too much wine,
and a cigarette would have been a good pacer. Exhaling clouds of
smoke, tapping or flicking ash off the end, and crushing the butt into a

receptacle or smashing it under the heel of my boot were all part of a language I felt homesick for. Having no cigarette made me feel the most naked. When I placed my forlorn hands in my lap or on my leg, I thought I looked suggestive. When I crossed my arms and legs and leaned back, I thought I looked defensive, not casual. My high school etiquette class simply hadn't taught comportment for the nude.

Several more people joined us, and we all sat and sipped wine in uncomfortable silence for a while. Eyes shifted restlessly about the room as we tried to spot an attractive sex partner of the appropriate gender and sexual persuasion. Nobody in my small group jumped into action immediately: "In a crowd like this," I thought, "you might as well save yourself for Misters Right. Or Mr. and Ms. Right. Or Ms. Right for the next ten minutes." I knew almost no one at the party, let alone anyone's sexual proclivities. If it's hard to spot lesbians and gay men in everyday life, it isn't any easier when we have our clothes off. We look shockingly like everyone else. If only we had a bit of lavender skin! I sat there, unable to recall which woman had arrived in which set of clothes. I wondered how people with specialized sexual tastes signaled them at events like this. No one had pockets out of which to drape a red or black hankie or belt loops from which to hang keys.

My speculations were interrupted by Pam and Rocky, two attractive lesbians I had briefly met the day before. I prayed they were not here to test their commitment to monogamy. I was particularly attracted to Pam, a woman about my age with welcoming eyes of an indeterminate color and an intensely warm smile. Her lover, a sergeant in the air force, called herself Rocky. The two women sat down near me on the floor and asked me how I knew Jeff, who had told them that this was my first party. They wondered how I liked the scene.

"Well, I haven't seen much action, but it's early, I guess."

"You're not going to see much if you sit here," Pam smiled encouragingly. "Let's take a tour."

In the red and blue lights of the bedrooms sweat steamed like fog off the glistening bodies, and faces were muted into handsome silhouettes. Ugliness would be discovered only at daybreak. There was a man fucking a woman while another guy mounted him from behind. There was

a heterosexual couple engaged in mutual oral sex—"sixty-
called it—while two bystanders massaged the couple's brea
tocks. A handsome young man was getting blown by one w
another woman inserted a dildo in his anus. Two guys wer
tercourse with a woman at the same time with circuslike c
Jeff was sitting cross-legged on the floor watching them w
quiet concentration.

By the end of the tour I felt that if I hadn't done ever
life, I had now certainly *seen* everything. But sex parties ;
gambling than a spectator sport. Few want to sit on the
watch others play craps, and so it is with sex. I had a fe
being asked to participate in anything at a place like this
worse than not being asked to dance at the high school p

"Look, there's a spot!" Pam gestured gleefully to an er
she had found a primo plot of sand at Coney Island in Ju
it!"

As I had just seen cum flying everywhere, I sat down
I'd plant myself in someone else's excitement. Could I sti
lesbian if any semen and I came into direct contact, e
know its owner? My ruminations were interrupted by P
was exploring my mouth so carefully that I wondered w
secretly counting my fillings. She pushed me back gently
and as she kissed me and stroked my breasts, Rocky wen
Being the sudden center of such tender attention made
ibly loved. I wondered for a fleeting moment why mor
do it three or more at a time as a group could provide
and stroking galore all at once. There was someone to
someone else was performing oral sex. I came and gral
I blessed Rocky's silky tongue.

My eyes closed in the floating world that follows or
a moment to guess which hands were Rocky's and wh
When I counted to five, I sat up with a jolt and saw th;
belonged to a man I had never seen before. "No!" I
"Down, Spot" voice. His hand flew off my hips like so
a hot stove, and he slithered away with a such a dejecte

I had noticed few bathing suit tan lines at the party: I was going to have to even out my tan at all costs. We paid a small fee and rambled down a rocky path that hid the ocean and nude bathers from view. We flung off our clothes and lay down on a tattered sleeping bag that we unzipped and spread out. (How many of these sleeping bags did Jeff have?) The sun kissed us everywhere, maybe even in a few spots Pam and Rocky had missed the night before, if that were possible. Before I knew it, I was asleep again. When I woke up an hour later, I hoped this wasn't the telltale start of narcolepsy. But where was Jeff? I spotted him down the beach near the water. He was frolicking with a little girl of about five years of age. I got up and strolled over. I liked the way he played with her, as if they were equals. He just sat there on the beach with her and dug around with her shovel and pail. Together they plotted castles. The little girl must have been to beaches like this many times before as she showed no concern about or interest in Jeff's nudity. When I was her age, my eyes would have popped out if I spotted some boy's weenie on the beach.

I waded into the water, but it was too rough to take a swim, so I returned to our spot and squeezed some lemon juice into my hair. I had heard that lemon juice lightens hair, but at the rate I was going, I would be blond by fifty—maybe. I sat fermenting my hair until it squeaked and hoped I was turning into a bronze California surfer girl.

The strength of the sun was fading, and so were we. We went back to Jeff's, where I waited for Rocky to pick me up. As we drove off in her old Chevy and discussed our day, I decided that "Rocky" referred to verbal ineptitude. She was an air force tech sergeant with what sounded like a boring clerical job. (Oh, great, now I was sleeping with a baby killer. Had I lost my scruples between the bedroom and the living room at the PVC party?) Her rotation was up, and the air force was about to ship her out, not to Vietnam, she hoped. She was in love with Pam and looking for a way to stay in the Bay Area.

Pam, Rocky told me, was a pharmacist. "Pam could work anywhere; I'm sure of it," Rocky lamented. "She should just come with me, wherever."

Sure, whatever. We went to Pam's house, which was on the north side of Berkeley. We ate at some cheap and undistinguished Chinese restaurant and then took up where we had left off the night before. I quickly discovered that though threesomes were new for me, they were a way of life for Pam. The more I slept with Rocky, the more I longed to have Pam alone. The more I slept with Pam, the more I knew Rocky thought three was a crowd. The more I slept with both of them, the more I knew Rocky would be crushed if Pam and I were to leave her out, even for one night. By the end of the first week I knew I wasn't a threesome enthusiast, despite having had such a good time at the party. The United States would have to find someone else to represent the country if this ever became an Olympic event.

Apart from spending busy evenings at Pam's house, I went to an orgy in the PVC center one night that attracted so many devotees that the first party seemed merely an appetizer for this main event. I found I was quickly becoming jaded. Two guys with a woman? Been there, watched that. Four guys sucking and fucking? Is this a rerun? The lesbians seemed too far and few between. One woman invited me to make love with her, only to ask her manfriend to join in at the last minute. Perhaps it was time to have "Only real lesbians need apply" tattooed across my breasts. I telephoned Pam and Rocky and got them to take me home with them; at least I could get some sleep. I *was* jaded, no doubt about it.

Actually I was jaded and infested. Pam started complaining about itching. I felt fine, but when the three of us performed a close inspection, we all had crabs. The fingers began to point in all directions, mostly at me.

"We didn't sleep with anyone but you. You must have given them to us," Rocky poked a thick finger where my triceps should have been.

"I didn't sleep with anyone but you, either," I stopped before I added, "Nya, nya, nya" and thumbed my nose at them. I offered a neutral villain: "Maybe we got them from the mats."

"Nah," Pam interjected. "You gotta spend a lot of time with them." Clearly, she had studied some biology on the way to pill dispensing.

"Well, there have to be lots of them at Jeff's." Oh, oh. Jeff's sleeping bag. Sure enough, it was the villain, so we coated ourselves with A200—

Pam had a handy supply at the pharmacy—and practically boiled the sleeping bag at the laundromat. Getting crabs out of my eyelashes was another matter. We tweezed all of the little critters out—ouch, ouch, ouch—and I was sure I'd be lashless by the end.

It was such a ghastly experience that I swore off sex for almost an entire day. I was hoping I hadn't picked up anything worse, though it didn't seem likely that I could get syphilis or gonorrhea from another woman. Anyway, I hoped not.

Though it sounds as if I was constantly busy having sex (okay, I was), I did visit the Bay Area political groups. Women's liberation seemed relatively well organized there. The local GLF, however, was not so well developed—only nine men were at the meeting I attended. I don't recall any women being present. The main issue, as in Los Angeles, was entrapment of gay men having public sex. Several men had been arrested in the men's room in the San Francisco branch of Macy's, and the group wanted to organize a picket of every Macy's in the country. This idea struck me as noble but overambitious. I could just picture myself out in front of the Macy's on Flatbush Avenue in Brooklyn, trying to stop all my mother's neighbors from getting to the sales' racks (a mere pit stop on their way to the real booty at Loehmann's around the corner). I knew a losing proposition when I came across one: The only thing in New York tougher than the Tactical Police Force was a group of Brooklyn sales mavens.

Meanwhile, the PVC was involved in its own brand of activism. When I returned to the PVC, Jeff told me that it and members of the SFL were involved in formulating a legal challenge to the sodomy laws in the state of California. They had a gay male couple and a lesbian couple who were willing to declare their interest in committing sodomy, but they couldn't find a married heterosexual couple to join the suit.

"Marry me and help us sue," Jeff said. Now that was indeed the least romantic marriage proposal I could imagine. But how could I resist? Since I didn't intend to get married for love or sex or children, why not get married in the name of sodomy?

So Jeff and I plotted our marriage the way we might organize a political action. We would drive to Reno or Tahoe, where marriage was quick and easy. So was divorce. Pam discussed getting married, too, since Jeff's friend Flower wanted a "cover" to shield his homosexual life from his conservative family. Flower had a Swedish friend named Stefan who wanted to get married so that he could remain in the United States. I suggested Stefan marry Rocky. We agreed we'd all head out to Nevada and have a triple wedding. Everyone's problem would be solved. Wouldn't my parents be surprised (if I ever told them, that is)?

At first it seemed as if everything would work out perfectly. Stefan was a hunk, and Rocky was delighted at this turn of events. Wouldn't the troops be amazed? She could see her future in the Bay Area coming into focus. But then the plan started to fall apart. Stefan got cold feet. He wanted his lover, a Presbyterian minister, to perform the services. Then he wanted Rocky to sign a prenuptial agreement because his family was wealthy. Sure, no problem. Then he thought about taking Sergeant Rocky to meet his family one day. Big problem. Though Rocky surely had a more demure first name on her birth certificate, her body language spelled "dyke" even in Swedish. The marriage was off. Stefan was lucky the days of suing for breach of promise were long gone.

I thought of a novel solution. Rocky could marry Jeff, and both their problems would be solved so long as Rocky went ahead with the suit. I thought myself extremely gallant to be giving up my "fiancé" to help out a friend.

Then Rocky discovered that Jeff's name was really Fuck Poland. She had thought it was some kind of nickname, not a legal fact. How was she going to face the colonel and tell him she was now Mrs. John Jefferson Fuck Poland? That would look just grand on her air force record. Rocky decided that she had only a few more years to serve, but it might take her longer than that to get rid of such a surname. She rejected Jeff's offer of matrimony, and none too kindly either.

I had given up the idea of marriage by then. I was getting restless and was fantasizing about lying on the beach in Venice again and getting back to my friends at the LA GLF. In those days we all would have claimed that my "vibes" did it, but just then Trish, Cindy, and Nick reappeared. As they were anxious to be on their way, without any hesitation I gathered my stuff, kissed everyone good-bye, and headed south.

⁂   ⁂   ⁂

In July 1980 Jeff, who had by then changed his name first to Jefferson Clitlick and then to Jefferson Freedom, had a sexual relationship with an eight-year-old girl, the daughter of some nudists. They presumably weren't aware of his intimate relationship with their daughter. Though Jeff's abuse of the girl ended in 1980, the police found out about it in 1983, and Jeff was charged with three counts each of "oral copulation" and "lewd and lascivious acts" with a minor. He fled the country and hid in various places until he was deported from Australia in 1988 and arrested when he got off the plane in Hawaii. After pleading no contest to only one count of fondling, he served less than a year in the county prison and was put on five years probation, part of which involved chemical castration with Depo Provera and therapy. Since Jeff was already impotent and interested primarily in oral sex, it's surprising the authorities didn't consider castrating the other end. In early 1995, having completed probation, Jeff petitioned the court and had the conviction set aside.

Recalling Jeff's fondness for children and his rebellious desire to break all conventions, I wasn't particularly surprised when I first read about his arrest on the Internet. I have since learned of another PVC member being accused of child molestation, a charge he avoided by moving far away. In retrospect, I see that a few of the people who talk about pushing the limits of consent have no respect for women or children and perhaps none for men either. Most of the people I interviewed from the naturist movement and the SFL in an attempt to verify the facts of Jeff's conviction became suddenly vague when questioned about his whereabouts, and those who knew him defended him as a "nice guy." No one expressed any concern about the little girl. Only Nikki Craft, a feminist whose post on the Net first brought the case to my attention, condemned his actions. Though its easy for pedophiles to hide behind claims of sexual freedom, liberation movements need to protect children, even when the enemy is one of us.

14

Changing Landscapes

After Trish, Cindy, Nick, and I camped our way back down to Los Angeles from the Bay Area, I realized that my summer in the sun was drawing to a close. Nevertheless, my stay in California had opened new vistas. My brief sojourn in the Bay Area would reshape my sexual attitudes for years to come. My only regret about the summer was that I had failed to connect with a radical feminist movement in Southern California. I falsely concluded that the struggle for women's rights was confined to New York and a few other cities. As a result, I was beginning to feel somewhat pessimistic about the future of the Women's Liberation Movement. Without a broad base of support all around the country, neither the radical women's movement nor the nascent Gay Liberation Movement would survive, let alone succeed.

Back in Los Angeles, I noticed that the local Gay Liberation Front was becoming more bourgeois: It rented permanent offices and allowed one member, Don Kilhefner, to move into them. Now it had an office just like any other mainstream organization. During my absence, the Peace and Freedom Party had vacated some office space upstairs at 577 $^{1}/_{2}$ North Vermont in Hollywood, which the GLF had taken over. Despite my misgivings about the direction the organization seemed to be taking, I volunteered to woman the hotline one evening per week. I always brought something to read at work: The phone could be busy, but there were also long stretches of silence. There was nothing to look at out the window, since all the stores were closed by the time I arrived in the evening. Sometimes another person would be there with me as well, but often I was alone. The office felt creepy and isolated.

The purpose of the hotline—the first one of its kind in the United States—was general. We just gave out whatever information or support we could to gay and lesbian callers, although most of them turned out to be men. We didn't have a lot of information to dispense, and our entire list of sympathetic doctors and lawyers as well as pertinent addresses was laid out in a loose-leaf notebook. Additional information was tacked around the desk. On a typical night we might get a dozen calls requesting information about gay liberation or the location of a bar, a half dozen calls about avoiding the draft, a few questions about treating venereal disease, and a couple of requests for crash pads. Occasionally, someone called to report police activity in a certain toilet or park. There were a few calls from desperately unhappy teenagers on the verge of suicide because they thought they were gay. Sometimes frantic parents called, wondering whether their children's homosexuality was their fault in some way.

We also got plenty of abusive crank calls. Some people just telephoned and hung up; some let loose with an obscenity or two and then hung up. Sometimes callers wanted to engage in conversation before getting down to hatefulness. One man started by telling me an elaborate lie about trying to cash a check in a gay bar. I could just picture that one: Who was going to hand over a driver's license along with a check imprinted with his home address in a gay bar? For that matter, what gay establishment took checks? None. A tavern or disco wasn't exactly the equivalent of the corner grocery. When I expressed some skepticism as to the veracity of the tale, the man let forth a stream of abuse.

"Eve's pussy sucker!" he yelled. Now that was original and rather perceptive, too. Because of my deep voice, most people assumed I was a gay man on the phone.

"I'm not as young as I once was, but Eve was a bit before my time!" I hung up.

Abusive callers would frequently try to let me know just how sick I was or how they could "rescue" me from my homosexuality. All I apparently needed was the right guy, someone just like them, who spent the evening making obscene calls to strangers. "If you're the alternative," I'd reply dryly, " I'll stick to women, thanks!" For those who insisted on detailing my moral or mental illness, I would point out that gay people didn't make harassing calls to heterosexuals. Who seemed more in need of psychiatric attention—them or me? My calm assessment of the flaws in their heterosexist assumptions would usually evoke a stream of obscenities and even threats on my life. People occasionally indicated that they knew the location of the office, and that made me feel vulnerable. Once a few moments after a caller announced he was coming after me and recited the exact address, I heard creaking on the stairs. I pulled out my Swiss Army knife, opened the largest blade, and prepared myself for the worst. When I sprang out from behind a door, the gay brother who was coming to relieve me shrieked, "Oh, Mary, you *are* a danger!"

Shortly after I returned from the Bay Area, Micki and Anita headed back to Kansas. My relationship with Micki had started out on low pilot and had just about sputtered out, though it might be more metaphorically apt to suggest that it had drowned in her beer. I wasn't entirely sorry to see her leave; I suspected I would miss Anita's car more than I would pine for Micki. She was generally unexpressive about her feelings and probably out of touch with them, so I didn't know how she really felt about me. I copied down her address and phone number, gave her my New York coordinates, and promised to visit her one day in the (very) distant future.

By now I had a reliable circle of friends who chauffeured me to meetings, bars, and parties, so even my slight sense of dependence on Micki was gone. After she left town, my trips to the beaches, bars, and meetings continued uninterrupted, though I was about to be kicked off disability, after which I would quickly run out of money.

The GLF continued to meet weekly, and there was lots to organize. On May 14 twenty members of West Coast GLF and Women's Liberation Movement groups had disrupted an American Psychiatric Association (APA) meeting on "sex problems": One paper promoted electric shock therapy to "cure" homosexuals. The activists yelled, "Off the couches and into the streets!" and demanded homosexuality be removed from the APA list of illnesses. Some LA GLF members began planning a second demonstration on August 24 to disrupt another APA meeting in San Francisco.

In August we moved the meetings to the North Vermont space. We made plans for a "camp-in" at the end of August in Sequoia National Park (which the Parks Department tried to block) and for the September 5 gay-in—the poster featuring me was still up all over town. We also planned an action at the Sewers of Paris, a gay bar on Cosmo Street. We summed up our grievances against the bar in an open letter: (1) discrimination against "trashy drags," hustlers, straights, strangers, and women and (2) failure to cooperate with the Christopher Street West Committee in promoting the celebration of gay independence. Both issues indicated to us that the proprietors of the Sewers were not responsive to the needs of the gay community they were supposed to serve.

Our letter went on to protest that bars exploited and profited from our community but never did "anything to fight the repressive laws, set up a bail fund to help gays who are busted, or start a Tavern Guild to protect the gay community." I wonder how many bars, even today, do more than offer a space in which to drink and/or dance and perhaps sponsor a softball team. Maybe a miraculous gay or lesbian bar with *lower* prices than nearby straight bars exists, but I have yet to locate it.

Once again I realized the shortcomings of the cultural reformers. Sure, it was important to have spaces where gays and lesbians could meet, drink, and play, but if we didn't own these venues, we would never really be safe, and we would just become another market niche, ripe for exploitation. Our utopian demands that the bars protect the community and funnel money back into it echoed protests on the East Coast. At least this protest was about more than unfair treatment by bar owners: The picketing and other actions taken at the Sewers of Paris may have been the first time that gay liberationists drew attention to discrimination within our own community. Before this we had taken for granted that in some large cities women were unwelcome in men's bars and vice versa. And even though I can't imagine that the gay bars discriminated against heterosexuals—after all, how could they tell who was who when our own gaydar often failed?—Blacks, Latinos, and Asians were routinely asked for extra identification at many gay bars. Moreover, despite our current glorification of men in drag (all types—from Dennis Rodman to Patrick Swayze—don sequined gowns and six-inch stiletto heels), real male or female transvestites and transsexuals then and now face discrimination from a few segments of the gay community as well as from the straight world.

In addition to trying to reform the community around us, we began to scheme to take over Alpine County, a sparsely populated area, with fewer than five hundred people, located east of Sacramento near the Nevada border. The fastest way to achieve true liberation, or so we believed, would be to find a place where we could all move and become the majority. Then we could pass laws that would benefit our way of life. Alpine would become the first American queer county. I could envision it perfectly: Laws would prohibit blatant displays of heterosexuality, such as holding hands or kissing in public. In some ways this was our cleverest idea, though I don't recall who first brought it up. Instead of trying to tackle the entire United States, we could transform one tiny corner of it. Since we looked just like everyone else—well, except for those liberation buttons, which we could leave at home—the locals would never catch on until we already owned most of the property. Despite the plan's utopian appeal, I suspected it was doomed. I never could figure out where all the money for Alpine County property was supposed to come from when we had only $100 in our treasury. The enterprise collapsed a few months later when word of the proposed takeover was leaked to the press in November. The local populace freaked out and threatened to shoot us on sight.

At the same time, we struggled with our own internal problems. The lesbians were becoming increasingly dissatisfied with male chauvinism and with the group's exclusive focus on men's issues and a corresponding lack of any concern for the substantive needs of lesbians. We protested that the gay men were treating us as their "wives" and that they took for granted that we shared common oppression and goals. The men tried to make a gesture toward compromise by nominating me to become the chair of the group in September, but I declined since I intended to head back east in mid-August. All of this eerily paralleled last winter's events in the New York GLF, except that at least the New York contingent had agreed to fund a women's dance.

Finally, one day in early August, though I don't recall exactly what action or word sparked it, the women had enough. Del Whan announced that the women were leaving the group. There was a rare long moment of stunned silence. I think some of the men might have been just as happy to see us go. Then they could tell themselves that they had worked hard to include women, but we had chosen not to cooperate. Without us, the gay men (greatly relieved) could return to their sexist language and behavior as well as to an unopposed male agenda.

Not all the men, however, were pleased. Sandy Blixton burst into tears. "Sisters! Sisters!" he cried, extending his arms toward us like a supplicant praying for forgiveness. "Please don't leave us! We brothers can change our sexist ways! Give us a chance!"

"Oh, shut up," Del snapped.

I was behind Del—both figuratively and literally—at that moment, ready to leave with her and the other women. I had no intention of being left alone with these fellows as their token woman. I crouched down next to Sandy's chair, put my arms around him, and gave him a long, hard hug. "Don't worry, Sandy; we have to do this, but we'll be back." Then we walked out.

Del was justifiably angry. She had worked very hard for the GLF and had been given little credit for it. But I don't think that she had any real plan for action. There were fewer than a dozen women in the Los Angeles group. The GLF had little money, but we had none. We had no place to meet, no phone line, no media connections. We needed the men as much as they needed us. We decided to meet at Del's house in Echo Park and discuss our options.

Meanwhile, the days were definitely getting shorter, and I started to make plans to return to New York. I missed June a lot. She was a witty writer, and her voice came through clearly in every letter. I had never missed anyone before, even when I had gone to summer camp at the age of five. When the other children cried because they were homesick, I thought they were insane. By the time I had left my parents' house in 1965, I had learned not to miss people. This aching for something I didn't have felt new and peculiar, especially in the wake of all the sexually satisfying experiences and other kinds of companionship I had had throughout the summer. I decided I must be in love.

Other aspects of my return to New York were more complicated. I didn't long to see my parents. In fact, I had hardly spoken to them all summer. Long-distance phone calls were expensive in the days of AT&T's monopoly. People of my father's generation considered interstate calls a luxury, to be used sparingly for events slightly less catastrophic than those requiring a telegram, which invariably brought news of a death. The few times my father called, I could imagine a three-minute egg timer dripping sand in the background. When the allotted time was up, he would begin clearing his throat and fidgeting until the conversation ended. The distance had given me such a sense of profound calm that I found myself sleeping for ten to twelve hours a night, a condition Meredith nicknamed "beditis." Between sleeping and sunning, the lines of illness and despair were gone from my face, and I was evenly bronze from head to bikini line. I looked younger than I had in high school or college.

I thought about returning to graduate school. It would be easy to reenroll. Despite all the activities of the previous years, the least of which seemed to involve studying, I had an excellent grade point average. I wasn't sure, however, that I wanted to continue. I couldn't see what use a doctorate in comparative literature was going to have in the coming revolution. Unfortunately, I didn't have a scholarship, so I was going to have to rustle up some work if school remained on the agenda—the courses at New York University were expensive.

I returned from California in late August 1970 to a changed personal and political landscape. The period that began with the Stonewall uprisings in June 1969 and continued through the summer of 1970 had been a long climatic surge of revolutionary fervor and personal satisfaction that began to fade as rapidly as it had developed.

The first transformation I came home to was a dramatic reconfiguration of the group of gay men I was sharing an apartment with on the Upper West Side of Manhattan: John, Jude, and Terry. While I was in California, John Knoebel had moved out of our apartment and joined three other men in what became the Ninety-fifth Street Collective. The four of them struggled intensively together to break down their patriarchal training. They reevaluated everything from sex to private property. As John later wrote in a 1972 essay: "We were the first gay male living collective in the country. We were experiencing something that had never been tried before, and this meant we largely had to create it as we went along." They split "everything equally: expenses, housework, ideas, and feelings." They held business and conscious-raising meetings together. The only barrier they were not able to break down was their own bodies—they went outside the group for sex partners. They were torn between sharing everything, including sex, and fearing that a strong relationship between any two of them would tear the commune apart.

Though I missed John's intelligent sensitivity and willingness to struggle with personal issues in ways that few men would even contemplate, I knew that this move was far better for him than staying in our precariously cramped living room. He might have been prompted to move by a serious development in our Upper West Side apartment.

When I came home, Terry was still living there. Although I was delighted to see him, I was upset to learn from Jude that over the summer Terry had become a heavy user of "recreational drugs." When Terry first moved in, I had been amused by his passion for pot, peyote, and LSD, one we discovered that my cat Ringo shared. One day Terry dropped several hits of acid onto the rug—the liquid drug was measured out onto small bits of blotter paper. Before we could snatch them up, Ringo had gulped one down.

"Oh well," Terry shrugged his shoulders. He popped a tab into his own mouth. "Can't let him trip alone, you know."

An hour later they were sitting on the couch side by side staring at the same blank spot on the opposite wall. Terry would point to something only they could see, and both their heads would follow it in unison. Oh great, even my cat was an acidhead. No wonder Ringo never showed the slightest interest in catnip—he was tuned into more potent mind-altering substances, just as the hippies I had adopted him from had forewarned me.

Terry and Ringo began tripping regularly, sometimes with acid, but more often they took peyote buttons. They always seemed to have pleasurable trips, totally in harmony with each other. As the cat was a consenting adult feline—no one was shoving drugs down his throat—I didn't think I could object.

But even before leaving, I had worried that Terry had no limits and no brakes. He didn't simply come out as a gay man—he exploded out of the closet, and before I knew it, he was sleeping with anyone who appealed to him. Once he came home after some rough sex with shredded clothing and a torn anus. I feared that drugs would do even more damage. When Jane Alpert went underground in May, I hoped Terry would fear arrest enough to cut down his drug use. It never occurred to me that he would actually contemplate a career as a drug dealer.

In my absence Terry and my ex-boyfriend, Mike, who had also developed an expensive pot habit, both lost their jobs in ways unrelated to drugs. Mike moved back into the neighborhood. He and Terry decided to sell some drugs to support themselves. By then Terry was addicted to a variety of substances. He took speed to get out of bed and Seconal to go to sleep. In between he smoked a steady supply of joints.

Lots of lefties were casual drug users, and some of them sold pot or acid so that they could get high for free. Few were professionals. Mike and Terry saw themselves as better than those selling heroin. They were rebels flouting American laws and capitalism by thriving in an underground economy, whereas heroin pushers sold lethal and addictive substances.

Terry was reasonably cautious. He sold drugs at GLF dances and discussed deals only from pay phones. Though he swore he kept his stash at Mike's place, one day I came home, opened the refrigerator, and discovered—standing out vividly against the moldy blotches of spilled and spoiled food that typically decorated the shelves—several blue cartons of speed and peyote tucked away in the back of the middle shelf.

We had agreed never to keep enough drugs in the house to allow the government to charge us with intent to sell. Now Terry had broken his word. My name was on the lease, and I could be held liable for his crime. I gave Terry a month to pack up and move out. I didn't care whether he lived with Mike or John, so long as he was gone. Smoking pot was one thing, but selling drugs and being political were a dangerous mix. I knew I had already attracted the government's attention: It was ridiculous to give law enforcement officials an easy excuse to arrest me. I was prepared to go to jail for a cause, but not for a drug bust.

Evicting Terry felt like a bitter divorce, the sad end of a relationship I had expected to last the rest of my life. I loved him more than I ever had Mike ("for sure," as Terry would have said). However, when I reached a difficult pass such as this, I refused to lose sight of my political convictions.

Still, I felt responsible in some way for what happened to Terry, as if I had encouraged him too quickly to come out without paying any attention to a glaring limitation: his addictive behavior. But what else could I do? Once he had moved out, I put him out of my mind. I was mad at Mike, too, for seducing the hapless Terry into his schemes.

Terry decided to visit his parents in Oklahoma. Perhaps I disrupted the partnership between Terry and Mike just in time. About two months later Mike was caught with a panel truck full of marijuana as he crossed the border from Canada into New York State. He had apparently been growing and drying his own marijuana all summer for resale in New York City. Mike told the judge that he wasn't a dealer—he intended to smoke all two hundred pounds himself. The judge was not convinced and sentenced him to ten years in a federal prison.

Over the summer June had sublet my room. When I returned from Los Angeles, she remained, and I discovered, much to my surprise, that I was living with a lover. Jude stayed on as well. Without the constant din of three to six other men cluttering the apartment, I started to get to know Jude better. He was a lot of things, but mostly he was never dull. He was impishly wicked in a way that I found hilarious as long as

I wasn't the butt of his humor. Once he stood in the kitchen a few feet behind the dining room table where I was serving dinner to a former publishing colleague, whom I was trying to impress. Realizing that she was slightly deaf, he campily criticized all the food at a pitch that she couldn't quite hear, while I could catch every word.

"This dinner is delicious," she crooned. "How could you afford shrimp?"

"She stole everything; that's how!" Jude sneered.

"What did he say?"

"Pay him no mind," I shot an evil look over my shoulder at him. I turned back to her, smiled sadly, and cupped my hands in her direction so that she'd catch my stage whisper. "He's slightly mad and mutters to himself all the time. Just ignore him—he's harmless."

Sometimes I gave myself the same advice. Whenever June or I asked Jude to perform some chore in the apartment, whether cleaning the bathtub or cooking part of a meal, he would rush to the phone and complain to the first person he could get a hold of.

"You won't believe it, John. These two butches are oppressing me again!" His tone was halfway between utter exasperation and an immi-nent bout of faintness. "Yes, yes, they are *both* ganging up on me. What's a girl like me to do?" His dire tone, accompanied by exaggerated ges-tures that only we could see, suggested he was about to be drafted for some dirty chore suitable for a prison trustee.

But the same campy wit, when aimed at outsiders, could be priceless. One morning as June and I awoke, I thought I saw a man, perched on the fire escape, opening our bedroom window.

"That's weird, June," I muttered. "I'm dreaming there's a man coming in our window."

"That's really weird. I'm having the same dream!" We looked at each other like two cartoon characters who suddenly realize they're sitting on a stick of dynamite. "Shoo! Shoo!" June said sleepily, waving the guy away.

We started to go back to sleep when we heard the window squeak. The culprit was back. "C'mon, scram!" June said.

"Don't worry; I'll take care of him." I hadn't been studying judo for nothing, and June's technique was more suitable for scaring scavenging pigeons. I went into the kitchen and grabbed my huge, square, Chinese vegetable cleaver.

The commotion had awakened Jude, who joined me in the kitchen. As usual he was stark naked. I told him what had happened, and just as I finished, we could hear June yelling at the intruder, who was back for a third try. Jude and I charged into the bedroom together. I was holding the knife over my head and yelling, "Banzai, scumbag!"

Jude shrieked as he ran behind me, flailing his arms: "Where is he, Mary? Just let me at him!" I don't know which one of us frightened the trespasser more, but he never came back.

Though Jude was often as moody and trying as he was comic, he did me a wonderful favor by introducing me to Allen Young that fall. Like so many other men, Allen was attracted to Jude's boyish charm and graceful dancer's body. Allen also appreciated Jude's humor and took him to an engagement party for two former classmates. Allen showed up bedecked in gay liberation buttons, while Jude's body language, clothing, and speech blared his queenliness. The Columbia alums, not slow learners, had to cope, but a few of the men couldn't bear to be in the same room with this openly gay couple, the first they had ever seen.

Their relationship didn't last very long, but during the time that they were going out, Allen was often at our apartment, and I got to know him better. Of course, I had seen him almost every week at the Gay Liberation Front. The first time I ever spoke with him, I decided that his hazel eyes were warm and sincere. Though he looked macho because he sometimes grew a dark bushy beard and wore work boots, I could tell that he genuinely liked and respected women. He would sometimes rebuke other men who interrupted women during meetings, and he generally went out of his way to talk to some women afterward.

But despite my sense that Allen was liberated, we had rarely spoken outside the meetings. People traveled in their own small subgroups and somehow didn't connect with people outside it. All I knew about Allen was that he lived in the Seventeenth Street Collective, which, like the Ninety-fifth Street Collective, Lois Hart's loft, and my apartment, was one of the centers of GLF activity. The Seventeenth Street Collective, which Allen shared with Carl Miller, Jim Fouratt, Giles Kotcher, and others, was on the eleventh floor of a commercial building. It was oddly sandwiched between the offices of *Screw* magazine and those of the Communist Party. Carl Miller, a fabric designer, was the original lessee of the loft, and Jim Fouratt and Craig Smith encouraged him to open it up for communal living, which was considered a desirable part of revolutionary consciousness. I don't think that they strove, like the Ninety-fifth Street Collective, to share absolutely everything, and most of the inhabitants weren't exactly enemies of the patriarchy. Like my apartment, the Seventeenth Street loft had almost no privacy, though it did feature a sort of cabinet with a bed in it, which was nicknamed the "Fuck Box."

Allen and I soon discovered that we had a lot in common. Among other things, we had both participated in the 1968 Columbia University campus uprising, where Allen was among those arrested. He had a journalism degree and was working for Liberation News Service. He told me that he was compiling a collection of gay liberation material. I had been gathering lesbian manifestos and writings for a possible anthology. I didn't see myself as a writer then. My mission was to collect and disseminate gay and lesbian material so that no one would grow up as I had—never seeing a word that named my difference. We decided to pool our resources and look for a publisher. We felt that by combining our archives with our writing and editing experience, we would be able to publish a wide range of material that would reach a broad audience.

Meanwhile, my relationship with June was growing more complicated. I was delighted by our reunion, but I was unprepared to be suddenly living with a lover. At twenty-three I didn't feel old enough to be "settled down," though I felt that some movement couples, such as Lois Hart and Suzanne Bevier, had a kind of status just for having formed the very sort of alliance that heterosexist society said was impossible. One of the common psychological axioms of the era was that homosexuals were doomed to sad and lonely lives, devoid of the kind of relationship that members of my parents' generation had idealized. But on some level I dreaded the very concept of marriage and had not imagined myself being part of a couple for another decade or so. I relished my newfound sexual freedom, and a committed relationship threatened to interfere with that. I told June before I returned from California that I had been involved with Micki and Pam, though I omitted others. I sensed limits to her belief in nonmonogamy.

June finally confessed that she had heard about me from both Samuel and Becky, back when she was living in Amsterdam. Both of them were writing to her about my exploits, and often two letters about me would arrive in the Netherlands on the very same day. Sure it couldn't be simply a coincidence that these two people who didn't know each other were so close to me, she concluded that it was her destiny to live with me. She returned to the United States to meet me.

To a point June was perfectly willing to accommodate my politics to ensure that our relationship worked. For me, both personally and politically, sexual fidelity was anathema: Monogamy equaled ownership, which reeked of patriarchal capitalism. On a more personal level the short time I had spent in the Psychedelic Venus Church convinced me that sexuality was a natural extension of friendship; in fact, it was often the precursor to friendship. Why not explore sexual attraction? If two women were turned on by each other, why avoid it in the name of some antiquated ideal of exclusivity? If the sex was wonderful, it would be part of the relationship. If the sex was uninspiring, friendship was still possible. I couldn't refuse the offer of sex once it crackled electrically in the air. My body knew how to relate to others with a sureness my words did not possess. And so even as June and I enjoyed our "honeymoon," I was marking and sealing the frontiers of our relationship. The seeds of its dissolution were already sown.

For the time being we turned out to be quite compatible in other ways. June adored animals, and she had probably saved Ringo's life while I was gone. Every time he saw me take out a suitcase, Ringo neurotically gnawed the fur off one rear leg until I threatened to change his name to "Baldy." Deciding that he had been abandoned, Ringo refused to eat, and June had to force baby food down his throat with an eye dropper. And even though Ringo could be picky and mean at times, he adored June.

A s we settled down into lesbian coupledom, the political world around us was shifting. Certainly, some of the schisms had already begun the previous winter when, in December 1996, some disaffected members of the GLF had left and started a new group, the Gay Activists Alliance (GAA). Arthur Bell, Arthur Evans, Jim Owles, and Marty Robinson helped carve out the politics of the new group, which was governed by a constitution, by-laws, a membership, and *Robert's Rules of Order*. In part, many GAA members opposed focusing energy on outside groups such as the Black Panthers, but they were equally disgusted with the general chaos of GLF meetings. GAA also had a clear agenda, which involved lobbying for civil rights legislation.

Race was a divisive issue within the GLF, and tensions about supporting the struggles of people of color escalated after my return in September 1970. A number of GLF members had traveled with the Venceremos Brigade to Cuba during the summer to help with the sugar cane harvest. They came back with glowing reports of Fidel Castro's revolution and felt that as white imperialists we could not criticize Latin American politics. Others, including Allen Young and me, objected to Cuba's horrible treatment of gay people, who were being imprisoned in "reeducation" camps. Angry debates over Cuba and the Black Panthers increased defections to GAA. Then as membership shrank, the remaining radical factions began to struggle with one another for control of the organization.

The GLF wasn't the only group with problems. The Daughters of Bilitis suddenly became more militant and more feminist when Ruth Simpson became its leader in the fall of 1970. There were some strange shifts in organizational configuration. An odd alliance developed between the DOB and Ti-Grace Atkinson, who had been booted out of The Feminists that June, most likely for refusing to abide by the lottery system she had set up. On the surface the New York chapter of the DOB didn't seem to have much to offer straight feminists. It tended to attract many politically naive or apolitical lesbians. Ti-Grace might have seen an opportunity to recruit and lead them.

Ti-Grace was getting decidedly weirder. A month before my return from California Ti-Grace spoke at a "Panel on Violence" at PS 41 in the Village and hailed recently murdered crime boss Joseph Columbo as a "sister," a protofeminist, a "star," someone who "fought for everybody else's rights." Had I been in the audience, I might have thought this was a joke, though no one ever accused Ti-Grace of having a sense of humor. By the time I returned from California, Ti-Grace had lost all her credibility, and thanks to her participation, the local DOB chapter was on its way to becoming defunct.

On January 4, 1971, Ti-Grace, speaking at the DOB, renounced feminists as "those dumb bitches who've taken up fiddling with the Man's supremacy." Though Ti-Grace was still not a lesbian, she told the packed crowd, including me, "I'm enormously less interested in whom you sleep with than I am in with whom you're prepared to die." Then she laid out a series of twenty-two charts more complicated than the grammar of her speech. Pointing to her diagrams, she explained that lesbians were the "buffer" between the patriarchy and feminists. Perhaps some of the lesbians were flattered to have been selected by Ti-Grace as her front-line troops, but I found the presentation bizarre, frightening, and confusing. I especially didn't care for the "prepared to die" bit and feared Ti-Grace was proposing a doomsday cult for lesbians.

After that, many of the DOB regulars took flight. Though not a member, I was among those who went screaming into the night. Simpson, however, was apparently totally entranced by Ti-Grace, and before long the DOB had become a front for Ti-Grace's activities and views. Some of the regulars even acted as her unpaid bodyguards. I'm not sure whether she was afraid of attacks from antifeminists or from other members of the women's movement.

Radical politics, however, was by no means dead. Demonstrations started up again not long after my return. I had no sooner unpacked than Elsie, one of my Redstockings sisters, told me she was organizing a prowoman action in Atlantic City around the Miss America pageant. Did I want to participate? Of course, of course. Through a connection in the flower wholesale market in Manhattan, Elsie purchased several dozen long-stem red roses. We loaded them into the trunk of a car she had borrowed, and five of us took off for Atlantic City. We stood on the boardwalk and told each woman who passed by that she was the real Miss America. And then we would hand her a rose.

Even though we did not attract any media coverage, this prowoman action went well until a Yippie Elsie knew told us that his group planned to release a stink bomb during the pageant that night. Certain that we would be blamed, we quickly handed out the rest of the roses and drove back to New York City. On the way we collected receipts at every toll booth and distributed them among us so that we each had at least one piece of evidence that we had left Atlantic City before the disruption took place. As it turns out, I don't think it ever did. Perhaps the Yippie was putting us on; perhaps the agitators got cold feet and called off their protest; perhaps it was simply not reported in the press.

About a week after that some of us held a sit-in at New York University. Ellen Broidy, whom I knew from the New York Gay Liberation Front, was an undergraduate involved with Gay Student Liberation (formerly the Student Homophile League) at NYU. Ellen had been trying to negotiate with the dorm council to allow a dance in the subbasement of Weinstein Hall. Other gay dances had been held there, including a Gay Pride Week dance sponsored by GAA. But this time the administrators told the gay group that homosexuality was a "mental disorder." The students would have to find a psychiatrist to disprove this diagnosis before we could hold a dance. Meanwhile, the university would consult another psychiatrist, who would present an opposing view. Then the university would decide which one to believe. Gay activists knew which version the university would choose: The American Psychiatric Association classified homosexuality as a mental disorder until 1973, so in 1970 we considered the entire medical profession one of our worst oppressors.

On September 20 Martha Shelley, Ellen, and other members of the New York group trying to hold the dance decided that a spontaneous sit-in was in order. "If we let people know in advance," Martha told me, "Weinstein Hall will be surrounded by cops. Let's take it over and hold it until the dance." A member of the student group went over to the nearby Fifth Avenue Peace Parade Committee (a group that opposed the war in Vietnam) to get some leaflets run off, while Martha asked the Gay Liberation Front to support the action. As usual about half the members supported the action, with the other half opposing it. I thought the sit-in sounded like a fun and worthwhile action. I figured that since I was registered at NYU, this was one action for which I couldn't be busted. With the tuition I was paying, NYU could hardly claim that I was "trespassing." A group of us trekked down together from the Church of the Holy Apostles to the Village, where we picked up some homeless street queens and poor gay kids, who saw this as a wonderful opportunity to sleep indoors.

The semester was just starting, and Weinstein Hall, a characterless red brick dorm that looked out on noisy University Place, tended to house freshmen who wanted to be as close to the university as possible during their initial year. About seventy members of GLF, Radicalesbians, and other groups stormed in and took over the subbasement. Most of the students were horrified. They had been in New York less than a week, and they were being overrun by radical faggots and dykes. One of them asked me whether we were really revolutionaries or part of a street theater group. Several made a dash to the pay phones to inform their parents that they were having their first "New York experience." Some of them were angry that we had invaded their space. Later some GLF members met with the students to explain that the dorm council had agreed to the dance in writing. If the university violated that contract, what justice could the students expect? "We're fighting for *your* rights," Martha explained.

Won over, some of the students gave us extra blankets and sheets, which we welcomed because the security forces turned on the air-conditioning as high as it would go to drive us out of the basement. We huddled together and generally tried to keep warm or find things to eat. I had been through this drill before at Columbia and on the steps of the Los Angeles federal building. Relatively speaking, the conditions here weren't as bad—at least the basement had a laundry room and toilets. But when I fell asleep, I had nightmares about the Tactical Police Force attacking me with clubs and horses. I believe in omens, so the next morning I left and went home.

Others stayed on, and I got the story from them afterward. The street transvestites who were there, including Sylvia Rivera and Marsha P. Johnson, were among the most militant. Sylvia left once, to ask GAA for help, but the alliance's executive committee decided that it was fine for individuals to participate but that GAA couldn't support the action as a group. Sylvia was furious. The protesters carried on by themselves. They continued to attempt to radicalize the students. Ellen Broidy was called into a dean's office and threatened with expulsion. According to an interview that Jim Fouratt gave to Martin Duberman for *Stonewall,* "A transsexual from Los Angeles . . . determined to out-radical everyone else" planted firebombs throughout the building. Jim had to remove them.

By the third day the air-conditioning had been completely turned off, and the protesters began to swelter in the windowless subbasement—they were going through ice and fire to be free. Students brought down blankets and cots and joined the sit-in and the games that the protesters played to pass the time. I'm surprised that the sight of radicals doing the bunny hop and playing charades didn't send them scurrying back to their books.

On Friday, four days after the occupation had begun, NYU, unwilling to wait as long as Columbia had, called in the TPF. According to Arthur Bell, a *Village Voice* columnist and GAA member, the twenty-nine remaining protesters were given ten seconds to leave. They did, but that night over four hundred angry gays returned to Greenwich Village to demand the gay dance. What had started as a battle over a student dance had escalated into a mini-Stonewall. There are stories of cops leveling their guns at demonstrators when clearing out Weinstein and during the angry demonstrations that followed. A few people were arrested, often on charges of drug possession. According to some reports, Sylvia was almost shot by the police. Street Transvestites Action Revolutionaries (STAR) was born out of the outrage over this.

The protests continued for weeks—I felt like a magnet for student uprisings wherever I enrolled. In some ways this riot was Columbia déjà vu, and in other ways it was another manifestation of this era of student uprisings. But this time, at least, there was some real support from within

New York University. Jim Clifford, an NYU employee (who died of AIDS in 1995 after working at the university for decades), helped the protesters write a leaflet with gay demands. The preamble noted that "NYU is located in the largest gay ghetto in the world" and therefore should provide a gay community center, free tuition for gay people, and equal employment opportunities for homosexuals. As NYU had a prestigious medical school, we also demanded that it liberate gay mental patients from Bellevue and provide free medical and dental care for gays. In those days our hopes were gargantuan. Today gay activists want to assimilate into institutions that haven't worked all that well for heterosexuals—marriage and military service, to name just two. But then we wanted to change the world.

For all the revolutionary fervor that fueled the Weinstein sit-in, it still suffered from the same old gender imbalance. Few women participated; it was too much a male event. Radicalesbians wasn't satisfied with this sort of action—to us, revolution meant forging a lesbian-centered world. The group had continued to meet over the summer, its numbers swelled by the Lavender Menace action, word of which spread throughout the city.

During the summer while I was in California, Radicalesbians had its first martyr. Lydia French, a thirty-one-year-old medical secretary who lived on the East Side, was found murdered in her apartment. She had been shot in the back, and there were no signs of forced entry. Lydia, whom several people described as naive and innocent, had begun attending GLF and Radicalesbians during the summer. Martha described her as "blond, slender, with graceful gestures," a woman who "talked with her hands." Lydia used to sit at meetings and draw people, with the skill of a sketch artist, and my ex-lover Becky had wondered at first whether Lydia was some sort of agent. When Becky discovered that they both attended Hunter College, they became friendly. It turned out that Lydia had never attended any gay group before and didn't realize that drawing people's faces might be an issue. Lydia was worried about her father, a retired army colonel: She told several members of Radicalesbians that her father had threatened to shoot her if she became a communist or a lesbian. Now she was a member of a Marxist lesbian group.

The killer was never found, and the police seemed more interested in Lydia's movement literature, which they removed from her apartment. Many of us saw their skewed priorities as a paradigm for the way in which we didn't matter when we were the victims of a crime.

Despite widespread outrage and grief over Lydia's death, the incident did not become a rallying point for the group. Radicalesbians failed to capitalize on Lydia French as a movement martyr as gay men, especially GAA, had claimed Diego Vinales. In a democratically run organization such as GAA, a majority vote ruled, but Radicalesbians operated by consensus. That meant *everyone* in the room had to agree to an action or a position. But if ten different opinions are needed, as the joke goes, just stick five lesbians in a room together. Any attempt to get several dozen lesbians to agree on any issue will cause a perpetual stalemate. Radicalesbians could come up with no unified position on Lydia's death, and when several members decided to cooperate with the police investigation, others left the group in protest.

Part of the rationale behind operating by consensus was to ensure equality. We saw star-tripping as an evil that the group had to avoid at all costs. When we met, we sat in a circle and went around and around the room. Each woman could speak only when the woman next to her had finished, though someone could opt not to speak. It was an exhausting—and to my mind, futile—process. We almost never came to any firm decision about anything. Any one person could block an action. In retrospect, I can see that consensus actually empowered the minority who refused to agree and probably encouraged some to take oppositional stances.

Therefore, even though there were no leaders per se, there was a lot of tension. People such as Lois Hart, who were used to holding sway in GLF, were clearly frustrated by the new arrangement. Some, including Rita Mae Brown and Martha Shelley, tried to promote a radical political agenda. Rita began to promote lesbian separatism—in particular, opposing cooperation with what she termed the "male-run media."

The emergence of separatist politics in Radicalesbians came at a particularly bad time for me. Allen and I were just beginning to shop around our book proposal for *Out of the Closets.* Furthermore, through

Allen and other connections, I had been taken on as a stringer for *University Review*, a newspaper distributed on campuses throughout the United States. The editors sent me off on a series of freelance assignments, not all of which they ran in the end. But in the course of my work I interviewed everyone from film directors to roller derby stars. I met such luminaries as Anaïs Nin, whose first diaries were just being published.

Though she had written other works, Nin was just beginning to emerge as someone important in her own right, not simply as writer Henry Miller's paramour. Because Nin made the kind of journal-writing women did both public and valid, she was considered a literary heroine in many circles. (Of course, since then Nin has been debunked as a fraud of sorts. It turned out that she had kept two sets of diaries—a public set, which I read in the early 1970s, and the kind of more intimate material found in *Henry and June*. She also had two husbands, one on each coast.)

In person Nin had the mesmerizing charm of someone who had to seduce—mentally or physically—everyone she met. She was not a typical beauty, though on top of her heart-shaped face, she braided some of the longest, loveliest hair I've ever seen (she sent me a photo of herself with her hair down). She wore a cape that Terry would have killed for, and from it emanated strong currents of Chanel No. 5. My primary reservation about her was her homophobia, which bubbled just below the surface. Every time the tape recorder was shut off, she launched into nasty tirades about male homosexuals—writers Marcel Proust and Truman Capote were among her targets. She denied vehemently that she had had a lesbian affair with June Miller, though as a gay activist I pressed her on this issue. Her later diaries confirm her erotic interest in other women. She saw lesbianism as a sort of narcissism. While challenging dual standards of sexual behavior for men and women, she believed the stock teachings of male psychotherapy. When I met her, however, I was taken in by her charm and by her interest in me. Indeed, when *Out of the Closets* was finally published in 1972, she persuaded magazines she was connected with to review it, and I was overwhelmed by her generosity.

Another media star I was sent to track down and interview was Jill Johnston. She had begun her career as a dance critic, but by 1970 she was writing weekly columns for the *Village Voice,* which she later collected in *Marmalade Me* (1971) and *Lesbian Nation* (1973). I liked some of her ideas, but too many of them were lost in her fascination with her own navel. I found her column almost impossible to read. Her dizzying, repetitious, grammarless style lacked a sense of the sound and shape of words. Her column, however, reached thousands of lesbians and gay men across the United States who otherwise wouldn't have heard of the movement. Moreover, Jill's wonderful sense of Yippie activism brought media attention to issues she wanted to raise. In the summer of 1970 she had taken off half her clothes and jumped topless into a swimming pool at a posh women's liberation cocktail party. At a famous New York Town Hall debate between Norman Mailer and Germaine Greer, Jill leaped onto the stage with two of her friends and started hugging them and rolling around on the floor with them. An uproar ensued.

Based on her columns and deeds, I was expecting a dynamic, engaging, sophisticated writer type, but as it turned out, she was rather skittish and strange and didn't have much to say. Jill insisted I meet her at Casey's, a popular Village restaurant that was way over my head financially, but I was flattered by the thought that Jill wanted to have dinner with me, cub reporter, so I agreed to the locale. She showed up in her "uniform"—denim pants and jacket. Around her neck were more metal trinkets than in a pawnshop window. I could have spent the evening trying to figure out what they were, but I didn't want her to think I was staring at her breasts. I knew that many of my friends idolized her, but I didn't find her horsey looks attractive. I was surprised to find her shy and suspicious about my motivations.

It was a long time before I could get her to talk about anything interesting. We ate our dinner and exchanged some meaningless chitchat. Just as I was about to snap on my tape recorder, she asked me to wait. "Hang on for a few minutes. I've gotta go take a crap," she said. Then she picked up her coffee cup from the table and sauntered downstairs to the ladies room. Ten or fifteen minutes later she returned. Finally, we talked about her life and writing.

When I wasn't interviewing people, I did other sorts of freelance writing and editing. I ghostwrote a few books, I screened manuscripts for agents and publishers, and I reviewed books and films. As the lowest tad on the pole, I was naturally assigned to the least promising films. I told myself, however, that it was all good writing practice; plus I needed the money desperately.

But the direction my career was going in was clearly contrary to the strictures Radicalesbians had imposed against media cooperation. Members who were early successes in the media or another profession were vehemently attacked. When the forthcoming publication of Kate Millett's *Sexual Politics* was announced in the *New York Times* on July 20, 1970, many activists hailed it as the first mainstream feminist analysis of literature, and Kate was anointed by the media as a new light. But to a few Radicalesbians, publishing in mainstream venues was collaborating with the enemy. When Kate appeared at one of the Radicalesbians meetings that fall, she was greeted by an unsigned leaflet (everyone I interviewed believed Rita Mae Brown to be its author) that had been planted on all the chairs before the start of the meeting. The leaflet accused Kate of several "crimes." First, the book was too expensive (as if she could price her own work). Second, Kate had "described herself as trying to be a bridge between Women's Liberation, N.O.W., and our group." The mimeo pointed out that since many members of Radicalesbians were also members of feminist groups, we didn't need her as a "bridge." Moreover, the unnamed woman who had authored the leaflet asked, "Who has decided that we want to work with these other groups?" Kate was dismissed as a married woman (that is, a fraud) who hadn't even sat through an entire meeting. The leaflet warned members that "if we do not establish policy on these questions [the media and our relationship to other movements] it means that any woman (or man in drag for all we know) can represent herself to the media as being a full fledged member of Lesbian Liberation and then go on to make statements that are tantamount to policy."

After the leaflet incident Radicalesbians escalated its attacks on Kate; the group determined not to let her become a media celebrity. That December Kate was "outed" (that word did not exist until the late 1980s) as a bisexual by Ann Sanchez of Radicalesbians during a talk Kate gave at Columbia University. During the question-and-answer period, Ann stood up in the audience and asked Kate more than once whether she was a lesbian; Kate finally but reluctantly admitted she was bisexual. Suddenly Kate was no longer the darling of the media. She didn't get tenure at Barnard College either. Now outing is fashionable, but at that moment I was horrified. Naming someone a lesbian in a public forum was damning, damaging, and irrevocable, once the "L" word was said aloud. Outing was something enemies did to us, not something we did to each other.

Even before Kate's public trashing, it was easy for me to conclude that publishing a book or achieving other forms of success could be dangerous in radical lesbian and feminist groups. I wasn't the only one to feel disgusted either. Barbara Love, a friend of Kate's and coauthor of the 1972 *Sappho Was a Right-On Woman*, recently told me that she left Radicalesbians around the same period. She felt that the group had developed a "fascistic atmosphere to the point of being absurd."

Members of the movement began to attack one "star" after another. This kind of "barracuda behavior" (biting anything that shines) continues to this day, which is one reason no unifying leader has ever emerged in the gay, lesbian, or women's movements. Few have been exempt from attack. In 1975 the few remaining Redstockings even attacked feminist activist and cofounder of *Ms.* magazine Gloria Steinem, accusing her of being an agent of the CIA. The only basis for this elaborate conspiracy charge was her attendance in 1959 and 1962 at two Communist Youth Festivals with the Independent Research Service, a group created by the U.S. National Student Association and, like it and other parts of the non-Communist Left, then supported by CIA-funded foundations. According to Carolyn Heilbrun's 1995 biography, *The Education of a Woman: The Life of Gloria Steinem*, "Most frustrating to Steinem was the fact that the Redstockings pretended to have 'discovered' facts about the Youth Festivals and the Independant Research Service that she had long ago made public and that had been published in newspapers and magazines." I publicly sided with Gloria and denounced the attack—Gloria's record of accomplishments for women speaks for itself. If the CIA had created Gloria Steinem, feminists would have begged the agency to make more like her!

I left Radicalesbians in disappointment in November 1970. By the end of the year Radicalesbians had pretty much dissolved, though a few women continued to use the name. I reevaluated my political commitments. Returning to Redstockings was one logical choice for my political energy. Unfortunately, Redstockings was also floundering. The founders, unable to persuade new members that Redstockings' manifestos and position papers contained the essential truths of the women's movement, lost interest in recruiting budding feminists or even in retaining the current membership. My C-R group had replaced a number of its original members, and I couldn't connect with the new ones, nor was I willing to start over again every time another woman joined our cell. I decided to limit my activities to a lesbian-only C-R group and spend more time on my graduate studies. I resolved not to become as burned out as I had the year before.

As the winter set in, I decided that more than anything else I wanted to return to sunny Southern California and settle there permanently. This time I no longer felt impelled to escape my family and bad health. I had learned to pace myself to protect my health, and my mother, withdrawn and silent, rarely called anymore.

June was initially opposed to moving. She had already lived far from home and was perfectly happy being back in New York near her family. After the dreary, dank winters in Amsterdam, New York seemed sunny and dry by comparison. Finally, she relented, and we decided to move to Venice, California, for the summer of 1971. We agreed that if we both liked it, we would stay on, but if June hated it, we would return east.

⁓   ⁓   ⁓

From mid-1970 through 1971 John Knoebel lived in the Ninety-fifth Street Collective. In 1972 he became one of the members of the Effeminists, a group of feminist gay men. Other members included GLF member Steve Dansky and poet Ken Pitchford (Robin Morgan's husband). Together they put out the first "male feminist" publication, *Double F.* In one issue the Effeminists labeled a number of gay men, including Allen Young and Craig Rodwell (owner of the Oscar Wilde Bookshop), "enemies of feminism." It seemed to me unfair to equate these men with rock star Mick Jagger (also proclaimed an "enemy"), and I didn't think that any man, including feminist men, should be deciding who women's enemies are. I was angry with the Effeminists and lost contact with John. After a couple of years John also abandoned Effeminism. He felt that all his political involvement had diminished his joy in being a gay man. He met a lover and moved to San Francisco with him. From 1979 to 1995 John worked for *The Advocate* and has since moved back to New York, where he owns a gay marketing company.

Jude Bartlett lived with June and me for another year or two. After he moved out, we lost touch with him. In the late 1980s June spotted an article about him in New York *Newsday* and telephoned me right away.

"Are you ready for this? It says Jude's a chef and owns a restaurant on the North Fork of Long Island. It says he liked to cook from the time he was a child."

"Huh? I don't remember him cooking anything for us? Do you?"

"No, of all people!"

The next time I heard of Jude was when his 1992 death from AIDS was announced at the twenty-fifth reunion of the GLFers in 1994. Shortly afterward I read a touching portrait of Jude's last moments in Doris Grumbach's 1994 memoir *Fifty Days of Solitude.* When Jude was dying, his sister had him brought to her home in Maine by ambulance. Grumbach was one of those who volunteered to take care of him. By then Grumbach saw him as a "gentle, sweet fellow," who didn't in the least resemble the feisty, campy queen who had been my roommate.

I saw Terry only a few times after he moved out of our apartment. He dropped out of graduate school and disappeared from the movement.

Of the three of us—John, Terry, and me—I was the only one to finish graduate school. One day a few years later he reappeared at my door. He looked gaunt and nervous. He had totally lost his sense of style, his wonderful Audrey Hepburn look. He was so obviously in a bad way that I let him spend the night. By then June and I were living alone, so we let Terry sleep on the couch. By the time we woke up the next morning, he was gone. A note indicated that he was leaving us two Black Beauties in return for our hospitality. As June and I had no use for speed, we went to toss them out, but could find only one pill. When Ringo started zooming around the apartment and tried to climb up the walls, we knew where the other Black Beauty had gone. The cat's heart was pounding horribly, and for hours we took turns trying to hold and comfort him. Ringo survived, barely. I was furious at Terry because he, better than anyone else, knew of Ringo's penchant for drugs.

I never saw Terry again.

I stayed in that same Upper West Side building until February 1977 when the apartment next to mine was torched. By then I was living alone. At one in the morning Ringo jumped up and down on my chest until I woke up. At first I thought he had totally lost his mind, as I had worked the chopping noises of the firemen into my dream. Ringo, Pooh Cat, and I were cornered for several hours in the hallway, along with the other tenants of the building. I didn't know we were trapped: We thought we were merely defending our possessions against the firemen, who had a reputation for loading their big pockets with other people's valuables. There had been so many fires in the building in recent years that everyone was nonchalant about the flames that were shooting through two stories of the building. "More water over there!" we would yell, urging the firemen on while we passed a bottle of rum back and forth to keep warm.

Finally, the firemen led us down the darkened stairwell while water and wet ash cascaded onto our heads. I saved only Ringo, Pooh, and some drafts of various books that were in the works, including my dissertation. I had packed everything into a large cat carrier as I soon as I realized the building was on fire.

I lost all my clothing and most of my possessions. Ringo, who was eight, never recovered from the fire, during which he suffered a heart attack. I took him to the best animal hospital in the city, but even my last money couldn't save him. Pooh Cat went crazy—she had never known life without Ringo to look after her. Pooh, who had always been terrified of leaving the house, ran away from her new location and was never seen again. I missed Ringo for years but never adopted another cat.

15

California Scheming

Looking forward to a summer of fun and politics, June and I piled into her old Falcon and drove to Los Angeles. When we arrived there at the end of May 1970, Del Whan housed us for a few days in a lesbian community center she and some other women had started in the Echo Park area near downtown. The first lesbian center in the country, it was used mostly for meetings and consciousness-raising groups. We were delighted to have a place to crash.

A week later we rented a furnished studio on Brooks Avenue in Venice, about a block from the gay beach. At first it was unpleasant to live there because a cold fog would roll in every night in May and early June and the only source of warmth was a tiny, inefficient gas heater.

We had very little money. Sandy Blixton, my radical brother from the LA GLF, advised us to get food stamps. He was an expert in these matters. He had qualified for Aid to the Totally Disabled by showing up at the welfare office with a roll of toilet paper, which he pounded into an unattractive, cone-shaped beanie. He hadn't shaved for a few days and had bitten his nails down to the quick.

"What am I going to do? What am I going to do?" he repeated over and over as the social worker stared. She assured him that he would be taken care of. Sensing he was gay, she asked, "Do you like men?"

"Oh, no," he answered. "I like boys."

"Would you like to see a psychiatrist?"

"Can he help me find some boys?"

"Why don't you ask him yourself?"

She made an immediate appointment for him with a shrink. On the way out, reassured by the social worker that he was going to get financial help, Sandy carefully tore off a small square of toilet paper and handed it to her.

"I would like to give you something because you were so nice to me. I only do this for people I like." She gingerly took the piece of toilet paper and handed him a card with his psychiatric appointment.

We appreciated Sandy's advice and his help with the paperwork, although we didn't have to resort to his tactics. Our income level was well below the poverty line, and we were fully entitled to food stamps. Even with assistance, we had to be clever to subsist on our small savings. We bought day-old bread from a store on Lincoln Boulevard that gave change in real money, unlike the other stores, which always handed us more food stamps. We joined one of the country's first food collectives, where a nickel would buy a head of lettuce or a pound of stringbeans. Lots of our friends gave us produce from their gardens or trees. Sandy was always bringing over oranges, grapefruit, and avocados from his yard.

June and I quickly encountered the suspicion and hostility with which the poor are treated. We learned, like the other welfare recipients, to avoid the cashiers who gave us a hard time. One cashier in particular—"Hilda," her tag read under a drawing of a smiling face—took special pride in questioning whether our purchases really qualified as food.

"So what's with these sunflower seeds? Ya got a parrot?" Hilda hoisted the bag so that the people in line behind us could judge for themselves.

"No, we eat them."

"This is bird food—I know it when I see it." Then she'd call over the manager and hold up the line, which would infuriate everyone behind us.

June and I hoped we might be able to eat grunions—small smeltlike fish that travel in large schools. The females beach themselves to lay eggs and then head back to sea on the next wave. Some of the local radio stations issued grunion alerts.

When we heard about the next grunion run, we set our alarm clocks and got up at 2:00 A.M. to be out on Venice Beach in time. There we stood with scores of hippies waiting for the grunions to arrive. Finally, two or three grunions beached themselves, hardly the school we had been promised.

"Let 'em go," a seasoned hippie advised us. "That's just the scouts. If you go for them, the others won't come up."

Sure enough, about ten minutes later small fish flipped like silver dollars all over the beach. It wasn't easy to catch them, since it was against the law to use a net or bucket. They were small, quick, and very slippery. Just when I'd think I finally had one, it would squirm out of my hands and race back to the sea. They turned out not to be worth losing a night's sleep over. They were too bony to eat.

I tried to find work, but the Southern California economy was very weak. When I went for a job as a meter reader for the gas company, three hundred people showed up for the few openings. I didn't get the job.

Finally, we decided just to enjoy ourselves while I worked on editing my half of *Out of the Closets,* which Allen and I had sold to Douglas Books, a small counterculture publisher and producer of record albums. I edited the lesbian essays, while Allen concentrated on those by gay men, though sometimes I worked on the material of male friends, such as Sandy. I edited articles or wrote my own material and correspondence in the mornings. After lunch we would walk barefoot to the boardwalk and join Tima and her friends on the gay beach. Not much had changed since the previous summer. Sandy, Tima, and everyone else seemed to have remained in the exact same spot, as if cemented there during the winter I was away. Everything else was the same, too—days of surfing in the waves, lying topless with the other women, and watching Tima deal drugs, while I worked diligently to perfect my tan.

We almost never left Venice. Even our political activity took place there. Sandy Blixton, Cherie Matisse, and others formed a Venice Gay Liberation Front in late 1970. At first the group met in Sandy's house on California Avenue. The meetings had a Venice counterculture flavor.

People would pick some of Sandy's pot on the way in and chew it or try to smoke it during the meeting, though fresh marijuana doesn't burn well. Sandy sat on the floor under a poster of Huey Newton, a Black Panther leader. Sandy always faced his door and rushed to hug and kiss people as they arrived.

By advertising in local papers, the group attracted a broad—and somewhat odd—array of people. Among them were two women, Tommi and Tammy, who were clearly from one of the richer neighborhoods on the West Side of town. I hadn't seen a butch/femme couple like these two since I stopped going to Kooky's bar. Tommi—and I do mean Tommi, because Tammy wasn't permitted to drive—rolled up to the curb in a large black Buick Roadster, the kind some of us associated with our fathers. I decided that someone must have oiled Tommi to squeeze her into her tight polyester suits. Her hair, shaped into a duck's ass in the back, smelled of Brill Cream. Tammy was all painted nails, permed hair, and frilly skirts. The first time they came through Sandy's door, we stared at them as if they were sisters from another planet.

It must have been equally shocking for Tommi and Tammy when they walked into what probably appeared to them as a den of homosexual terrorists. They didn't seem to be aware that we considered "role-playing" a freely chosen imitation of heterosexual norms. Today I realize how oppressive the early post-Stonewall movement was to people like Tommi and Tammy who had butch/femme identities. Most of us couldn't see that butches and femmes were trying to be themselves, just as the rest of us were. But even though I regret our prejudices, I also resist the current fashion to idolize these same women for bucking the "mainstream" gay ideology of the era. As a group they were no more or less heroic than anyone else. There were so few of us who were publicly gay that we all faced danger, whether we were butch, femme, or androgynous radicals.

In any case, after we recovered from our shock, and Tommi and Tammy recovered from theirs, it turned out that we were a good fit. Tommi and Tammy were extremely warm women, and we were delighted when they decided to stay. They were excited by the idea of C-R and eagerly joined the group. They had a great sense of humor, and

Tammy brought wonderful things to eat, such as cookies from a bakery instead of a Nabisco box. The Venice GLF was small enough to make us want new people to feel comfortable, whatever their backgrounds.

However, aside from being lesbians, they had almost nothing in common with the rest of us. They weren't radical at all. Once they loudly objected to our calling one another "brothers" and "sisters" when we weren't blood relatives, and anyway they were terms that "only Black people used for their friends." Terri, an African American woman and a Venice GLF regular, wondered aloud what their problem was. After a few weeks in the group Tommi, who worked as a printer, proudly produced some lavender stationery with gilt lettering that she had had made up for us. We were embarrassed beyond words by this bourgeois excess.

There were other points of contention. Tom, Tam, and some of the others were uncomfortable about meeting in Sandy's house. Some worried that the pot growing in the front yard made us vulnerable to arrest. Still others protested that it was more professional for a group to meet in a neutral space. Others didn't like the poster of Huey Newton hanging over them. As in other GLF groups, the Black Panthers became a hot topic of debate. The TV news was filled with footage of Panthers being routed out of their homes and stripped before the television cameras or framed for crimes they had no part in. Some of us felt the Panthers were the vanguard of radical activism and deserved our support. We wanted the Panthers to visit us. Eventually, Panther Joan Ringo spoke at one of our meetings.

But others disagreed with our position that gays and lesbians were engaged in the same struggle feminists and the Panthers were. They didn't see much connection between gay rights and women's liberation and even less to "far-out" groups such as the Black Panthers or to the philosophy of the Chinese Communist leader Chairman Mao. At heart we were facing the same ideological struggle that had rent the New York branch of the Gay Liberation Front. Most homosexuals wanted to be what we called "isolationists"—that is, they wanted to work only for gay interests. As a result of our debate over the Panthers, a number of our members left the group.

These days single-focus groups are the norm. Maybe we've sacrificed a lot by losing sight of the oppression of others in our myopic quest for our own rights. If all queers can get married, if gay men can get the AIDS drugs they need, or if we can have military careers, it no longer seems to matter to most of today's leaders that people of color die from poverty, indifference, and violence every day and have little chance of getting the medication they need. Children go to bed hungry in this country and elsewhere. We are poisoning a planet all of us live on—no matter what our sexual orientation. I'm by no means suggesting that I've abandoned or neglected gay, lesbian, bisexual, and transgender rights. I can't, however, turn my back on the environment, war, poverty, homelessness, crimes against women, and racism.

The desire to shut out the rest of the world to concentrate on our own rights had its roots in the homophile movements that preceded Stonewall, but single-issue politics became entrenched again within a year after the uprising. Some gay men and lesbians had the nerve to denounce lesbian separatism without noticing that they were equally self-involved.

Those of us who remained in the Venice GLF tackled these divisive issues as delicately as possible and tried to focus more on our commonality. We agreed that meeting at Sandy's house made us too dependent on his goodwill and unfairly empowered him. Eventually we moved to the local office of the Peace and Freedom Party. However, the PFP office sported posters of Eldridge Cleaver, the author of *Soul on Ice* (1968) and the PFP presidential candidate. Some people, turned off by Cleaver, quit the group. Our numbers were diminishing. As in New York, the West Coast movement seemed in decline.

Despite our cultural and political differences, we all continued our struggle to be unified. One afternoon a gilt-edged envelope arrived in the mail for June and me. It was an invitation to Tom and Tam's "wedding" the following month in the Metropolitan Community Church. I quickly telephoned Sandy. He had also received an invite. We debated whether it was our revolutionary duty to oppose this patriarchal event.

Sandy had nothing but contempt for Troy Perry, MCC's pastor, and called him "another opportunist" who had cleverly created "a supermarket chain of 'community' churches in and around Los Angeles." We all objected to the sexist language of patriarchal religion, and we didn't want, as Sandy put it, to encourage "people to marry, to play husband and wife roles, even though the marriages were female/female and male/male." We finally concluded, however, that Tom and Tam would be crushed if we didn't turn up on their big day. We felt we had to attend as a show of support.

On the day of the "union"—in those days the term "commitment" was not yet being used—Sandy drove us over to MCC, which was in its new "mother house." I hadn't seen Troy Perry since he and I had protested together at the federal building the summer before. It felt odd, almost creepy, for me to be sitting in a church waiting for a wedding (however outside the bounds of the law) to take place. Whenever I saw people tossing rice at newlyweds, I was the one who would shout, "Another woman sold into slavery!"

Troy was the first one down the aisle. When he passed us, we noticed that he was wearing sandals underneath his ecclesiastical robes. Tommi was next, dressed in a black tuxedo, followed by her best dyke. And then Tammy, in a white satin dress, was led down the aisle by a gay man. The service was mercifully brief, and luckily Troy didn't ask whether anyone had reason to oppose the union.

Afterward we walked to a reception in the church annex. The goodies laid out on the buffet clearly cost more than the three of us spent on food in a year. Despite the plenty, there was little for vegetarians to eat. A huge white cake was rolled out, with a bride and groom on top, and the happy couple cut the cake. Tommi and Tammy said they were glad we had come, but we weren't thrilled to be there. We couldn't figure out why they needed to spend so much money to prove their love for each other. Hadn't they been just as happy a few weeks earlier? Now, in our eyes, they were simply several thousand dollars poorer.

Not that all weddings had to feel so antithetical to our ideals. Indeed, there must have been something in the salty Venice air that summer. The next day on Venice Beach Sandy, June, and I were chewing over the wedding when Tima announced that Peaches and Sybil, two of the beach regulars, were going to be united at her house in less than two weeks. She scrawled down her address on some Zig-Zag paper she used to roll joints. There was no gilt announcement this time.

On the day of the wedding, Tima greeted us at the door and handed each of us a film canister.

"What's this?" June asked.

"Party favors." Tima winked. Inside each package were a Black Beauty, a Seconal, and half of a fat joint.

"Great. Thanks," I said, pulling June into the house before she insulted Tima by handing it back. "And June," I whispered, pointing to the buffet, "trust me, whatever you do, don't go near that watermelon. Definitely skip the oranges. As a matter of fact, don't drink or eat anything unless it comes sealed." I had forgotten to warn June about Venice's drug-enhanced fruit. As I spoke, I spotted Tima pouring white powder into the punch; it probably wasn't confectioner's sugar.

All sorts of people showed up. One man wandered around dressed in a Santa Claus suit; he was my first pick for the "undercover narc award." A hippie with long hair and a beard wore a beige suit and rep tie. I wondered whether he had just stolen the outfit and was wearing it as a lark. A Black man in a dashiki had the largest afro I had ever seen. Standing on the lawn, he looked like a topiary. Peaches, Sybil, and the entire bridal party wore wreaths made of carnations and orchids. Peaches wore a halter top, and Sybil wore a scoop-necked blouse. Both wore cut-off jeans and matching beaded necklaces and bracelets. They were an identical lush shade of bronze from the beach.

As the moment for the ceremony drew near, Tima ripped off her T-shirt and insisted that she would perform the ceremony bare-breasted. Others took this as a signal to join in and tossed their shirts into a pile.

Tima had just begun her opening remarks when we heard the unmistakable sound of helicopters. Uh, oh—La La land's finest pork was coming to bust our chops. Pandemonium broke out. People started to stampede in all directions. I grabbed June's hand, and we fled through the bougainvillea, wrecking part of the bush and our pants in our flight. We followed two other party guests up an alley between a row of houses. When the choppers landed in Tima's yard, and we felt certain the cops couldn't see us, we circled back to our car.

No one was arrested. Blouses and T-shirts were tossed back on in time, though not always on the backs they had flown off. The cops were concerned about complaints of noise; they weren't aware of drugs on the premises. They had no search warrant or reason to search, and after years of riots in the Los Angeles area the Venice police were usually just as happy not to enter someone's house.

However, Tima's luck, and that of her companions, was running out. One day while June and I were taking a visitor sightseeing, the gay beach in Venice was raided by the police. Tima, Sybil, Peaches, and five other regulars were arrested for indecent exposure. Sandy, who witnessed the police raid, later told me that when the cops descended onto the beach, they became totally transfixed by the women's breasts. The pigs refused to allow the women to put their tops back on and took them into the Venice station handcuffed and half-naked.

"Take me! Take me, too! I'm topless," Sandy taunted. But the police left him behind.

Though the women bailed themselves out the same day, we were all outraged at the fate of the Venice Eight, as we called the women. At first Tima and the others were determined to fight the charges; they had the support of the Venice GLF and other groups. Local radical lawyers offered free legal representation.

I urged Tima and the others to take their battle all the way to the top courts. Then, as now, I strongly supported the inherent right of women to dress—or undress—as men do. I hated the hypocrisy. Breasts could be shown in films—why not on the beach? And although nude bathing may not seem a burning (pardon the pun) issue to many, its illegality represents part of a puritanical disdain for women's bodies encoded in American law and thinking. Our right to control our bodies is, even now, hemmed in by laws ranging from restrictions on abortions to dress codes.

Tima and her friends initially enjoyed their new status as politicos and regaled everyone with their tale of a seminude day in the precinct. They had been allowed to put their tops back on for night court. In the end, however, they wanted to avoid a close inspection of their lives and illicit activities that a court battle would surely involve. They had more to hide than to gain. And so they copped a plea and paid a fine.

The days of the nude lesbian beach came to an abrupt and unpleasant end. Tima became too paranoid even to smoke dope on the beach, let alone sell it. After she and the others sobered up, the party atmosphere dissipated like summer fog on a sunny day. People didn't want to hang around them anymore; they didn't even want to be around one another.

The group dissolved into unhappy clumps scattered over the beach. I felt bad, although June didn't really share my regret. By now June had had enough of the beach anyway—she didn't like to swim and hated sitting in the sun, as she burned and peeled instead of tanning. She felt that Venice was more dangerous than pleasurable—she disliked the overabundance of drugs and crime in the area. She missed her family and demanded that we return to New York. With no job prospects on the horizon, I could hardly argue against returning east. In fact, I had even received the offer of a teaching assistantship in French at NYU's Bronx campus for the entire year.

Despite the brighter prospects in New York, I was sad to leave Southern California. I felt an emotional attachment to Venice that I have never had for any other city, despite having spent most of my life in New York City. I felt had found my true home, a place where I was happier than I was anywhere else. No day was so bad, no political failure so dismal that it couldn't be cured by a short walk to the beach to watch the blazing red sun, in all its glory, dip into the Pacific.

☙　　☙　　☙

Sandy Blixton remained active in gay and leftist politics. Later he became involved in AIDS organizations in Southern California. In 1986 he was diagnosed with full-blown AIDS. He battled a plethora of illnesses, including Kaposi's sarcoma, pneumocystis pneumonia, cancerous lesions on his liver, and peripheral neuropathy. When medical "experts" urged those infected with HIV not to keep pets, he became a poster boy for PAWS, a group espousing the benefits of animal companionship. No matter how sick he was over the years, he was always upbeat and fervently interested in the world around him, especially political events. From time to time he would repeat his unwavering determination not to die until he had personally bankrupted the patriarchy. Now with new multiple therapies and the Chinese herbs he swears by, he seems remarkably healthy. By August 1998, when he turned seventy-one, he was one of the people who had survived AIDS the longest.

16

Consciousness-razing

The one thing I learned from my year at New York University in the Bronx in 1971–1972 was that I never wanted to teach French again. The first semester I taught a section of beginning French to a sleepy group of freshmen who showed up for their nine o'clock class in pajamas and slippers. The text, *Mise en train*, had been written by the French absurdist Eugène Ionesco in an attempt to drive French professors mad.

Intermediate French during the spring semester was better. The more advanced students were engaged in the material; I discovered I liked teaching. The experience convinced me to pursue my doctorate, although I might have thought better of it had I realized I would spend more than a decade working as a migrant laborer in the fields of academe, with part-time positions at several different universities. At the time the position at NYU had more perks than I had ever had before, including a small salary and a tuition remission.

Teaching, course preparation, and graduate courses left me no time to write and little time to interact with my parents. When we did talk, I whined about my work and my father talked of his own troubles. He and his partners were having a hard time. The St. Lawrence Seaway had been widened, after which a good part of his business had literally gone up the river. The development of containerization, which moved products from the manufacturer to flatbed trucks or trains and then onto ships for export, made marine carpentry obsolete. The corporation decided to sell the land the lumber was stored on. Then the partners moved their remaining business onto an old, shaky pier. Meanwhile, my parents' neighborhood in Brooklyn was declining so rapidly that it had been nicknamed "Mugger's Row." Fearful of remaining there, my parents began to plan a retirement in south Florida because many of their relatives had already moved there. My father sarcastically called Miami Beach "God's waiting room," and my mother hated both heat and sunlight. Despite their reservations, they were resigned to abandoning the borough where they had both spent almost all of their lives. I felt they would be far safer in Florida, and they would have a better support network of other seniors in addition to our relations. Furthermore, if they lived over a thousand miles away, they wouldn't badger me to drop by.

I found myself without any outlets for my political activism. None of the groups I had been involved with was still operating. Redstockings had ceased functioning in fall 1970, and now the Gay Liberation Front had disintegrated as well. Their problems were similar in many ways. Both saw themselves as broad "umbrella" groups that spoke for an entire "class" of people—that is, women or homosexuals. Like other radical American groups, both had tried to pattern themselves after revolutionary movements elsewhere, adapting Chinese and Cuban class analysis to forge solidarity among American women and homosexuals. But they failed to consider the internal divisions and tensions that ran counter to these class identities. Radical groups disintegrated as people were drawn into new or conflicting causes. The breakdown of the GLF was one instance of the fragmentation and fracturing that happened for good reasons but broke the movement's momentum, or pointed to the impossibility of defining a movement at all. Gay women withdrew from the GLF and Women's Liberation Movement to form the Lavender Menace and then Radicalesbians; gender benders began STAR; people of color put their energy into the Third World Caucus and the Salsa Soul Sisters. Less radical members of the GLF fled to their archrivals, the larger and better organized Gay Activists Alliance. Without these constituencies, gay white men could hardly claim to represent *all* homosexuals anymore. After the GLF had become less diverse, ideological zealots and violence-oriented individuals dominated the group. Along with some of the marginal crazies, they drove both newcomers and older members like me away.

The demise of GLF saddened me, though I thought I understood exactly why it had happened. I still believed that GLF's radicalism and its two-pronged political and cultural approaches to activism were the best routes to gay liberation. I did not—and still do not—choose to put my energy behind the legislative thrust of groups such as GAA and their descendants. The quality of life is not substantially better in states where homosexuality has been decriminalized. Queers are bashed and murdered from New York to Wyoming. Conversely, pockets of gay culture flourish in states where consensual sodomy is still a crime. I suspect that gaining the right to marry (though I applaud anyone who wants to) might fuel a homophobic backlash. Also, in our zeal to assimilate we may be losing a valuable opportunity to rethink and reformulate what it means to relate to others, maybe as a couple, but in a myriad of other ways as well.

This radical view of wanting to change gay people's hearts and lives, rather than legalize their behavior, kept me then and now from embracing the call to legislative reform. Creating cultural alternatives and demanding respect for lesbians and gay men have always seemed the better paths.

So now, in the absence of Redstockings and GLF, my last remaining political connection was a consciousness-raising group I had helped start the previous fall. When Barbara Love and her lover, Sidney Abbott, pulled out of Radicalesbians in late 1970, they set up twenty-six C-R groups. I helped organize Group 8, which met on Tuesday nights. When I returned from California in September 1971, the group was still meeting.

Since the early days of Redstockings, consciousness-raising had expanded all over the country, but the process had undergone some changes. The basic tenet of using Marxist analysis to understand women as an oppressed class had disappeared because participants were more into a socially oriented rap session or even a social group. By the time Barbara and Sidney called for the formation of lesbian C-R groups, some women were joining because they were needy or lonely or simply had a free night per week that they wanted to fill. Many viewed the groups as dating services.

I should have realized early on that Group 8 was headed in the wrong direction. At the very first meeting that fall a heterosexual woman, April, took off her top; we didn't know what to say to her. I couldn't fathom what she was doing in our group. Then there was Lorna, who supplemented her welfare check by selling pot. She wanted the C-R group to be a social gathering. When she wasn't drinking or forcing drinks on others, Lorna was spilling them in my lap. Protesting that vodka and politics didn't mix just made me seem like a bad sport. At the time I thought Lorna was passive-aggressive, but in retrospect I realize that she was simply drunk, and when she wasn't, she was stoned. For me, consciousness-raising was meant to be a political activity, not a happy hour. As much as I had disagreed with some of Redstockings' philosophy, I still believed that the function of C-R was to examine a common core of oppression—in this case, what it meant to be a lesbian.

The participation of Marge and Sarah, two therapists who were also lovers, raised a different issue. Lovers were not supposed to attend the same C-R group, yet partners often insisted on being together. Some were terrified that the intimate revelations and the closeness that naturally develops among women who share their deepest secrets would draw their lover into another relationship. Though nonmonogamy was the politically correct line, jealousy was still rampant. Even when no one was flirting, the presence of two lovers stifled honest discussion about relationships, sexual identities, and other important matters. How could a lesbian admit that sex was lousy or nonexistent when her lover was sitting across the room? Even when lovers were not in the same group, the politicized lesbian community was so small and inbred that we knew the people we were supposedly discussing anonymously. We typically knew their ex-lovers and their ex-lovers' lovers, or else we *were* their ex-lovers or their ex-lovers' lovers. I've always said, "There are really only sixty-nine lesbians in the world, and it's all done with mirrors."

I went on with my polyamorous encounters outside the group but never shared them with the others. Once I was pursued by a flight attendant who told me during a candlelight dinner in a gay restaurant that she could never go out with someone like me because I wouldn't possibly understand her erratic schedule. After I had graciously accepted her comments as a rebuff, she leaped over the dinner table and started shoving her tongue down my throat in front of the startled diners. Later she practically ripped my clothes off in her car but refused to go somewhere safe to have sex. In the end I was more bothered than hot. Had I discussed this story in my C-R group, it would have reached June in a flash. So I kept my sex life separate from my C-R group, supposedly the core of my political life—and that felt all wrong to me. Wasn't the point to be able to integrate them both?

Though Group 8 turned out to be more of a support group than a true C-R group, I remained in it because I liked most of the women and because I thought that C-R was an important process to stay in touch with. Every time I considered quitting, we'd have a fascinating discussion, and I would return home with some new thoughts on lesbian life. Even though the narratives often lacked political analysis and were more on the level of gossip than revelation, Group 8 still presented me with an opportunity to swap stories with other lesbians.

But in the end the negatives began to outweigh the positives, and one particular incident after I returned the second time from California finally pushed me over the edge. By this time Marge and Sarah had come to dominate the meetings. With their psychoanalytic backgrounds, they transformed C-R into group therapy sessions focused on helping individuals with their problems rather than on understanding the underlying class oppression we all suffered as gay women.

In truth, Marge and Sarah wanted attention paid to their own problems, which became clear when Sarah went into the hospital for an appendectomy. Finally alone in the group, Marge insisted on telling us about her relationship with Sarah. I objected vociferously. It was not the role of the C-R group to get involved in Marge and Sarah's relationship. Marge, however, persuaded the others that this was her only opportunity to open her heart to us because Sarah was usually present.

Marge proceeded with a long tale of woe. They shared a large, if messy, house. Sarah had recently become involved with Brandy, a siren who was destroying their relationship.

The following Tuesday Sarah, clutching her stitches, showed up where we were meeting, at the West End Avenue apartment of a Group 8 member named Louise. The windows of the apartment were just about pavement level. As we talked, we had a picturesque view of passing feet and of dogs making their evening deposits on the sidewalk. Sarah had heard (probably about ten seconds after C-R had ended the previous Tuesday) about Marge's monopolization of the group.

"I demand equal time," Sarah announced. A political career was in her future.

Do not ever assume that lesbians will turn down a juicy story in the name of politics or common sense. Almost nobody will, I suppose, as television and radio talk shows prove every day. Only two other women and I objected to the turn the group had taken. What were we going to do about Marge, who was also present? The majority voted to ask Marge to go out for an hour and then return. I silently wished her lots of luck finding a cup of coffee in our neighborhood.

Looking wan from a week in the hospital, Sarah launched into her own tragic tale. If we had an applause meter to reward painful stories, like the old television show *Queen for a Day*, Sarah would definitely have won at least a toaster oven. She had been driven into Brandy's consoling arms by Marge's sheer cruelty. She accused Marge of battering her. We all knew that Marge had a black belt in karate, so this sounded pretty awful. Now Sarah was afraid for her life—Marge had a handgun and had threatened to use it on Sarah if she tried to leave.

By the time Marge reappeared outside the window to ask permission to enter, we were all bug-eyed. Sarah had more to tell, however, so we sent Marge off for a second cup of coffee. Sarah filled us in with more nightmarish details about Marge's abuse, including the story about how she had allegedly slugged Brandy at a party. Suddenly Marge was back, this time less than twenty minutes later. She demanded to be let in. We asked her to wait.

A moment later Marge was at the front door. We refused to open it. The next thing we saw were her hands flying right through the thick wood of the door. Louise took Sarah and her stitches into the kitchen, which had two doors, one facing the entrance, the other facing the living room. She hid Sarah in a large gap behind the refrigerator.

Unfortunately I was among those left in the living room. The other women thought we should try to calm Marge down until Sarah could be spirited out of the apartment. If not, we should defend Sarah. *We?* I had started studying karate at a nearby dojo, but at that moment I was a very white belt. Even were I more proficient in martial arts, I wasn't about to get involved. The way I saw it, they had both set us up, used and abused us. Was the state giving licenses to psychopaths to practice therapy on others?

I backed into a corner behind Louise's couch. As a devout pacifist I didn't believe in fighting, except in self-defense. I hoped I wouldn't freeze if Marge went for me. After rapists and serial killers, I'm most afraid of enraged women and cockroaches, in that order. If I had had any shred of religious fervor, I would have prayed.

Before we had a chance to construct more of a strategy, the remains of the door flew into the room. Someone would have a dandy toothpick collection later on. Marge, in a karate stance, her hands showing not even a splinter, advanced into the room.

"Calm down, Marge," Rusty, the most athletic member of our group, said. "This isn't going to solve anything."

"Where's Sarah?" Marge had tunnel vision.

"Try to remember that she just had surgery. We don't want any more accidents here."

"Get outta my way!" Marge picked up a straight-backed chair to emphasize her point. Her eyes were wild and almost rolling. When Rusty didn't budge, Marge swung the chair at her. Rusty ducked, but Louise would soon be shopping for a new chair and coffee table. A melee broke out, and several of the women were punched and shoved as they tried to hold Marge back. Several moments later two police officers entered the front doorway and stepped over the shards of the door into the living room. During the fight Louise had snuck around Marge and called the cops from her bedroom.

"Which one of you ladies broke down that door?" one of the cops asked. Five index fingers pointed at Marge. The cops handcuffed Marge. Louise demanded to know whether Marge was willing to pay for a new door, locks (few New York apartments have just one), and furniture. I imagined Louise was thinking of a steel door. After all, how safe could she feel after Marge had come flying into her apartment with apparently little effort? Marge refused, so the cops detained Marge for breaking and entering and malicious destruction of property. Marge retaliated by asking the police to arrest most of the others for assault and battery. The others pressed countercharges. Several squad cars arrived and removed almost the entire group.

Ellen (another group member) and I were not taken into custody because we hadn't participated in the fight. We walked over to the nearby Twenty-fourth Precinct, just in case we had to bail out the group. I always kept $100 at home at all times to bail out friends, but it wouldn't pay for the whole group. I made a mental note to skip Marge; in fact, I would have bribed the cops if I thought they'd keep her in the tank.

They made Ellen and me wait in the precinct lobby for about an hour. When I looked at my watch, I realized it was midnight. I spotted a pay phone and called June.

"Where the hell are you?" she shrieked. "It's after midnight." I'm sure she was imagining me involved in an orgy with the entire C-R group.

"I'm over at the Twenty-fourth Precinct."

"What are you doing there?"

"I'm bailing out the C-R group. Gotta run. Ellen will walk me home later. Bye." I hung up before she could demand details.

Finally, Ellen and I were ushered into a conference room in the back where a detective sat with Marge and the others. Marge was calm, using her most soothing therapeutic voice. Doors wouldn't melt in her mouth. I wondered whether she was more schizophrenic than my mother.

Marge was given a desk summons, after which we all went home. The next Tuesday we met without Marge or Sarah. I was trying desperately not to become my mother and yell, "I warned you this would happen!" I believed that both of the therapists were to blame and that each, in her own way, had used the group. Most of the women felt that Sarah was blameless and that we should expel only Marge.

The episode put me in an untenable position. Even though I expected violence from the outside world, a C-R group was the last place where I thought it would erupt. I didn't become a feminist to get into a brawl with other women.

I was also appalled that Louise had called the cops. I still thought of myself as a tough revolutionary who denounced the police as the repressive agents of the patriarchy. I certainly didn't want to run to them at the first sign of trouble, especially when lesbians were the source of the problem. The inaction of the police over the murder of Lydia French had proved their insensitivity to the value of our lives. In order to transform the world, we had to learn to mediate our own problems first. Some of the women in the group lacked feminist ideals, or they never would have chosen a good story over their principles.

Disillusioned and disgusted, I decided to take a break from political activism and C-R groups and turn to my writing to raise people's consciousness and stir them to action. It seemed to me that I would accomplish more by writing one great speech like Sojourner Truth's or one germinal pamphlet like Thomas Paine's than by sitting in C-R groups for the rest of my life. Indeed, when *Out of the Closets: Voices of Gay Liberation* was finally published at the end of 1972, gay men and lesbians gave it an enormously positive reception. People wrote us that somehow the book had reached them in mental hospitals where they had been incarcerated by families determined to make them into heterosexuals. The essays about psychiatry made these lesbians and gay men realize that they weren't sick, and they walked out or escaped from shock treatment and aversion therapy. Others had less dramatic but equally important revelations: They discovered that they weren't the only ones in the world attracted to members of the same sex. All too many of us had grown up alone and isolated, sure that only we felt the way we did. A few wrote us that they were contemplating suicide until they discovered this anthology, which assured them they were normal. About two years later when *Out of the Closets* was the first book of its kind printed as a mass market paperback, it appeared at the front of supermarkets and in bus terminals where people who didn't have access to liberal bookstores grabbed them up. One man told me of buying the book and reading it lying down in the back seat of his parents' car on the way home from a vacation. He was terrified that they would see what he was reading, so he ripped off the cover and title page. Others simply used the list of gay organizations at the end of the anthology to locate a gay organization or bookstore.

Although Allen and I initially hated the phrase *Voices of Gay Liberation,* a subtitle imposed by the publisher, I see now how right he was, for in a way *Out of the Closets* was not entirely our or the contributors' creation. Rather, it was a way to give voice to a rebellious generation, one that refused to be silenced or to remain invisible.

Out of the Closets marked the beginning of a different kind of political activism for me. Although I joined a number of other political groups later on, writing and public speaking became my main tools for activism, for addressing the burning questions of the times. Now there are shelves of works by and about queers, but then, before we had any books about ourselves, we had only each other and our dreams of the revolution that never came.

சு   சு   சு

In 1992 Allen and I embarked on a tour of England and Scotland to celebrate the first publication of *Out of the Closets* in the United Kingdom. I was glad to be on the road again with Allen, twenty years after the initial publication of the book, and to still have our friendship intact.

In Manchester we found ourselves on the wrong side of the road, in every sense. Much to our surprise, we discovered that our British publisher had booked us into a straight leftist bookstore. After eating dinner standing up in the stockroom of the store, we presented the book. Just as we started, four young lesbians marched into the bookstore, leafed through a copy of the book, and then sat with defiant scowls and linked arms in the front row. After we spoke, they pointed out that, though they weren't born when the anthology first appeared, they were certain that we should have revised the volume to remove the words, experiences, and ideology of the 1960s that they found offensive.

They'd never understand it, but to rewrite my history would have been the simpler path. I could have sprung from some supportive leftist family that cheered me as I entered the fray. I could have created parents who were more sympathetic. In my freshly minted past I would have embraced the movement wholeheartedly and unhesitatingly. I wouldn't have had doubts about where the women's and gay liberation movements were headed. I might have sacrificed sun and sex for social change. And maybe I could have insisted that American radicalism didn't fade in the 1970s into Reaganism and the "me" generation.

But truth exists outside the fashions of the time. Allen and I were no longer radicals, and we weren't going to pretend we were just to peddle a few books and win the hearts of this particular audience. In the early 1970s we might have engaged in a heated debate, but now we sat back and let the Marxists slug it out with the Maoists as we looked on in bemused silence. And when the opposing factions had shouted themselves hoarse, Allen and I linked arms and went home.

Epilogue

It is hard for me to explain how the protagonist of this memoir emerged as a tenured full professor and director of women's studies. It took me sixteen years to complete my degree. After all those years I thought New York University would present me with a retirement present rather than a doctorate. I toiled for many years as an adjunct professor, and now I've been at Pace University in New York City for a quarter century. A preppie academic in Brooks Brothers blazers, blouses, and flannel pants, I bear little resemblance to my younger incarnation. Instead of plotting the peaceful overthrow of the system, I sit through endless committee meetings where some colleagues visibly cringe at words like "precedent" and "change." My evenings are spent hunched over unmarked term papers and drafts of scholarly essays. In my spare time I scan the Internet for stocks that will speed my way to a capitalistic retirement in a gentle climate. Nowadays a night of debauchery is likely to entail a trip to a gourmet emporium to fondle the grapes and sample the extra virgin olive oil. My drugs of choice are not marijuana and hashish, but Motrin and caffeine.

As I revisited the exploits of the lesbian/feminist radical with the unkempt hair and utopian ideals, I often felt I was writing about someone else, some long-dead, distant relative whose name escapes me. I am no longer the person at the center of this political autobiography, not even vaguely. Though I sometimes laughed or cried as I recalled poignant memories, I felt little connection with the person I was writing about, and I could not explain, even to myself, how I had eventually shed the person I was, like an empty snakeskin, and embraced a middle-class identity.

The more personal and painful aspects of this memoir will be news to those who have known me for the past twenty years. I can't very well turn to friends and protest, like a "perp" in a liquor store hold up, "It wasn't me who did all that; it was someone else who looked just like me!" Moreover, I don't want to deny my younger self. I'm not ashamed of anything I did. No one was injured in any of our actions. Amazingly, I was never arrested, though many of my friends were. I realize how lucky I was to be young in an era when the worst thing a lesbian could catch was pubic lice or scabies. My story might have been very different had I grown up in the age of AIDS, genital herpes, and venereal warts. Today the sexually active lesbian should be encased in plastic armor: latex gloves, dental dams, Saran Wrap, condoms. If I had to wear all that, I'd feel as erotic as a wrapped, leftover pot roast. I embraced midlife and monogamy at the right time.

Writing this memoir felt like coming out all over again, except that this time it was much more painful. When in the wake of the Stonewall uprisings I first confessed my homosexuality to friends and relations who were certain that I was heterosexual, there was naturally some embarrassment. But now I've spilled the beans about myself and my family. Friends and my partner know about my colorful past, but I have generally kept my family in a dark closet. My mother's mental illness was a fact of life that I accepted, and feminism made me much more sympathetic to her plight as a woman ignored by the medical establishment. Still, writing about my mother's illness and my father's role in pathologizing her felt like treason: I had betrayed my parents, exposed them to the world in all their cruelty and vulnerability. In my generation children of the mentally ill learned very early on not to invite playmates into the house and not to let word of bizarre goings-on seep into the outside world. Consequently, I feel as if I've opened a second closet door, revealing contents much more starkly dangerous than an admission of sexual variation. Perhaps my account will comfort those who also suffered in silence for fear of damaging the image of the movement. Perhaps it will give them permission to speak of their pain without fear of condemnation. But I still worry: Will I now be held accountable not only for my own behavior but also for that of my ancestors? The next time I lose my temper with friends or disagree with colleagues, will people whisper to each other, "Aha, madness runs in her family"?

But what about the other people I write about, those who cannot speak for themselves? All too many of my contemporaries are dead and not necessarily from AIDS-related illnesses, as one might suppose of someone with a raft of gay male friends. Murder, suicide, and fatal illnesses speeded by poverty and a distrust of the patriarchal medical establishment took an inordinate toll on leftists. But in a memoir the dead and the living remain, fixed like butterflies in their glass cases. The living have no chance for rebuttal, no opportunity to insist that they, too, are different people today.

To the degree that members of my generation will recognize—and identify—with my experiences, struggles, aspirations, and failures, I can claim that this memoir represents not just me but also many young radicals of the Vietnam War era. But my experiences are also shaped by the particulars of my race, class, religion, and familial background, and I hope, in the original spirit of consciousness-raising, that my account will encourage others to give voice to their own.

Realizing that the radicals of yesteryear are now no more likely than I am to zap corporations or take illicit drugs, I disguised some major characters and consolidated minor figures. No one, except perhaps politicians and felons, should be pilloried for the sins of the past. I resisted the impulse to fictionalize events, for fear I would diminish those larger, more reckless times when the war in Vietnam raged and the hot winds of revolution blew at my back. Unlike Anna Quindlen, whose 1997 *New York Times* "Bookend" essay fretted over the impossibility of capturing small details with any accuracy, my goal was to portray the spirit of the times—the "feel" of the era—rather than worrying over whether a particular individual wore horn-rimmed or wire eyeglasses. I wanted people to know what it was like to live then and what some of us did to forge social change.

Now, thirty years after members of Redstockings barged into legislative hearings on abortion and after gay men rioted at the Stonewall Inn, things have certainly changed for the better. The young women I deal with at school agonize as much as my contemporaries did when they face an unexpected pregnancy, but they have legal remedies to choose from. Feminists and homosexuals have our own presses, magazines, music and film festivals, and community centers. The "Ellenization" of television has caused an explosion of gay and lesbian characters in a variety of shows. No one need grow up, as I did, identifying more with Jack London's *White Fang* than with other humans.

Once the patriarchy controlled the bodies and everyday lives of women, homosexuals, and transgendered people with an iron fist. The struggle is far from over, and reactionary forces miss no opportunity to reinstate their dominance through legislative efforts and sometimes even terrorism. Today our lobbyists and activists seem more reactive than proactive. Back then the colorful actions of radicals captured not just headlines but also the imagination of an entire generation yearning for equality. Though the grand revolution we were expecting never came, we are all freer today because of the courage of many individuals who were willing to risk everything for gender justice.

Acknowledgments

I have a lot to be thankful for, not least of which are the gay and lesbian pioneers of the Mattachine Society and the Daughters of Bilitis who paved the way for the modern gay movement, as well as the suffragettes and early members of the National Organization for Women who opened the door, although sometimes grudgingly, to the radicals who came after them. I am particularly indebted to Phyllis Lyon and Del Martin, who have always been unstintingly generous with both wit and wisdom, and to the late Jim Kepner, pack rat extraordinare and master of magnificent facts and arcane gossip.

Alternative newspapers and magazines gave me my first writing opportunities, and earlier accounts of some of the events recounted here appeared in *Rat* and *Win* magazines. *The Harvard Gay and Lesbian Review* first published "Lesbian New York," an analysis of the first lesbian dance, in the winter 1995 issue.

Many people gave me both their time and material to help me write a memoir that they hoped would reflect their experience. Those who agreed to be interviewed or who generously helped me out with information and research questions include Ros Baxandall, Jessica Biondi, Sandy Blixton, Mimi Bowling, Ellen Broidy, Nene Brown, Susan Brownmiller, Chelsea Dreher, Martin Duberman, Sandra Fields, Michela Griffo, Kali Grosberg, Margaret Jeffres, Marlene and Richard Kasman, Chuck Keeton, Constance Knapp, John Knoebel, Barbara Love, Phil Mattera, Robin Morgan, William Offut, Irene Peslikis, Margo

Rila, Martha Shelley, Alix Kates Shulman, Ellen Shumsky, Madeline M. Smith, and Ann Tobin.

Research assistance was provided by H. Claire Jackson, Heather Lukes, Renée Savin, and Phil Tarley. Access to archives and photographs was generously provided by the Manuscripts and Archives Division of the New York Public Library, Rutgers University, the June Mazer Collection, and the ONE Institute/International Gay and Lesbian Archives, where John O'Brien and Misha Schutt were particularly generous with their time. I am forever indebted to the librarians of Pace University, smart and helpful all. My thanks go to the Women's Studies Program at UCLA for inviting me to be a visiting scholar in residence during the fall of 1996. A sabbatical, Summer Research Grants, funding from the Scholarly Research Committee, and course releases from Dean Charles Masiello and Dyson College, Pace University, all helped me find time for this project. The support of my Pace women's studies colleagues and of Professor Sherman Raskin, chair of the English Department, has meant more than I can express. I owe much to the Pace University students in my course "Women Writing About Their Lives: From Fact to Fiction." Exploring autobiographical writing with them gave me the courage to speak of my own life. The Pace University Design and Development Department provided helpful technical assistance.

Juliana Nocker believed in this book enough to persuade me to stay at Basic Books. I thank her for her faith in me and am indebted to Jo Ann Miller for returning to Basic, where she and Libby Garland enthusiastically embraced this project. Richard Fumosa and Jan Kristiansson guided this book through production.

This memoir has been improved by the support and helpful feedback of Linda Gardiner, EJ Graff, Marny Hall, Naomi Holoch, Libbie Sherman, and Allen Young, all of whom read various sections or all of my manuscript. Sydelle Kramer of the Frances Goldin Literary Agency provided perceptive editing and sound advice. Most of all, I am forever indebted to two individuals for speeding me toward the completion of this work. Bertha Harris took me under her none-too-maternal wing to help me edit and revise my chapters. Bertha turned out to be both seer (forecasting readers' reactions) and football coach (cheering me on from the sidelines with 6:00 A.M. faxes urging me to punt or run for the goal). And then there is Deb Shoss, queen of the Internet, who can locate historical information, ranging from global events to minutiae, all within hours. I remain astounded by her research capabilities, by her range of knowledge, and by her unflagging goodwill.

Last but never least, my love goes to Karen F. Kerner, my life partner, devoted lover, playmate, and in-house editor.

Photo Credits

Cover photograph of Gay-In III, by Lee Mason, Los Angeles, 1970, from the collection of Karla Jay.

Photograph of Karla Jay, Brooklyn, New York, 1964, from the collection of Karla Jay.

Photograph of Karla Jay, Brooklyn, New York, © Jill Posener, 1995.

Photograph of Abraham and Rhoda Berlin, New York, 1948, from the collection of Karla Jay.

Photograph of Karla Jay, 1956, Pennsylvania, from the collection of Karla Jay.

Photograph of Karla Jay and unidentified companions at college prom, New Haven, 1965, from the collection of Karla Jay.

Photograph of first lesbian dance, New York, 1970, © Ellen Shumsky, 1970. Reprinted by permission of Ellen Shumsky.

Photograph of *Ladies' Home Journal* action. Photograph by Ann Alter. Reprinted from *Rat*, April 4–18, 1970, with permission of the photographer.

Funky Dance cartoons by Tona Derosa, Los Angeles. Flyers reprinted courtesy of ONE Institute/International Gay and Lesbian Archives. (Attempts to locate Tony Derosa have been unsuccessful. The author encourages anyone to contact her who knows the whereabouts of Tony Derosa.)

Photograph of Lavender Menace action, May 1, 1970. Diana Davies Papers, Manuscripts and Archives Division, New York Public Library, Astor, Lenox, and Tilden Foundations. © Diana Davies. Reprinted by permission of Diana Davies.

Photograph of Karla Jay and three friends at Griffith Park. Photograph by Lee Mason, Los Angeles, 1970, from the collection of Karla Jay.

March on Albany, New York, 1971. Diana Davies Papers, Manuscripts and Archives Division, New York Public Library, Astor, Lenox, and Tilden Foundations. © Diana Davies. Reprinted by permission of Diana Davies.

Allen Young and Karla Jay, 1972, from the collection of Allen Young. Reprinted by permission of Allen Young.

Index